HAWORTH HARVEST

THE STORY OF THE BRONTËS

By the same Author

MARY QUEEN OF SCOTS
THE PRIVATE LIFE OF HENRY VIII
THEA
BREAKERS
SOLITAIRE
THE GOWK STORM
WHEN THE WIND BLOWS
THE STRANGERS
THESE ARE MY FRIENDS
THE WINNOWING YEARS
THE HIDDEN FAIRING
THE KEEPER OF TIME
THE FOLLOWING WIND
THEY NEED NO CANDLE
THE OTHER TRAVELLER

HAWORTH HARVEST

The Story of the Brontës

N. BRYSSON MORRISON

Author of "Mary, Queen of Scots," etc.

New York
THE VANGUARD PRESS, INC.

Standard Book Number 8149-0670-2
Library of Congress Catalogue Card Number 78-89661
Copyright, ©, 1969, by N. Brysson Morrison

4-70 C A— 695

Manufactured in the United States of America.

CONTENTS

ILLUSTRATIONS

Pages from Charlotte's earliest known manuscript, about 1824
Brontë Collection, Haworth

Part of a letter from Charlotte to William Smith Williams; January, 1849
Bonnell Collection, Haworth

'The Emigrant.' A poem in Branwell Brontë's hand, signed 'Northangerland' and dated May 26th, 1845
Brontë Society Collection

BOOK ONE

SEED-TIME

I

Whole years, collected in time's glass,
In silent lapse, how soon they pass,
And steal your life away!—

                                        Patrick Brontë

THE REVEREND Patrick Brontë, the new incumbent of
Haworth, was a handsome man with all the impetuosity of
the Irish, his walk a stride. He had covered a considerable
distance since he had been born, forty-three years before on
St Patrick's Day, to a humble farmer in County Down. Nine
brothers and sisters had shared with him the name of
Brunty, but he changed his when his hero Nelson was
created Duke of Brontë. By that time he had left his childhood home far behind and, a young man driven by ambition, was making his way towards Cambridge. He arrived
at the university with seven pounds in his pocket and
departed four years later with a Bachelor of Arts degree.

He was not unfamiliar to his new parishioners since for
some months he had walked across the moors from
Thornton, a distance of six miles, to take the services, but
this April day in 1820 was the first occasion they had seen
his wife and family. Their tall parson looked even taller
beside his diminutive wife and a daisy-chain of six children,
the eldest of whom was six, the youngest three months. The
children indeed were so small that the carrier said he could
have put them all under a clothes-basket.

His parishioners were to remember after a lifetime the
eight carts with the new parson's furniture and gear that
laboured up their village street that day. By then, some

forty years later, the outsider, the incomer, the foreigner, had become part and parcel of the place. 'They kept themselves very close,' Haworth was to remember from the beginning about the parsonage.

So did Haworth. Every family in the unprepossessing village was a single unit, every household in the solitary, inhospitable dwellings marooned on the sea of moors was a community by itself. They judged their parson as a rare good one if he minded his own business and did not trouble himself with theirs.

Their religion was not deeply embedded; Yorkshiremen, their roots ploughed back to the heathen ways of their Norse ancestors. They were heavy drinkers, their manners rough to rudeness, their voices hard, their spirit sturdy and unyielding. None was poor; for centuries the clacking of looms had been heard in the village as cloth was woven from the wool of the grey moorland sheep that grazed right up to the back of the parsonage. Coal and the number of streams in the neighbourhood made it productive for manufacture, and Haworth lived on its mills.

Its square church tower was like a signpost to the approaching family. The track had begun to climb ever since they left Keighley, and they could see their destination in the distance, clinging to the skyline, the only sign of human life in that featureless landscape. It was April, but there was little bloom of spring about the district, no subtle gradations of colour as the treeless wasteland rolled into the horizon. A curious monolithic greyness flattened everything, making space and undulation monotonous and harsh.

The same greyness chilled the village, where the barefaced houses, built of a local stone called grit, looked high because of the slant and narrowness of the scaling street. The flagstones which paved the steep brae were placed endways, to give horses' hooves a surer grip. Haworth had the scoured, uncompromising drabness that even sunshine cannot brighten. At the braehead were the inn and the church, and the strain on the horses eased. To the left waited the last house in the village, the parsonage, like a door-stop to the moors beyond.

It stood, in a moat of gravestones, straight and unadorned as a child's drawing on a slate, a house against whose unsheltered walls the wind slapped. The garden was an oblong directly in front and grew some currant bushes and a cherry tree. A rough unused doorway at the foot led into the graveyard with its table tombs and tilting stones so close together, one of these six children was to note with her bright eyes, that the rank weeds and coarse grass had scarcely room to shoot between them.

The eastern light, unimpeded by tree or building, laid bare the interior of the house. Because of the parson's dread of fire the windows were unscreened by curtains. They practically all faced to the front, and through the lower could be viewed the church linked to the parsonage by the graveyard, while from the upper storey was glimpsed a stretch of moorland.

Its new mistress was of gentle birth. She had been twenty-nine when she met and married the vehement Irishman, and twenty-nine was old in those days for a woman to marry. Her letters to him during their brief engagement reveal her as both candid and charming, a pleasing combination, and him as a spirited wooer. 'My Dear Friend' becomes in no time 'My Dear Saucy Pat'. She was, like him, a Methodist and, as in all letters of her period, the shadow of eternity falls across her page. 'I look to Him Who has been my unerring guide through life, and in Whose continued protection and assistance I confidently trust.' 'I firmly believe the Almighty has set us apart for each other; may we, by earnest, frequent prayer and every possible exertion, endeavour to fulfil His will in all things.'

It was unlikely that the closeness of the graveyard disturbed Mrs Brontë: a parson's wife would take for granted these symbols of mortality. A nine-room house, the Haworth parsonage was commodious compared with the one they had left behind in Thornton's Market Street. That was why her husband had moved, because of his expanding family and because Haworth was thought to be higher and healthier for them and his wife. She, never strong, had borne six children in seven years of marriage and was now ill.

The new home was large, the rooms good, the windows wide; she had brought two young girls, the Garrs sisters, as nurses for the children, and there were local servants to do the work. But she, as a Cornish woman, found it cold with its stone-flagged, uncarpeted floors: stone was plentiful in the district, timber scarce. After the benign climate and near-tropical vegetation of her native Penzance, her new habitation must have struck her as inclement, the place bald, austere, on the edge of the world.

Not only she but her husband missed the sociabilities and hospitalities of Thornton, the tea-parties, the delightful dinners at Kipping House, the companionship of their equals. It is difficult to appreciate what the lack of communication meant not so very long ago: Haworth might have been on the moon for all Mrs Brontë was to see of their friends in Thornton only six miles distant.

But the husband had compensations denied to his wife, the work of his far-flung parish for one thing, and the release for his energies in long walks on the moors where something in him responded to the wildness around him. She must have been conscious of the wind as was no one else in the parsonage.

Even in summer it sounded round the house, which was roofed with heavy flags to prevent the gales stripping it bare as they pitched against it like the sea. The wind could not have the same effect on Mr Brontë as it had on his wife, for storms were his element: they were the *leitmotif* sounding again and again in his letters and sermons. As for their children, the wind formed part of their background, an accompaniment they heard without the need of listening, to which in later years their poetry was to be strung.

Even before his wife died, within eighteen months of their arrival at Haworth, Mr Brontë began to take most of his meals by himself. It was a habit he retained to the end of his life and which began to form now as a necessity to withdraw from the harassment of the daily round. The digestive trouble he suffered from was psychological rather than physical, requiring him to have quiet for digestion and those who looked after him to be careful of his diet. After all, he lived to be eighty-four and survived all his children: his long walks over rough country prove he had all the hardiness of the peasant.

He was a puritan and an Irishman, a mixture that acted on him with the force of fermentation. The puritan must have been uppermost when he cut the sleeves from one of his wife's gowns; the Irishman walked into Keighley and brought her back a new one. The Irishman, however, could do nothing about the row of little coloured boots, warming on the hearth for his children when they returned with wet feet, which the puritan thrust into the fire as fripperies. The stories of his pistol shooting from the kitchen door are not so spectacular as they sound: it was not unusual for men to carry firearms in his day, and as a young man at Drumballyroney he practised pistol shooting. At Haworth it was not a safety valve but a matter of keeping up his eye that became as much a daily habit with him as winding his watch. As far as temper was concerned, the puritan had the Irishman well in check. When displeased, he walled himself into silence, so that his wife could be grateful that he never gave her an angry word. When pleased, he could be approachable, even genial. 'Nancy,' he entered the kitchen to demand of one of the Garrs sisters, 'is what I've heard true, that you are going to marry a Pat?'

Maria, the eldest of the family, slipped into her mother's place even before her mother died. She was a wise child who would shut herself up with her father's newspaper and then recount all she had read, including debates in Parliament, to her brother and sisters. Their father, passionate about everything he felt, was violently Conservative, and his children were reared on his politics.

Our first picture of the small Brontës is of them walking hand in hand on to the moors behind the parsonage, the older ones mindful of the younger. It is their togetherness that is important to remember. Like peas in a pod, they were linked to one another, sharing the same shell, yet each separate, solitary, housing a world in herself.

No one would have known there was a child in the parsonage, because Mama was ill in one room and Papa was writing his sermons in another. As there was no bad temper or irritability amongst them when they grew up, so there were no tantrums or moods when they were small. 'There never were such good children,' a servant was to remember when she was old, 'such still, noiseless, good little creatures.'

The mother's illness declared itself as an internal cancer. She loved her children and longed to hear of them, but she did not want them to see her changed with suffering, so they were seldom allowed to enter her room and then only one at a time.

All six fell ill with scarlet fever, and the father feared he was going to lose both wife and family. His children recovered, but not his wife; while the crisis lasted her sister, older by some seven years, arrived to take charge of the household. Even after she came Mr Brontë would not permit anyone but himself to do the night nursing, which he did devotedly. The best medical advice available was called in, but the patient was beyond human aid.

She used to ask to be lifted so that she could watch her hearth being cleaned, because the servant did it as it was done in Cornwall. She died moaning, 'Oh God, my poor children—oh God, my poor children.' Her husband suffered with her the months of agony she endured; the parson in him noted that she died, if not triumphantly, at least calm in her belief.

For the first time since they had taken possession of the

parsonage, the gate at the foot of the garden was opened as the funeral procession moved from the house through the graveyard to the church vault.

Mrs Brontë's death caused her children to cling to one another even more, strengthened their compositeness as a family. They did not and could not draw from one another the protection and assurance they would have had from their mother; what they knew unconsciously was that they were all in the same boat, amongst the winds and waves and rocks that tenanted their father's world.

The three younger children were unable to remember their mother. Charlotte hoarded her few memories. She could recall her playing, in the evening light, with Branwell in the parlour. The picture glows with the gold sheen that could shine only from the other side of the grave.

Mr Brontë found his loneliness as a widower well-nigh insupportable, and his children only added to his distress by reminding him of their mother. 'Had I been at Dewsbury I should not have wanted kind friends', he wrote soon after her death; 'had I been at Hartshead, I should have seen them and others occasionally; or had I been at Thornton a family there who were very truly kind would have soothed my sorrows.' But he was at Haworth, a stranger in a strange land.

He had as little wish for his sister-in-law, opinionated and dogmatic as himself, to become a permanency at the parsonage as she had to make it her home; and his thoughts turned, as it was natural for them to turn when he looked at his motherless children, to second marriage.

He approached young Elizabeth Firth, a member of that family who were 'very truly kind'. Her home was Kipping House in Thornton, and her diary abounds with entries about the Brontës when they lived in the parsonage in Market Street: more than one records 'Mr. Brontë in the evening' or 'Mr. Brontë called', 'Mr. and Mrs. Brontë to dinner', 'Mr. and Mrs. Brontë to tea'. She was godmother to three of the children, and amongst her accounts appears

the disbursement, 'Gave at Anne Brontë's christening £1';
another details, 'Frock for one of the Brontës 16/-'.
Probably it was she who gave the little coloured boots
whose gaiety disturbed the father.

The transition from god- to stepmother would not have
been an unkindly one, but fate and Elizabeth Firth decreed
otherwise. She became engaged to the Vicar of Huddersfield, and Mr Brontë had to look elsewhere for a second
wife.

As a handsome young curate from Blarney-Land, he had
been irresistible and susceptible to the opposite sex. For
three years before he married, during his first curacy in
Essex, he had courted a Mary Burder, the niece of his landlady. There had been an engagement from which he appears
to have extricated himself because, the impression is
created, he felt he could do better. Now, after a lapse of
some fifteen years, he set about restoring this relationship.
The Brontë children inherited their shrinking sensitivity
from their mother, not their father.

He wrote a preliminary letter to Mrs Burder, inquiring
closely after her family, whether they be married or single.
For his part he gave financial details of his curacy at
Haworth, which was his for life and which no one could
take from him, telling her he had a good house rent free,
that no one had anything to do with the church but himself
and his congregation was large. He mentioned his marriage
with a very amiable and respectable lady, who had been
dead for nearly two years, but did not say anything at this
juncture about offspring.

Mrs Burder kept him on tenterhooks for months before
she replied, when he wrote to her daughter. He began by
telling her, certain of his words emphasized by the heavy
underlinings of his era, that he thought for *years* past it was
highly probable she was married, but that, at this moment
of writing, he experienced a very agreeable sensation at his
heart to reflect she was still single. He was selfish enough
to wish her to remain so, even if she would never allow him

to see her. 'You were the *first* whose hand I solicited,' he recalled, 'and no doubt I was the first to whom *you promised to give that hand.*'

However much she might dislike him now, he was sure she once loved him with an unaffected innocent love, and he felt confident that after all she had seen and heard she could not doubt his love for her. He warned her that the long interval of time was bound to have effected many changes, and admitted he was looking older. But he trusted he had gained more than he had lost, and hoped he could venture to say he was better and wiser.

His brood of six was mentioned for the first time to the hoped-for stepmother with the words, 'I have a *small* but sweet little family that soothe my heart and afford me pleasure by their endearing little ways'. He added in the same sentence that he had what he considered a competency of the good things of life, which he detailed as being settled in a part of the country *for life* where he had many friends.

He wanted but *one* addition to his comforts, and then he thought he should wish for no more on this side of eternity. He wanted to see a Dearly Beloved Friend, kind as he *once* saw her and as much disposed to promote his happiness. If he had ever given her any pain, he only wished for an opportunity to make her ample amends, by every attention and kindness.

All that he requested at present was that she should be so good as to answer his letter as soon as convenient and tell him candidly whether she and her mother would have any objection to seeing him as an *Old Friend*. He could not tell how *she* might feel reading this, but he must say *his* ancient love was rekindled, and he had a longing desire to see her.

Mary Burder did not keep him long in suspense to let him know what she felt on reading his letter, for she answered it within four days. The accumulated rancour of fifteen years gave an edge to her pen which she used as a stiletto.

She thanked that wise, that indulgent Providence which

had watched over her for good in the past and withheld her from forming in very early life an indissoluble engagement with one whom she could not think was altogether clear of duplicity. Acidly she remarked that she was happy she had not been the ascribed cause of hindering his promotion or preventing any brilliant alliance. 'Nor have these great and affluent friends that you used to write and speak of withheld their patronage on my account, young, inexperienced, unsuspecting and ignorant as I was of what I had a right to look forward to.'

'Many communications were received from you in humble silence,' she continued, 'which ought rather to have met with contempt and indignation ever considering the sacredness of a promise.' She assured him that she had never betrayed his confidence, strange as was the disclosure he once made to her. (This may refer to his humble birth.) She asked how he could possibly think that she or her dear Parent could give him a cordial welcome as an *old friend*? 'Indeed, I must give a decided negative to the desired visit. I know of no ties of friendship ever existing between us which the last eleven or twelve years have not severed or at least placed an insuperable bar to any revival.'

Her present condition, upon which he was pleased to remark, had hitherto been the state of her choice. We can sense the satisfaction with which she tells him of the handsome competency she now enjoyed—'teased with no domestic cares and anxieties and without anyone to control or oppose me, I have felt no willingness to risk in a change so many enjoyments in my possession'.

Because of the death of a beloved aunt, she could truly sympathize with him and the poor little innocents in his bereavement, but pointed out the Lord could supply all his and their need. Her letter ends: 'Cherishing no feeling of resentment or animosity, I remain, Revd. Sir, sincerely your Well Wisher, Mary D. Burder.'

Mr Brontë continued to press his suit. He told her that when he looked at her letter, breathing such a spirit of disdain, hatred and revenge, he appeared to be in an unpleasant dream. 'However you may hate me *now*,' he wrote, 'I am sure you once loved me—and perhaps, as you may yet find, better than you will ever love another.' He entreated her at least to let him call in the spring or summer. 'If you cannot see me as a *friend*, surely you can see me without feelings of revenge or hatred and speak to me civilly. . . . It can do no one *living* any harm, and might, I conceive, be productive of some good.'

If Miss Burder replied, which is not likely as she had said all she had to say, her answer has not been preserved. A short time later she changed her present condition by marrying the dissenting minister of the little village where she had lived all her life. They had four children.

A third attempt at remarriage proved equally abortive. The young woman in Keighley whom Mr Brontë approached was daunted by his lack of fortune and six children into the bargain. He had to bow to the inevitable and prevail upon his sister-in-law to become a fixture at the parsonage. His children had no stepmother, and the pattern for their future life began to take form.

To the small Brontës, Papa in his study and Aunt Branwell in her room were like two outposts. They breakfasted with their father and he joined them sometimes in the living room for tea, when he either sat silent or regaled them with fantastic stories of his Irish days and weird Celtic tales emphatic with the supernatural. These were interspersed with real-life stories he heard as he moved about his moorland parish, of village violence, family tragedies, suicides, blackmail, even murder. His audience listened to him with enormous gusto: he was like a seafarer, bringing to the landlocked parsonage the salty tang of trackless oceans and other climates.

He was not only a clergyman but a Victorian father, the pivot of the household, deferred to and considered in every instance, but there is no evidence that his family went in fear and trembling of him. Indeed, there is an early story of

Charlotte rushing into Papa's study to tell him she had seen
an angel standing by Anne's cradle, but when they went to
look it was gone. Self-centred, he had neither interest in
nor liking of children as children; nevertheless his small,
big-browed audience was a necessity to him. He conversed
with Maria, his eldest, on the leading topics of the day with
as much pleasure and freedom as with an adult.

It does not matter that his poems, published at his own
expense, are puerile. What matters is that the urge to write,
which was to take possession of his children like a passion,
manifested itself in him.

An evangelical parson, he preached on the sin of un-
regenerate man and the Saviour's redemptive grace. His
religion crackled with purging fire, but it was not steeped
in the gloom of his sister-in-law's. We know that one of his
Thornton parishioners, who suffered greatly from depression, was made happy as he lay dying, by God's grace and
Mr Brontë's conversation.

Aunt Branwell took up permanent residence at the
parsonage only through a strong sense of duty. Her public-
spirited family had been identified with Penzance for
generations, and had supported the Society of People
calling themselves Methodists from Wesley's day. In
Haworth Elizabeth Branwell was exiled from the chapel
meetings and the pleasant social round she knew so well
where she, as an elder Branwell daughter, had shone. In this
arid desert she fed herself on her reminiscences of happier
days and on outdated early Methodist periodicals.

She wore pattens to protect her feet from the chill
dampness of the stone floors, but as time wore on they were
heard less and less about the house. She took over the room,
the brightest, where her sister had died, and here she
taught her nieces sewing. Despite her strong Methodism,
which enjoined no gold or jewels, no curling of hair or
costly apparel, no superfluities, Aunt Branwell wore silk
dresses, shawls and laces, and a front of bright auburn
curls, and took snuff out of a pretty gold box. She poured

tea from a lustre pot with the text glazed on it, 'To me to live is Christ, to die is gain'.

Between the two outposts a state of armed neutrality existed. Miss Branwell, entrenched behind her financial independence, matched her brother-in-law's obstinacy with her own. As they aged, each became more exaggerated, her caps growing larger and larger, and his neckcloth more and more voluminous.

Beyond these two outposts the Brontës lived a life of their own, gathered round little Maria who mothered and taught them their prayers. They no longer crept about the house because Mama was ill, but were lively and joyous, occupied with their day's doings. Seldom can any family, Victorian or otherwise, have had their liberty. When they were not being taught by their father they spent their time in the short narrow room without a fireplace above the front door, where the little girls slept at night. The small Brontës did not play like other children, they were grown-ups who never had to put away childish things, but they drew on the walls pictures of heads and pieces of people. Or they would gravitate to the kitchen, warm with firelight, where the sisters, Nancy and Sarah Garrs, despite or perhaps because of their youth and inexperience, made much of their nurslings.

And they would take the track behind the parsonage on to the Yorkshire moors. They were the seedfield for the Brontë genius, those children with their Cornish mother and Irish father.

This was their nursery. It shook with the shock of the elements, a world so spacious even the tumult of storm had its proportion, of light and shade and colour, change and movement, established as eternity.

Here everything was giant or minute as a flower head. Clouds, swollen with rain, were driven across the sky by wind that rustled amongst the grasses at their feet like the pages of a book.

2

She lay with flowers about her head—
Though formal grave-clothes hid her hair!
Still did her lips the smile retain
Which parted them when hope was high,
Still seemed the brow as smoothed from pain
As when all thought she could not die—

Branwell Brontë

THE PROSPECTUS of the new school, written by the clergyman founder, ran: 'It is truly painful to reflect how many Poor Clergymen are utterly unable to bestow that on their female offspring to which their rank in Society entitles them ... I have already engaged professional teachers of more than ordinary talent.' The singing mistress bore the appropriate name of Finch, and allied to her musical duties were those of scourge mistress, an employment which in the Brontës' day was taken for granted. The education comprised history, geography, the use of the globes, grammar, writing and arithmetic, all kinds of needlework, and the nicer kind of household duties, such as ironing. Additional charge was made for the accomplishments of music and drawing.

The fourteen pounds a year for each pupil did not clothe, lodge, board and educate her; the remainder was raised by subscription, so that the school had to be run on careful lines. Mr Carus Wilson, a clergyman and one of the twelve trustees, was also treasurer and secretary. He took so active an interest in the establishment that, being a zealous man, he stamped his personality on every department.

Mr Brontë, with his passion for education and five female

offspring in his motherless home, leapt at such an opportunity. His two eldest had been sent to the good school Miss Firth had attended, but had to be withdrawn after a very short space because the fees were too heavy. Now he enrolled them at Cowan Bridge, but they missed the first term in January because of an epidemic of whooping-cough and measles which swept like a plague through Haworth. None of the small Brontës escaped, and it was spring before they were strong enough to recuperate in their nursery of the moors with its strengthening air. Maria and Elizabeth seldom accompanied them on these expeditions as Aunt kept them sewing in her airless room in preparation for their new school.

Papa took them to Cowan Bridge himself, in time to join the second term in July. The year was 1824 and Maria between ten and eleven, Elizabeth a year younger. The school was not so very far from Haworth, a cluster of cottages situated on the main road between Leeds and Kendal, but bad roads and infrequent coaches separated place from place as though seas, not land, lay between. Papa had to stay overnight, and was so impressed with what he saw that he returned with Charlotte the following month. Emily was not sent to join her sisters until three months later, perhaps because she took longer to recover from the sickness of the previous winter.

Four children at boarding-school must have strained Mr Brontë's finances considerably, but to him what his daughters were receiving made the sacrifice worth while. He paid extra for Maria to have French and drawing lessons, his little wonder of a Maria who, when she was seven, walked with him from Thornton to Bradford and, seated on a high stool at the printer's, helped him to correct the proofs of his books.

Thus the compact unit of the family was broken up into its six component parts, with only two remaining at home. They were their aunt's favourites. Both were Branwells and Anne, the youngest, belonged to her maiden aunt as none of her sisters did. She was a contented pretty little thing whose eyes retained the blueness of baby-hood, who, because she was the youngest, always appeared to her sisters as so much their junior. From her earliest days she loved flowers, pondering down at them as they hugged the earth, discovering in the pale face of a single primrose a whole world.

Beside his small still sister, Branwell, nearly three years her senior, was always on the go, every red hair of his head electric with excitement. Aunt, who was not the spoiling kind, spoiled him because he was a boy and because of his endearing Irish ways.

A happening they were always to remember took place before Emily went to boarding-school. The three children were walking early one evening on the moors with their nurses. There had been weeks of wind and rain but, at the beginning of September, the ground was still flushed with heather. It was a day only September could produce, with a high blue sky, still and radiant.

Papa in the parsonage was startled to hear clap upon clap of thunder while lightning forked like tails into rooms suddenly unnaturally darkened and unnaturally silent. Alarmed at the thought of his children, he went upstairs and saw the sky a fierce red colour over the moors, with dusty clouds driven before the gale whipping up round the parsonage. From the blackening sky a few large drops of rain began to fall.

When the storm broke, the children, with Nancy and Sarah, were in a little valley, but this was no ordinary squall. Not only were the heavens above splitting with thunder, crackling with lightning and discharging thunderbolts of rain. Something was happening to the very ground beneath them.

There was the sound of an explosion muffled by distance. Crow Hill, unable to carry any longer the waters pent inside it, literally burst, and the bog, black and sticky, came churning down the valley, uprooting and bearing on its relentless tide everything in its passage.

It was a sight to inspire awe in the beholder, this up-heaval of the earth itself, this shaking of the foundation, this moving of the immovable. Papa not only preached a sermon on it but printed it. His text was: 'His lightning enlightened the world; the earth saw and trembled. The hills melted like wax at the presence of the Lord.'

Miss Branwell considered the Garrs sisters, who did not like her, wasteful young servants. When Nancy left to be married Sarah went with her. It was decided one elderly woman would be more economical than two young ones. Mr Brontë was a good and generous master; he gave the Garrs ten pounds when they left.

In their place Tabitha Aykroyd walked in. She was a Haworth woman, a widow, Yorkshire born and bred, with a sharp tongue in her head and wholesome as bread. Her face was not unlike a cottage loaf, every bump with its hollow. Over fifty, she was active and bustling with the unexpended energy of the countrywoman, attuned to seasons, not the fret of a clock, and she made the kitchen her domain with its bright fire, scoured floor and utensils polished with cleanliness. The children were welcome enough in her realm, but on her terms; they were to know with the acceptance of subjects what was expected of them and from her.

The seeds of consumption were already planted in Maria and Elizabeth when they journeyed to school with their father, and the superintendent was not anxious to admit them as she did not consider they were sufficiently recovered to mix with the other pupils. But Cowan Bridge was situated in a charming sheltered green valley, picturesque enough to be idyllic, and the change of air from exposed Haworth was thought to be beneficial. Its garden glowed with flowers, and its broad path was bordered by little plots, gay with pink thrift and crimson double daisies, each of which had as its owner a pupil who was encouraged to tend it.

Taken from a home so quiet the tick of the clock in the

hall could be heard in every room, the two parsonage children were now herded amongst girls of all ages with whom they did everything. The buildings taken over for the school, with low ceilings, stone floors, windows difficult or not made to open, narrow tortuous passages, were unsuitable for an influx of inhabitants, and the sanitation was primitive. No longer the good thick York-shire oat-cake made on the griddle at home for their daily bread but a dry, hard-baked clap-bread. To the Brontë girls, accustomed to the simple meals at the parsonage, the school food, prepared by a dirty cook, was revolting. The porridge was often burnt and the meat unfit for eating, while the milk tasted of the unclean utensils in which it had been kept.

The two children had to adapt themselves to rules and regulations and set lessons. Cowan Bridge pronounced their sewing, over which they had bent in Aunt Branwell's room throughout the long summer days, very bad—they had reached Aunt Branwell too late. The school found that Maria, the sage companion of her father, could read and write tolerably, do a few sums, knew a little grammar, geography and history, but that she worked very badly.

Because she was ill she was unable to make any effort and was in consequence considered slatternly and not to be trying. She day-dreamed when she should have been concentrating on her lessons. Sometimes the unfamiliar sounds around her, the teacher's voice, the drone of someone reading aloud, the low, vague hum of a crowded schoolroom, all mingled into the running waters of the beck at home, chuckling over stones. Little separated heaven from home in Maria's mind, which was calm with acceptance. When it came to her turn to answer the teacher's question she had to be prodded awake by those next to her, not knowing what she had been asked.

The pupils were called by their surnames, as in a boys' school. Since it was summer when the two Brontës arrived, they wore buff nankeen dresses with short sleeves and high necks, white cotton stockings and strong shoes. When Emily joined her sisters it was winter, and they were all in thick purple dresses and black woollen stockings. Holland pockets tied on in front served as workbags. Their country black shoes and coarse straw bonnets worn in summer, and white cotton gloves supplied for church, were the only articles of apparel they did not make themselves. Not only their uniform but the way they did their hair, pulled back from their faces and flattened against their heads, made them all appear alike. Hair long enough to be braided or curled was not allowed by Mr Wilson, for in his eyes it encouraged vanity and a waste of time. Even at night the girls looked alike as candles with their snuffers, for all wore nightcaps.

In less than a month Charlotte joined her sisters. She might write indifferently, but she sewed neatly and could do a few sums. She might know nothing systematically, nothing of grammar, geography, history or accomplishments, but the school noted she was altogether clever for her age, which was eight. She was so tiny she looked even younger.

Charlotte, unlike her elder sisters, was a rebel. Giant emotions stormed through her at the sight of injustice and cruelty. Her world rocked on its foundations when she saw Maria, the adored eldest sister who was mother to them all, who knew everything and could do no wrong, punished and pilloried before the whole school, made to wear the 'untidy' badge on her arm.

Everything about Maria Brontë irritated one of the teachers, the neat, punctual, particular Miss Andrews: her drooping head, her habit of standing on the side of her shoe, her preoccupation with her own thoughts, her forgetfulness of rules, her reading when she should have been learning her lesson.

Charlotte thought her heart would burst when she saw Maria dismissed from her class in disgrace and made to stand in the middle of the large room, the mark of the whole school. How could Maria, who was nearly eleven, stand such ignominy? Why, when Miss Andrews told her she was a dirty disagreeable girl who had not cleaned her nails that morning, did Maria not tell her that neither she nor any of them could clean her nails or wash her face because the water in their ewers had been frozen?

Perhaps it was her adult forbearance that tried her teacher more than anything else. It was unnatural in a child that no matter how severely she was punished no improvement was noticeable. In such circumstances the only remedy a limited Miss Andrews found at her disposal was to double the punishment, which only served to double Maria's gentle submissiveness.

When no one else in her history class could answer questions about the reign of Charles I, Maria could supply tonnage, poundage and ship-money without difficulty. She had always been interested in Charles I, pondered on how a man who wished to do right could act so unjustly and unwisely—poor murdered king, whose enemies were so much worse than he. Miss Andrews was not impressed, but irritated by those stray signs of attention which merely proved that Maria could but would not.

The school found that Emily read very prettily and was able to sew a little. The reason why the two younger Brontës' reports were more favourable than the two older ones was that they benefited from Aunt Branwell, whose advent in the parsonage imposed a certain regularity upon the children's day. She was particular about time-tables, and inculcated into her nieces the habits of order, punctuality, neatness and obedience. Also, although none of the Brontës was robust, neither Charlotte nor Emily was harbouring consumption as were Maria and Elizabeth. The hardships they endured in common with the other pupils were taken for granted in their age and regarded as necessary discipline to equip them for the hardest lesson of all—life. The bad food was due to a slovenly cook; the establishment, in its first year, was undergoing teething troubles, but the education it provided even then was excellent.

None of the four Brontës caught the low fever which spread through the school early in February, but Maria by that time was obviously ill. The school authorities realized that something was very wrong and sent for her father. It was the first intimation Papa had received that Maria was ill and the sight of his small daughter appalled him. He took her home in the Leeds coach, the girls crowding out to watch her go.

Maria at home again—to eight-year-old Branwell she might never have been away as she became once more the centre round which his life revolved. No matter that she was now in bed in Aunt's room and never rose from it, that she talked of a journey she was about to make with a happy ending—everything was as it should be now that Maria was home again, everything was as it always would be.

It was spring when Aunt Branwell took him in to see his eldest sister in her coffin. When he was a grown man he was to remember every detail of that terrible day. The tolling of the church bell which warned there was to be a funeral, his heart pounding as he looked down at his own black clothes, desolated by his feeling of loneliness, straining his ears for the reassurance of some everyday sound, hearing only silence in the sunny house; his gasp, the sickening chill as he realized that was Maria lying there, her shroud concealing her bright hair, with flowers about her head. He hid his peaked face, like a small white kite, in his aunt's skirts.

Discipline for the healthy pupils at Cowan Bridge relaxed as the fever turned the school temporarily into a hospital, and they rambled like gipsies through the lush, green flowery countryside. The bad cook fled, afraid of infection, and the woman who took her place was a motherly person. Charlotte found a broad flat stone in the middle of a stream which she reached by taking off her shoes and stockings and wading across to it. Here she would sit, in this leafy fastness, listening to the sound of the stream like the sea she had never seen. Sometimes she shared her island kingdom with her friend, a good-natured Creole some years older, who would not allow the big girls to tyrannize the tiny Charlotte.

The school authorities saw Elizabeth sickening as Maria had sickened and, thoroughly alarmed, sent her home in the care of the housekeeper, a Mrs Hardacre. At the same time, as the hum of summer beat to its noon-tide, Charlotte and Emily were taken to Mr Wilson's seaside house, 'The Cove', at Morecambe Bay. They arrived at night and were put to bed in a room at the back. The house faced the sea waiting for them in the morning.

The expenses of Elizabeth's journey home are recorded in the school account book and show that she was sent by private coach. 'Elizabeth's fare home, guard and coachman, 13/-; Mrs. Hardacre's fare 8/-, horse, gig, pikes and men, 2/6. Mrs. Hardacre's bed at Keighley, 1/-; two letters, 1/4½.' The letters were those forwarded to Haworth to inform Mr Brontë that Elizabeth was on her way home.

The sight of his daughter told the distracted father she was dying. He did not rest until he had removed his remaining two children from the school: the very next day he journeyed to Morecambe and brought Charlotte and Emily home before they had time to see the sea.

Elizabeth did not tarry. She was put in the bed Maria had vacated and within a fortnight followed her through the gateway at the foot of the garden, to be buried beside her mother and sister in the old church with its black pews.

3

We wove a web in childhood,
A web of sunny air;
We dug a spring in infancy,
Of water pure and fair—

Charlotte Brontë

THE HOUSE, facing east, was swept by the morning sun when the doors opened with that suddenness of doors that have been shut all night. Towards evening it became flecked with slants and glimmers of light, and when the lamps were lit it did not so much shut out the outside rocking against its uncurtained windows as cradle its own stillness. The sounds it housed belonged to it as much as its tick belongs to a clock: Papa tapping the weather-glass on his way upstairs to bed, the click-click of Aunt's pattens on the stone floor, the reverberation of Tabby's movements in the kitchen.

This was home to the four remaining Brontës where everything was familiar yet even everyday had something special about it. It was not a rigid household, and the excitement and exhilaration of living tossed through it, intensifying the most ordinary happenings.

Charlotte, at nine, succeeded Maria as the eldest, but if Maria had slipped into her mother's place, Charlotte did not slip into Maria's. She was the leader rather than little mother; with her passionate child's heart she craved to be mothered herself. But she accepted responsibility, and her father came to treat her as though she were adult, as he had treated Maria.

She was ten when she was given her mother's copy of

The Imitation of Christ, which she read regularly, unconsciously drinking in its beautiful cadences while she consciously set herself the task of moulding her conduct on the Augustinian monk's teaching. Her rejection of the world for union with God became in the aspiring Charlotte's case a tug of war between duty and what she yearned to do, and it was duty that won with her. She was to turn away from and distrust even what was innocent because she wanted it, and force herself to embrace instead what was austere and demanding.

The children trooped to their father's study every morning for their lessons. He had been a schoolmaster before he went to Cambridge and wrote in the sixpenny notebooks he supplied, 'All that is written in this notebook must be written in a good and legible plain hand'. Sixpence was a large sum in those days even outside a thrifty parsonage, but he knew what it was to write, when hours glided by pleasantly and almost imperceptibly, full of indescribable pleasure such as he could wish to taste as long as life lasted.

And his children took after him. Writing came to them more naturally than talking. There was not enough paper in existence for all they had to write down. They wrote in minute script to get as much on to a page as possible, fifteen hundred words squeezed on a single sheet measuring 2 inches by $1\frac{3}{4}$ inches which cannot be read now without a magnifying glass and sometimes not even then. They stitched the sheets together to make them into proper books, binding them with the coarse blue or brown paper wrapped round the sugar that came to the parsonage, each little book—and there are more than a hundred of them—with its own elaborate frontispiece setting out its title and author and other works from the same pen. So many books that they used different *noms de plume*, names they invented themselves or those of famous men they admired. Verses, plays, magazines (they were not only the contributors and editor, but the public who wrote to him to air their views), ghost stories, essays, romances, fairy-tales—they ranged this world and the supernatural for copy—*Meditations while Journeying in a Canadian Forest, Reflections on the Fate of a Neglected Genius, An Adventure in Ireland*. But these did not suffice; each chose a real island and populated it with renowned as well as invented characters. The islands expanded into archipelagos, the archipelagos into worlds, for this was creation.

From Aunt Branwell her nieces learned to be neat to the point of fastidiousness, and methodical. It is the exception if a poem or manuscript is not dated, and the habit of writing at stated intervals a diary or 'regularity paper' can be traced to their Methodist aunt's upbringing. For the good of their souls she made them sew and sew and sew. They stitched and seamed in her room, listening to Papa or Branwell reading from the newspaper and to Aunt disputing with Papa afterwards about what they had heard. Discussion would be continued later over tea.

Each girl had her own household duties allotted to her. As Aunt Branwell grew older and retired more and more to her own room, they continued to do their own duties, but in their own time. The routine of every day acted on them with the normality of a wound clock which went neither too fast nor too slow, but which kept time.

It was a discipline Branwell did not undergo. An only boy, he was not sent to school, but was brought up with three sisters, a maiden aunt, an elderly servant and an ageing clergyman father whose bedroom he shared.

He was effervescent, like an unstoppered bottle. We have a picture of him sitting at the kitchen table speaking rapidly as he tightly held his nose and wrote down the sounds he made. Naturally left-handed, he liked to show off by writing with both hands at the same time. He and Charlotte were painfully short-sighted. They were very close to each other; Charlotte signed her early poems UT, Us Two. They referred to their make-believe existence as the infernal world or the world below, and their output was prodigious.

That Emily supplied grist for the Brontë mill is shown
in the thirteen-year-old Charlotte's *The History of the Year
1829* when she wrote: 'Emily's and my best plays were
established the 1st December 1827; the others March 1828.
Best plays mean secret plays; they are very nice ones. All
our plays are very strange ones. Their nature I need not
write on paper, for I think I shall always remember
them.'

There was no royal oak in the garden, only the cherry
tree of which their father was very fond. They made do with
it when they enacted the flight of Charles II after the battle
of Worcester. Emily was dressed up as the king because she
was the tallest and hid in the cherry tree, which she reached
from her father's bedroom window, while the three others
spent the day looking for her. Unfortunately she broke a
branch, which upset both king and troopers, for Papa
greatly prized his cherry tree and the break was very
obvious. Tabby, however, came to their rescue and supplied
soot from the kitchen chimney to be rubbed on the raw
broken end. Papa discovered it but not the culprit.

Tabby was now part and parcel of the parsonage. There
had been a time when she had run down to her nephew's
cottage crying, 'William! William! Yah mun goa up to
Mr Brontë's fur aw'm sure yon childers all goo'n mad!'
But now she accepted their ploys and plays and make-
believe as the natural course of events. The villagers, who
felt there was something queer about their Irish parson and
his children, had expected Tabby to be communicative
regarding the parsonage family, who after all belonged to
the community, but no stray scraps of reminiscence or
crumbs of gossip fell from Tabby's table into their laps.
She told them what she thought was good for them, which
was precisely nothing.

A church trustee once invited the four little Brontës to
one of his children's parties. They came in a bunch and
stayed in a bunch the whole evening, tongue-tied with
shyness and scared at what was going on around them,

unable to join in because they knew no games and so could not hunt the slipper or go round the gooseberry bush. The best moment of the evening came for them when it was time to go home.

All the children inherited their love of animals from their father, but it was Emily who was chiefly responsible for the procession of pets which passed through their hands. That was the one battle, and it was a running one, waged between them and Aunt, who did not consider the parsonage, where everything was so spotless it looked beautiful, a suitable place for dogs or cats, hawks, pheasants and geese.

Emily was the one most like her father. She and Anne both showed signs of growing tall, but Emily was the only Brontë amongst them. The other three were Branwells, Charlotte and Branwell diminutive as their mother had been. Both were overconscious of their lack of inches, and Branwell, when he grew old enough to accompany his father to the barber's, would persuade him to crest his red hair, of which he had a shock, as high as possible to make him look taller. Everything about Charlotte was little except her brow, which took up the major part of her tiny face, a brow, big enough to write the Ten Commandments on. From her earliest days she was conscious of her plainness, which she exaggerated, of her too big brow and too big nose and crooked mouth, but she had fine eyes and pretty hands and brown hair.

All three girls had pretty hair, but the pity was they wore it frizzed and tightly curled in the unbecoming fashion of their aunt's youth. Aunt was also responsible for their clothes, which were antiquated even by Haworth standards. The hands on her clock had stopped decades before when life lay in front of instead of behind her in Penzance.

Emily was the liveliest of the three sisters, her large eyes kindling and glimmering with her thoughts. She was sallow, like Charlotte, but in summer she looked all brown, even her thin wrists. She would talk to the rabbit or bird she held and it made no bid to escape from her hands. If Hetopadeca was right that religion was compassion for all things that have life, then Emily was religious.

She was blithe as the day was long, and the day was never long enough for all they had to do in it. It started with family prayers, breakfast and lessons with Papa. Early dinner divided morning from afternoon, and in the afternoon, either before or after tea, came the walk on the moors where sky met earth and the horizon knew no bounds, where the wild cotton was like drifts of snow in the distance. On the moors they ran wild, joyous with freedom, jumping from tussock to tussock, and Emily could always take the longest leap. After tea they did their daily stint of needlework in Aunt's room. Emily, who despite Aunt and unlike her sisters, was poor at sewing, was working her second sampler, using black wool on a neutral ground for the word of Agur the son of Jakeh: 'Surely I am more brutish than any man, and have not the understanding of a man. I neither learned wisdom, nor have the knowledge of the holy . . .' Still using black wool, she finished the sampler with the four lines which were rolled up in her mind with the sun, lark song and plover cry that gladdened the rough earth of Higher Withins:

> *Ye saints on earth, ascribe, with heavens high host,*
> *Glory and honour to the One in Three;*
> *To God the Father, Son and Holy Ghost,*
> *As was, and is, and evermore shall be.*

When their sewing was folded for the day they joined Branwell in the kitchen, made splendid by its fire, and tried to coax Tabby to light a candle. The winter winds drummed on the windows and shrilled like fifes in the chimney, while winter rains flailed against the pane. But it was not always winter; there were spring, summer and autumn, each with its own guerdon. The most dismal hour of the twenty-four sounded when the clock struck seven, for then they were all packed off to bed, even the fourteen-year-old Charlotte.

Anne suffered from the frightening paroxysms of breath-lessness that accompany asthma. She was the prettiest of the three sisters, with her violet eyes and her light brown hair curling naturally on the nape of her slender neck. She had what her sisters lacked, a fair clear complexion that added to her air of delicacy. Her aunt's favourite niece, she slept with her in the same room where Miss Branwell ruled throughout the day.

Methodism was divided into two camps: those who believed, like Calvin, in predestination, and those like Wesley who did not. Unhappily for her nieces and nephew, Aunt Branwell, unlike their father, belonged to the former: it could never be said of her as it was of Charles Wesley that she went on a merry jig to heaven. She believed that eternal punishment or eternal happiness was immutably fixed by God for each individual soul before birth. Only the sinless would escape damnation—and who was sinless in this evil world?

Thus from the beginning of her life Anne came under the influence of a mind of uniform tone, a mind like an organ whose player used only one set of pipes, the three particular stops of Sin, Death and Judgment.

Their existence when they walked the moors, made the beds and helped Tabby in the kitchen, was one existence. The other was when each was a Chief Geni, Talli, Branni, Emmi, Anni, with fire flashing round their heads. They possessed a magic fluid which forced a talker to speak the truth whether he wanted to or not and they had the power to bring back to life characters they had previously des-troyed. They might live in both worlds concurrently, but the sisters did not substitute the dream for the reality as the brother was to come to do.

In 1830, when Charlotte was fourteen, another world impinged on her, near with necessity and foreboding with unfamiliarity. Her godparents offered to send her to boarding-school.

4

If the shower will make the roses bloom,
Oh, why lament its fall?
Rapidly, merrily,
Life's sunny hours flit by,
Gratefully, cheerily,
Enjoy them as they fly!

Charlotte Brontë

MARY TAYLOR watched the arrival of the new pupil as she emerged in outlandish clothes from the covered cart which had brought her to Roe Head School: for all the world like a little old woman, thought the amused girl. It was January and the landscape was covered with snow, but surely even January could not be responsible for anyone looking so cold and miserable. Mary listened to their kindly headmistress greeting the new girl and heard her voice as she replied. Where on earth could she come from—was that Scots, or an Irish brogue?

Charlotte was the second pupil to arrive that day after the others. Ellen Nussey, also new, felt quite at home in this large, well-appointed house, and as she entered an empty room thought it very nice and comfortable for a schoolroom.

Hearing a sound, she realized she was not alone, and looking behind the curtains saw a girl on the window-seat. Ellen did not notice then her ugly old-fashioned dress or hair screwed into tight curls or pale face made sharp with thinness. All she, the youngest of a family of twelve, saw was that someone was crying, and her warm heart went out to comfort her.

But Charlotte was not comforted. Everything about this

girl was pretty, her dark ringlets, brown eyes and charming frock; everything spoke of a cosseted existence in a sheltered world foreign to the undemonstrative parsonage child who viewed its carefree inhabitants with a critical eye. Her first impression of Ellen Nussey was that she did not like her.

She wondered how she was going to live through the days to come, divorced from her home on its windy uplands, from Branwell, whom she loved even as her own soul, from Papa and Emily and Anne and Tabby. But she had come to learn and learn she must; her godparents were paying her fees, not a penny of their money or a minute of her time must be wasted until she could return home equipped and fitted to teach Emily and Anne all she had been taught and to earn her own living.

This handsome mansion standing in its own grounds was no Cowan Bridge, and to Charlotte's unaccustomed eye there was opulence here. Instead of over fifty fellow pupils, their accents varying as far as Cumberland, there were eight, all girls from wealthy homes more or less near the school. Charlotte had come the furthest distance not only in mileage but in custom and environment. Here she was not called Brontë but Miss Brontë, nor did she look exactly the same as everyone else but quite different. And what did it avail Miss Brontë that she had read everything she could lay her hands on, had written a complete library of books herself and annexed the whole of Africa as writing territory, when she was more ignorant than the youngest girl at Roe Head because she knew no grammar and practically nothing of geography?

Instead of Aunt Branwell, in her mauve shoulder shawl and daisy-fresh cap, rustling in her black silk, clicking in her pattens, there was Miss Wooler and her three sisters. But it was Miss Wooler who held the centre of the picture at Roe Head, moving amongst them in her white embroidered dresses like an abbess, the sweetness of her voice disguising the maturity of her judgment. She recognized that the slightest deviation from routine acted on her new pupil's nervous stomach, and that leaving home was a major disturbance. For the year and a half Charlotte was at Roe Head a special dish was prepared for her every day. When the odd little newcomer wept as though her heart would break at being told she must be placed in a lower class until she had caught up with girls of her own age, her head-mistress allowed her to join her contemporaries and to overtake them by extra study.

Instead of Branwell and Emily and Anne, engrafted into her very existence like shoots on the one branch, there were girls who laughed because she was so short-sighted her nose nearly touched the book she was reading, and who laughed still more when, told to raise her head, she jerked the book up also. They laughed at her because she did not know how to play any of their games, nor did she want to join them. For she had not come to Roe Head to toss about a ball she could not see properly: she had come to learn. In their play hours she sat by herself or read a book; in the playground she stood under a tree, perfectly happy looking up at the branches spreading above her, glimpsing the sky between them, noticing the differences in barks and growth.

She began to make a niche for herself at her new school. She did not look at a picture like the rest of her fellow pupils, she examined it. They used to ask her what she was seeing and were surprised at what she revealed. She knew all the school poetry they knew, and a great deal more besides, could tell them who wrote what and all about him. She was forever talking about clever people, painters and their pictures, writers like Johnson and Sheridan, whom she spoke about with the familiarity of neighbours. 'Now, you don't know the meaning of clever', she once told them. 'Sheridan might be clever; yes, Sheridan was clever—scamps often are, but Johnson hadn't a spark of cleverality in him.' Someone said there was no such word as cleverality and that was the end of that. Charlotte knew the Bible so well she was like a concordance. Accustomed since she could remember anything to making up stories, she would regale her schoolfellows with her latest when they were all in bed and the lights out. Once, hearing a disturbance, Miss Wooler rushed upstairs to find a pupil having violent palpitations after listening to one of Charlotte's best ghost stories.

When it was too stormy or wet to have their usual out-door exercise, Miss Wooler would join the girls and talk to them. She was a born *raconteur*, but her material was not insubstantial as make-believe but of the stuff of reality, of history enacted on the lanes and roads and heaths round Roe Head, of men gathering in the dark to march against those who were overthrowing their monasteries and taxing their land, and, within living memory, of mill-hands, blue with woollen dye, destroying the machines they believed would take from them what could scarcely be called a livelihood.

As she talked Miss Wooler would walk up and down the room for exercise, and her pupils would walk with her. The coveted position was of course next to their headmistress, but those unable to win it paired with a friend. Charlotte had two boon companions, good-looking fair-haired Mary Taylor and, after her first reaction, pretty ringletted Ellen Nussey. Unlike the astringent Mary, Ellen was bland. She was like a pillow, she gave with you; Mary was like a bolster, resistant to pressure.

When the girls gathered round the fire in the evening, Charlotte had her brother and her sisters Emily and Anne, Maria and Elizabeth, to talk about. Mary Taylor concluded that Maria and Elizabeth must have been wonders of talent and kindness from Charlotte's description of them. 'You know what you are all like?' she once exclaimed. 'Growing potatoes in a cellar.' There was the ache of a pause before Charlotte replied, 'Yes, we are.' It was the outspoken Mary who told her she was very ugly, an opinion Charlotte received with the acquiescence of a grace.

But it was to Mary, one morning early, that Charlotte,

still disturbed by her dream, related how she had dreamed she was wanted in the drawing-room, and when she went in, who should be waiting there but—Maria and Elizabeth. 'What happened?' Mary demanded avidly. 'Go on, tell me. Make it out. I know you can.' But Charlotte said there was no more to tell; only she wished she had not dreamed that particular dream. Maria and Elizabeth were so changed; they were very fashionably dressed for one thing and had forgotten what they used to care for, criticizing the Roe Head drawing-room and other things as well.

Charlotte was now seeing her home from the outside as it would strike others. This had nothing to do with her love for it, but meant that for the first time she was conscious of it as apart from herself. 'In the little wild, moorland village where we reside', she wrote to Branwell from school.

She wrote home once a week, and usually to her brother, because she found the most to say to him. In spring he walked ten miles to Roe Head to pay her a surprise visit and ten miles home again. She admitted that what used to excite her wildly had now a more temperate effect. Politics, for instance—she had imagined she had lost all interest in them, but the extreme pleasure that she felt when she heard from him that the Reform Bill had been thrown out convinced her that she had not, as yet, lost *all* her *penchant* for them. She hoped that the present delightful weather would contribute to the perfect restoration of their dear Papa's health.

The state of their parent's health caused Charlotte and Papa the greatest disquiet. He was in and out of bed, having to be taken care of and to take care of himself. Charlotte was haunted by the fear that something would happen to Papa, that one day, instead of being so weak he could not rise without assistance, he would be unable to rise at all. Then what would happen to them all when they had to move out of the parsonage, which was their home, their shield and bulwark, to make room for the new man? She must provision herself to meet such an eventuality, stock herself with learning, develop her drawing however hard it was on her eyes. She was the one upon whom her father depended, the eldest of the family, and so responsible for what happened to them all until Branwell was old enough to take his place as breadwinner. He was studying Latin and Greek with Papa, and so brilliant at everything that undoubtedly he was a genius. Branwell would save them all.

Charlotte's letter to her brother concludes with the hope that the present delightful weather might give Aunt pleasant reminiscences of the salubrious climate of her native place. Aunt's harping on the well-known string of the pleasures of Penzance was like a refrain in the Haworth parsonage.

Roe Head was not cut off and solitary like Haworth, but standing in picturesque rolling green Robin Hood countryside, populated with residences and manor houses, and a new hazard opened up to Charlotte which she was never to meet without trepidation—visiting.

Her godparents not only paid her school fees, but invited her to spend week-ends with them. There were invitations from both Anne's godmothers, Mrs Franks who might have been their stepmother, and her friend Miss Outhewaite, both of whom were kindly disposed to all the children of their one-time parson.

None of his children except Branwell inherited their father's Irish gregariousness or the give and take of social genialities. The thought of having to pay even an afternoon call blighted Charlotte's days as it approached; the actuality was an agony and the memory of her tongue-tied shyness a misery and shame, all of which increased rather than lessened as she grew older. There was one quite terrible visit during her Roe Head days when a stranger, assuming from her size that she was much younger than she was, took her on her knee as though she were an infant. None of the four Brontës was ever to feel at home except in the Haworth parsonage. In Branwell's case this developed into a love-hate condition, when hate strangled the love for what he could not do without.

He was fifteen now, and the first thing noticed about him was his shock of tawny hair under which he vibrated, shivered and pulsated like a nerve. He missed his partner and confederate in the elaborations of their Glass Town creation. The sea none of them had ever seen sounded through all their juvenilia and Glass Town was a confederacy of islands. There magic empires were given the actuality of a political economy, schools, government, capital and other cities, their topography and geography mapped out and charted in detail.

Branwell was passing through the sanguinary stage of male adolescence while Charlotte was at school. The confederacy of Glass Town shuddered with war, battle after battle raged and blasted, revolution overthrew. Death was everywhere, on the battlefield, the scaffold, before the firing-squad. His hero, one Alexander Rogue, Member of Parliament, had red hair, was well over six feet and a man of action, whether he was abducting peeresses or provoking civil war, and was shot dead by a firing-party to whom he himself gave the order to shoot. But Branwell could not bear that this magnificent projection of himself should disappear into oblivion. The next thing heard about him was that he had returned from no one knew where and was living like a prince in a fine house in George's Street.

Emily and Anne grew heartily tired of Branwell waging his ceaseless gory wars. They invented a country of their own, a vast world that heaved itself out of the North and South Pacific in the territory of their minds. It was called Gondal. They wrote out its particulars for Charlotte on her return from school, a *dramatis personae* of the rival kings and queens and lesser nobility. This period was Anne's Golden Age; Emily's was still to come.

Charlotte left Roe Head after eighteen months with the silver medal for good conduct and three prizes. She was now sixteen, and on her last day longed to feel like a schoolgirl, to play games and run about like the others; so she suggested to her companions that they should all run round the front garden. Perhaps something tremendous would happen that she would remember for all time. Nothing did. They met no one and were not even fined.

Charlotte home again, not just for the holidays but for good, was like a traveller opening his pack to show what he had been able to gather on his journeyings. Never had she and Branwell been nearer to each other than now, never their collaboration more close. She might teach Emily as she taught Anne, and Emily's spelling might be more like a ten-year-old's than like a fourteen-year-old's, but Charlotte always accepted her as an equal. Emily, whose face could sparkle with mischief, sport and glee, was already a character in her own right, with as absolute a sway over her own opinions as she had over any of her Gondal characters, whereas Anne was tractable and conciliatory, very much the youngest of the family.

Emily and Anne thought their eldest sister wonderful. It was exciting to hear all about school, and Ellen and Mary, and Martha, who was Mary's younger sister and such a great rattle she was known as Miss Boisterous, younger than Emily but older than Anne. They began to do in the parsonage things that Charlotte had done at school, such as walking round the table as they talked when they had the sitting-room to themselves at night.

Charlotte's Roe Head art lessons rekindled their enthusiasm for sketching and painting, and his eldest daughter prevailed on their father to let them have a drawing master. Perhaps one day, if they became proficient enough, they could make money by their sketches.

William Robinson, the portrait painter, came from Leeds to the Haworth parsonage to give them regular lessons. Papa paid him two guineas a visit. This was veritable cornucopia; and before long Branwell was painting in oils. Why should he not become a portrait painter like Mr Robinson? Vista after vista began to open dizzily in front of them for Branwell, and his facility became inflated in his own and his family's eyes into achievement.

London was to be his venue—that was where the Royal Academy was, and the Academy schools. Mr Robinson had arrived in London twelve years before when he was twenty-one with nothing but a letter of introduction to Sir Thomas Lawrence, who agreed to teach him for nothing because, being a genius himself, he recognized one when he saw him. And look where Mr Robinson was today—a famous artist who had painted the portraits of Wellington, the Duke of York and Princess Sophia.

And music. Branwell could play the organ and flute. Listening to music transported him to another plane where all was sublimity. Mr Sutherland, the organist of Keighley Church, walked up the steep brae to the parsonage to give the vicar's children music lessons, and a year after Charlotte's return from school a piano appeared in Mr Brontë's study. Emily was its cleverest exponent, her fleet fingers running up and down its keys.

In September of the year she left school Charlotte made the journey to Birstall to stay with her school friend Ellen Nussey. Branwell escorted her in the hired Haworth gig. Never had he seen anything like this: the sweep of avenue leading to 'The Rydings' with its battlemented roof, the gardens, lawns, rookery, orchard, the superb chestnuts, each fitting into the landscape with the inevitability of a picture. Everywhere he looked he saw something to exclaim at, something he wanted to paint. He could not contain his admiration and excitement. When later that day the time came for him to say goodbye he said to Charlotte: 'I leave you in Paradise.'

But no paradise was perfect for Charlotte. Mrs Nussey, since her husband's death, lived quietly enough amongst her younger sons and daughters, yet there seemed a great many unfamiliar faces for Charlotte to accustom herself to. When a stranger led her in to dinner, she trembled so she could hardly walk and nearly burst into tears. But her friendship with Ellen ripened and they agreed to correspond in French to improve their use of that language. Ellen, however, let the French idea lapse almost at once, and Charlotte soon followed suit. Their correspondence was to last a lifetime.

Next summer the incredible happened. Emily gave up her bed in Charlotte's room to sleep in a spare one beside Tabby, for the parsonage was to have a visitor.

Ellen Nussey drove over to Haworth in her mother's carriage, accompanied by a manservant, for a stay with her friend Charlotte.

5

. . . Summer days were all too short
For all the pleasures crowded there—

Anne Brontë

Miss Nussey, Charlotte's friend, had arrived. They looked
at each other when Aunt went upstairs with her to show
her to her room. Papa was taking care of the manservant,
finding out he had been a sailor, arranging about fodder for
the horse. She was very, very pretty, Charlotte's friend,
with her pleasing expression and slim neck, very ladylike.
And she had come on a visit to stay with them all.

It was quite different from anything Ellen had ever seen
before. She had not known until she came to Haworth that
such places existed. Brought up in a conventional, well-to-
do home, visiting the comfortable, well-to-do houses of
relations, neighbours and friends, with their thick curtains
and hangings, and upholstered furniture, the parsonage at
first struck her as stripped, even bare.

No draperies anywhere, because of Mr Brontë's fear of
fire, or carpeting, except a little in the dining-room and the
parson's study, which was also known as the parlour. No
sprigged or patterned wallpaper, instead all the walls painted
the same dove colour whose plainness framed each shadow
and every reflection. Yet there was such a sparkle about
everything that nothing looked scant and everything
appeared fitting.

And the garden. It was nearly all grass as far as Ellen
could see, with a few thorns and shrubs whose stunted
forms told of the tussle they had with the winds whose

playground it was. But before she left Ellen thought of the garden as a kingdom to them all, with Papa's cherry tree and Emily and Anne's currant bushes.

The parsonage's inhabitants too were quite different from anyone Ellen had ever met before, with a reality about them that was almost startling on first acquaintance. Miss Branwell, for instance, might be small and wear outrageously large old-fashioned caps, a front of false red curls and dated silk dresses, but there was nothing relegated about her. She was quite formidably on the spot, whether she was laughing at your discomfiture when she presented you with her gold snuffbox or—and Miss Branwell was always at her liveliest at tea time—enjoyably arguing with her brother-in-law. And Tabby, the old servant, as much one of the family as any of them. And Mr Brontë himself—he seemed venerable to Ellen (everyone in this household except her contemporaries was very, very old) with his snow-white hair and throat muffled in a cravat. His courtesy made Charlotte's friend feel an honoured guest. He should have been a soldier, that's what he should have been, instead of a clergyman. Perhaps it was the pistols that he discharged every morning between six and seven that made her think that, or because he was so upright, sitting on a plain, uncushioned chair straight as a ramrod.

And Charlotte's brother and sisters. It was not only Branwell's bright red hair which made him unusual looking but the fact that he wore it long, as befitted a poet or genius or artist. He could be very voluble, just as he was on the day he escorted Charlotte to 'The Rydings', his face keen with intelligence. But no spark seems to have glanced from him to waken response in his sister's friend. She and Charlotte and Emily and Anne laughed and made fun of one another and settled to call themselves the quartette; there was no place for a fifth in a quartette. Ellen and Charlotte walked round the table arm in arm in the parlour at night as they talked, just as they had done at Roe Head, with Emily and Anne following suit.

The walks on the moors were the highlights of the day. Not strolls or the circumspect exercise they used to take at school. This was more like release. When Mr Brontë did not send Branwell to accompany them Tabby came to see that no harm happened to her 'childer'. Ellen became one of her bairns too, never to grow up in her eyes. It was high summer, a sea of heather round them, blue heaven above, and the sun brightening on their uplifted faces as they walked.

At school Charlotte used to tell them all she was seeing in an ordinary picture; on the moors it was Emily gleefully pointing out every moss, flower, grass, shade and form. She and Anne forded the streams that crossed their paths and placed stepping-stones for their more sedate sister and her friend. The short-sighted Charlotte was terrified of wild animals, and Emily in high delight would lead her towards some cropping sheep, laughing at her horror when she discovered its nearness. She and Anne took them to a hiding-place they had discovered which they called The Meeting Of The Waters. It was a small oasis where large stones served as chairs for them among the dancing little springs.

Emily was tall and not yet full grown, but it was her eyes you noticed particularly, they were so large. Only she did not look at you much—that was because she was reserved, as Charlotte warned Ellen. Ellen noticed that Charlotte rather deferred to Emily as though she, not Charlotte, were the elder. Certainly she did not talk much, except on the moors where she seemed to be in her element, so that when she did speak her slightest remark did not sound slight but had the force of assertion. Reserve was different from shyness. Reserve was to keep for future use or emergency. Anne was shy, but, given time, you could get near a shy person.

Anne was much the prettiest of the Brontë sisters, with her lovely complexion, not sallow like Emily or Charlotte, naturally curling hair and eyes the colour of certain blue pansies. Emily was fifteen now and beginning to have the disposal of her own time, but Anne was still very much under the surveillance of their aunt. The odd thing about the Brontë girls was that you would notice them, every one of them, but not because they walked about in ugly strong shoes and hideous coloured stockings and clothes that had never been fashionable. Miss Nussey could not quite make that out. It was not as though any of them shone in company, quite the reverse. The only place they shone was at home.

After the parsonage, 'The Rydings' seemed ordinary, a little dull and rather stuffy. And at Haworth Ellen was missed; everyone had liked and admired her. Charlotte, who was lonely and flat without her, wrote to tell her so: 'Emily and Anne say they never saw anyone they liked so well as you.' The only one she did not mention was Branwell.

Charlotte was not only the parson's eldest daughter but the substitute for his wife. She taught in the Sunday School, became a visitor at the day school and inspector of needle-work. Over-conscientious herself, she was particular about the children's work; three threads for each stitch was her rule. Her Sunday School pupils were to remember when they were old women that Miss Brontë could be very sharp-spoken.

It was humiliating to be so poor that your friends had to pay the postage on your letters. The Brontës never had any money to spend. When they wanted frames for their best pictures they gave Mr Wood, the village carpenter, some of their own drawings and paintings in exchange, which he good-humouredly stuffed into a drawer, to be cleared out when it became too full. Presents embarrassed them, they did not know how to accept them, and when Ellen sent her clothes Charlotte went stiff with pride.

The winter was wild and stormy. They were sealed more or less in the house by days of lashing rain or by snow that stoppered up the bridle-path and made impassable the moors. There were so many funerals that the clang of the passing bell was heard with monotonous regularity. Papa was ill and Aunt articulate about the climate she was called upon to endure. But in the dining-room brother and sisters sat in the glow of the firelight planning what was to happen to themselves and plotting the lives of kings and queens.

Charlotte and Branwell were still partners, still using the same writing territory. Out of Glass Town had evolved their own country of Angria, just as Gondal was the creation of Emily and Anne. Branwell's Alexander Rogue was now glorified into Alexander Percy, Earl of Northangerland, still unbelievably tall, still with red hair, and leading a voluptuous life as totally unlike that of his two historians as Elrington Hall with its balconies and archways and exotic flowers was unlike the parsonage. But no longer did Charlotte and Branwell sign themselves WT and UT—We Two and Us Two. They had split into two separate individuals, each seeing the other apart from himself and herself.

The attitude of the only brother to his sisters is revealed in an Angrian story by Charlotte of this period, precious because not only does it reveal the taken-for-granted superiority of the male by the male but Charlotte's unprecedented questioning of that superiority. It is precious also because it echoes the friendly give and take of family parlance in the parsonage.

Asked about his sisters, Branwell replies they are silly creatures not worth talking about. Charlotte is described as a broad dumpy thing and Emily lean and scant with a face the size of a penny. As for Anne, she was nothing, absolutely nothing. 'What! is she an idiot?' he was asked. 'Next door to it', came the brotherly response.

Charlotte's portrait of one Patrick Benjamin Wiggins betrays no trace of the schoolgirl's brush. Its banter is pointed with satire, its good humour barbed with the cutting edge only a home truth can have. Branwell, interested in himself alone, sees his sisters from the outside; Charlotte, interested in everyone and their motives, sees Branwell outside in.

Unerringly she describes him as a lad of sixteen with the face of a man of twenty-five; his hair red, his features not bad, for he had a Roman nose, small mouth and well-turned chin. His figure, though diminutive, was perfectly symmetrical, and of this Patrick Benjamin Wiggins seemed not unconscious from the frequent and complacent looks he cast down at himself. A pair of spectacles garnished his nose, and through these he gazed constantly at the King of Angria's boxing-master, whose breadth of shoulder appeared to attract his sincere admiration, and he pushed out his own small contracted chest to make it appear broader. As a musician he was greater than Bach, as a poet he surpassed Byron, as a painter Charles Lorraine, and as a rebel he snatched the palm from Alexander Rogue himself. Alexander Rogue had as much reality for Charlotte as Bach, Byron and Charles Lorraine.

Emily and Anne's Gondal might be located in the North and South Pacific, but its climate was that of home, swirling mists, trackless moors, hill, dale and mountain. It was his soil that bred the Gondalian, that made him fundamental as the ground he trod, not the handsome cities, cathedrals and palaces shadowy in the background. Country came before love in his loyalties, and treachery was the darkest crime man could commit. War was war, leaving behind its sickening aftermath of death and devastation, exile and imprisonment, ruined countryside. It had none of Angria's trumpet pomp and panoply and chivalric pageantry. And death was death. No magic potion in Gondal to restore hero or heroine to life, no Geni to come to their aid. Each man or woman was his or her own Geni.

Branwell stated he was not satisfied with being a sign painter in the village as Charlotte and 'them things' were with being sempstresses. But Charlotte was not satisfied with her daily routine of walks, sewing, writing, reading and drawing. Ellen went to London, and her friend's imagination became restless with the thought of that great city, apocryphal as Babylon or Nineveh or ancient Rome to her, the glare, the glitter, the dazzling display of London. To be awed by St Paul's and Westminster Abbey, to be in St James's and see for yourself the palace where so many kings had held court, to look on pictures painted by the living hand of the artist, perhaps to glimpse some of London's great personages. She asked Ellen if she would be kind enough to tell her how many performers were in the king's military band—Branwell very much wanted to know.

Music was one of his enthusiasms, and enthusiasms with Branwell had the strength of passions. He would walk into Keighley to hear Spencer's popular band, and sacred music which he heard at orchestral concerts in Leeds, Bradford and Keighley raised him to the peak of ecstasy. Boxing was another enthusiasm. He was a member of the village boxing club which met in the Black Bull Inn, and he could talk knowledgeably about London's great boxers and their form. Indeed there was very little t'vicar's Pat could not talk about, and he was always sure of an admiring audience amongst the villagers. His sisters they seldom saw and never knew, his father strode amongst them on his parochial business, but Pat Brontë (their harsh voices pronounced the surname as one syllable) was their star performer.

They were all on the threshold of life, where the future sweeps to meet the present and the present overtakes the future. Branwell waited for everything to happen, when he would go out into the world and take his place in it, when every moment of the day would tingle with the living of it. A threshold can be a draughty place, and Charlotte sometimes found herself standing still and trying to take stock: doors were shutting behind her, but what was opening? Emily and Anne were waiting for nothing—life was brimming over as it was, so much to do, so much to see to, so much happening every single moment.

The 24th of November 1834 was a Monday—just like any

other Monday. Emily was sixteen and Anne rising fifteen. Emily fed the pheasant known gloriously as Rainbow, Diamond, and Snowflake, and Jasper the dog. Branwell went down to Dr Driver, who lent them *John Bull* and *Blackwood's Magazine*, and brought back the news that Sir Robert Peel was to be invited to stand for Leeds. Emily and Anne had been peeling apples for Charlotte, who was going to make an apple pudding, and nuts and apples for Aunt. Charlotte said she made perfect puddings and that she was of a quick but limited intellect. Was Charlotte referring to Aunt? Tabby told Anne to peel a potato, and Aunt came into the kitchen and said, 'Where are your feet, Anne?' Anne answered, 'On the floor, Aunt.' Papa opened the parlour door and gave Branwell a letter, saying, 'Read this and show it to your aunt and Charlotte.' The Gondals were discovering the interior of Gaaldine. Sally Mosley from the village was washing in the back kitchen. It was past twelve o'clock and Anne and Emily had not tidied themselves yet, or made the beds, or done their lessons, and they wanted to go out to play. They were going to have boiled beef and turnips for dinner, potatoes and apple pudding. The kitchen was in a very untidy state. Neither Anne nor Emily had done her music exercise—B major. Emily waved a pen in Tabby's face to explain everything, and Tabby said she should stop pottering and start peeling a potato. Emily replied, 'O dear, O dear, O dear, I will directly', and took a knife and began peeling. Papa went out a walk. Mr Sutherland was expected.

It is all there, no punctuation, badly spelled and *staccato* with capitals, tumbled on to a scrap of paper folded even smaller to fit a little black pin-box, the first of the four diary papers kept by Emily and Anne. It is written by Emily but signed by both and illustrated by a bit of Lady Juliet's hair done by Anne which just gets on to the tiny sheet.

'Anne and I say I wonder what we shall be like and what we shall be and where we shall be if all goes on well in the year 1874—in which year I shall be in my 57th year and

Anne will be going on in her 55th year, Branwell will be going in his 58th year And Charlotte in her 59th year hoping we shall all be well at that time we close our paper Emily and Anne November the 24 1834.'

Forty years hence—what *would* have happened to them all? But what did anything matter, tomorrow, next week, a month to come, when they had today and everything was happening in the one glorious moment—Sir Robert Peel, the Gondals and Sally Mosley doing the washing in the back kitchen.

The deep raisin and prune shades of November gave place to the vibrant greens and yellows of July. In his study Papa wrote to Mrs Franks, the woman he had wanted to make his second wife, recommending to her his daughters Charlotte and Emily who would shortly be living near her at Roe Head School. His dear little Anne he was keeping at home for another year under her aunt's and his own tuition. His son he was sending to the Royal Academy for Artists in London—his correspondent knew how much he was indebted, under God, to her and other kind friends for their help and every act of kindness. It was Mrs Franks's stepmother, Branwell's godmother, who was paying for her godson's training as a painter and for his expenses in London. He ended his letter on a personal note by telling her his health was very delicate, indeed he had never been well since he left Thornton. Thornton, where his happiest days had been spent, was to him what Penzance was to his sister-in-law. For a delicate man he had weathered the past fifteen years remarkably well with many a mile over rough country.

About the same time Charlotte was writing to her very best friend Ellen Nussey: 'We are all about to divide, break up, separate. Emily is going to school, Branwell is going to London, and I am going to be a governess.'

BOOK TWO

HAY-TIME

I

We sowed in youth a mustard seed,
We cut an almond rod;
We are now grown up to riper age:
Are they buried in the sod?

Charlotte Brontë

THE DRAFT of a letter written to the Royal Academy asking where a probationary student should present his drawings still remains, three fragments of poems scribbled on the back of it. But if Branwell submitted himself at the school with his specimen drawings, he was not admitted. The likelihood is that he did not, for the effect the metropolis had on him can be mapped out by the account he wrote on his return not of Alexander Rogue or the Earl of Northangerland but of one Charles Wentworth. Some have doubted whether he ever reached London. The certainty that he did does not rest on a manuscript but on more than one conclusive proof, such as meeting later a Mr Woolven who saw him first in a tavern in High Holborn.

For the first time in his life the parson's son had money in his pocket, plenty of it to support him in the months to come, and letters of introduction to those able and willing to help him. It was two days' journey from Haworth to the mightiest city in the world where he was to begin a life that was worth the living. The parsonage with its tombs, his family, uncouth Haworth and its uncouth inhabitants—he had left them all behind to start on his greatest adventure. Every revolution of the coach's wheels was bearing him nearer to the London he had all his life looked upon as a fountain of happiness where all his thirsts would be satisfied.

His father's parting advice that no one could have real happiness without working for it turned itself over in his mind. 'Exertion', he had said, 'is the nutshell which holds pleasure; crack it, and it can be found. Otherwise, never. And the harder the shell, the better the nut.' But why should he labour? There were plenty of paths in life, the problem was to know which he should take.

The farther he travelled from home and the deeper he penetrated into the unfamiliar autumn landscape, the unsteadier became his equilibrium. This was something for which he was quite unprepared. He should be mounting each moment, savouring it to the full. Instead he found every peak of jubilation had its sickening descent. What if happiness did not consist in his dreams coming true but in the dreaming of them?

On his arrival he made his way to the Chapter Coffee House in Paternoster Row—his father had drawn out a rough plan to guide him to its whereabouts. He felt a thrill of excitement when he was shown to his room, but that ebbed almost at once, leaving the shore of his mind cold and wrinkled. He longed for supper, which he had in the coffee room, and although tired after so much travelling he sat up all night instead of undressing and going to bed.

In the morning it was wonderful to reflect that he had not a relation in the city. No Papa to tell him he must not go about doing nothing and caring for nothing but building air castles, no Charlotte to shame him with her assiduous energy. He took out all his letters of introduction, read them over, folded them up again, thought of the money in his pocket and his new independence, had breakfast and went out into the streets of London.

Amongst these passers-by he felt wild in his country clothes, as though he had not a penny in the world, a sixpenny bit to his name. But no one troubled to notice him, each was too intent on his own business to look his way. He threaded the dense and bustling crowds and walked for hours, neither eating nor drinking nor calling a coach, in too much of a turmoil to stop and examine anything. He had that uneasy feeling when rest is torment and ease begets stupor, but sparks struck from his mind as he saw names and recognized places that recalled glorious events, associations, personages. He wandered to a bridge, leaned on the parapet and, the sun shining full upon him, watched for hours the traffic of merchant ships on the river below.

Then the tears came, spurting from his eyes. The flashes of glory which he had felt when he recognized streets and buildings were only flashes—nothing made up for the years of dullness that preceded today. Instead of exaltation and exhilaration he was filled with dejection. He looked down at the oily grey waters of the Thames and thought of the clear waters of the becks and burns in their summer loneliness at home. When at last he turned to retrace his steps he did not raise his head. He entered the Chapter Coffee House, stretched himself on a sofa and lay there, unsleeping, until it was dark.

The following day passed very like his first. He delivered none of his letters of introduction nor went to show his specimen drawings at the Academy School.

On the third morning he found himself outside St Paul's, its enormous dome swelling into the cloudless sky, but he was unable to enter in case it did not come up to expectations. Realizing that his instinctive fear was of ending his pleasure by approaching reality, he suddenly dashed through his dread, walked up the grand flight of steps and entered.

He lost all sense of time while he glided about in the still shadow of coolness beneath the vast roof and sublime dome. He looked up at it until it seemed to rise and soar beyond his sight. He lay down on his back and still looked up at it until he thought it would thunder down in ruins on his head. From nave to aisles he moved, beneath the chancel screen with the gilded organ pipes above, into the choir to the high, dark, aged mass of original stone near the altar. When the stunning crash of the bell struck one it did not so much break as express yet more silence.

He had believed that if he had the free range of the British Museum, including the library, for a week he would feel he was in Paradise. But Paradise was all about him and not limited to a week or to libraries, picture galleries and museums, and instead of being inspired he was overpowered by the genius and achievements of other men. He trailed through the passing days, in his aimless wandering coming across certain localities and notable buildings. Then he knelt on the lowest step of the museum and kissed the stone. But he knew that these acted on him like little squibs of rum which served only to make him more depressed.

His best evenings were those spent in the snug Castle Tavern in High Holborn run by the retired champion boxer Tom Spring. Here, where pictures of famous pugilists with blacksmith arms hung next to equally famous racehorses, there was conviviality, stir and cheer. You rubbed shoulders with your fellowmen instead of slipping unnoticed between them, flitting like a ghost through the reality of London; you heard your own voice and, sweeter still, others heard it too; you were even called upon to act as umpire when an argument arose about the dates of certain battles.

What was bound to happen happened. The money to keep him in the months to come with which he had left Haworth dwindled to near vanishing point. For the first time since he had arrived in London he hurried through the crowded and troubled streets to reach the Chapter Coffee House, packed his belongings, made himself respectable for the journey he was about to undertake and drove to Trafalgar Square to catch the mail home, his letters of introduction still undelivered.

T'vicar's Pat was home again. Haworth could scarcely believe it when they heard, it was but the other day he had left first thing in the morning in the carrier's cart to catch the Keighley coach. Before he even reached London he had been set upon by sharpers and robbed of most of his money—that was the information that filtered from the close-lipped parsonage. He was slight as a bairn, t'vicar's Pat, and would be an easy prey for artful dodgers. It was said his father had to send money to fetch him back to Haworth, for he had been well and truly skinned of near every penny.

Home again in the parsonage amongst the tombs. Charlotte was away governessing at Roe Head School—he must have been glad of that. There was plenty to face without her when he related his sharper's story to Papa and Aunt, when holes began to be poked through it, when there was no corner into which he could escape from his father's blue eye.

Charlotte and Emily had left for Roe Head before his departure for London. Only Anne had been at home to speed their brother on his way.

Ellen Nussey said Emily and Anne were so close they might have been twins, and without Emily Anne felt as bereft as though cut off from her other self. It was she who had changed, not the places they both loved, because she was alone. No Emily to bump into on their walks as they discussed what they were going to make happen next in Gondal, for the moors were to them what the stage was to an actor rehearsing his part, trying out his voice, getting into the feel of it. Shyness locked the youngest Brontë into herself even from her own family, except from Emily. With Emily alone she had that blessed taken-for-granted closeness of two parts of a whole.

Christmas, when Charlotte and Emily would be home for the holidays, seemed very far away, but as it happened Emily returned in October, long before Christmas, unable to endure for even less than three months her homesickness. An alarmed Charlotte wrote to Papa that Emily was going into a decline and he, like Charlotte, remembering Maria and Elizabeth, sent for her at once. It was arranged that Anne should go to Roe Head in her stead. Emily had scarcely returned when Anne left to fill her place.

Thus Emily, not Anne, was the sister with Branwell in the

months to come. Between the one who had returned to her Promised Land and the other who had turned his back on his was an acceptance characteristic of Emily's few relationships. To her the individual was inviolate, to be accepted as he was without criticism or questioning, as she expected to be accepted.

To her, severance from home had been like annihilation; return was restoration that healed and repaired her sense of failure. To Branwell the return to the ordinariness of everyday, the staleness of familiarity, was well-nigh unbearable. From his desperation at finding himself back where he had started came the best poems he had yet written, with the revealing titles, 'Misery', 'Memory', 'Still and bright, in twilight shining', 'Sleep, mourner, sleep!' At the same time he employed himself with his boyish Angrian tales and in writing to the editor of *Blackwood's Magazine*. When reading these letters, with their incipient grandeur mania, and certain other writings of Branwell, one recognizes that his feelings and hallucinatory sensations are like symptoms of a functional disease such as epilepsy. It is known that he was bitten by a mad dog when he was eight and that the wound was not cauterized.

Not through his art but through his writing was he going to make his name. All he needed was an outlet for his work, and what better than *Blackwood's Magazine*, which he had revered from childhood? With one letter he enclosed specimens of his work, in another he asked to be given a subject upon which he could write to show his prowess. He stated that he had thought of a series of articles the design of which was superior to anything they had yet printed, offered to make the three-hundred-mile journey to Edinburgh to see them, and wrote that the idea of aiding any other periodical was horribly repulsive to him.

The editor was adjured, cajoled and invited not to act like a commonplace person, to be a man and prove that what his correspondent wrote was true. Did he think his magazine so perfect that no addition to its power was either possible or desirable? His correspondent was not one of the wretched writers of the day: he possessed strength to aid *Blackwood's* beyond some of its authors. They had just lost through death one of their finest contributors, James Hogg, the Ettrick Shepherd. As these men died, *Blackwood's* would decay unless their places were supplied by others like them. He concluded: 'You have lost an able writer in James Hogg, and God grant you may gain one in Patrick Branwell Brontë.'

Blackwood's answered none of his letters, which they thought were written by a lunatic, but kept them in their files as curiosities.

Both Charlotte and Anne suffered from acute home-sickness at Roe Head, but they were different from Emily, to whom her native environment was as necessary as air. Miss Wooler had not taken to her, she was a difficult pupil whom they had been unable to help however kind they were. Anne, despite her shyness, was much more likeable, able to conform to school routine, to benefit from her lessons. But she did not make a niche for herself as Charlotte had done when she was a pupil, and she formed no friendships. Anne had no Ellen Nussey or Mary Taylor.

Charlotte had understood only too well how Emily felt, removed from the existence she had always known to a school humming with its own activities, time-tables and supervision. She knew that every morning Emily awoke, the vision of home and the moors rushed upon her. But she had less understanding of her younger sister, perhaps because naturally enough she did not realize that the tractable Anne called for understanding.

It was a pity too that visiting took so much out of Charlotte, for she was unable to make a way for the younger girl, and no enjoyment was reaped from what should have been pleasurable. There was the fatal invitation from Mrs Franks, Anne's godmother, to spend a whole long pro-tracted week of their precious holidays with her before they escaped to the bliss of home. In desperation Charlotte wrote that Papa would not be willing to dispense with them for so long. But Papa, always pleased for his children to have what he would have enjoyed, wrote to their hostess telling her to keep them for the suggested time.

Charlotte was a born writer, and her efforts to suppress her creative longings took as much toll as enduring the agonies of childbirth without being able to bring forth. Teaching was totally uncongenial to her, and the conflict between doing what she hated, her duty, and her longing to write, temptation, made her a battleground. Duty won, but this was no victory; this was attrition.

No one would have guessed by looking at Miss Brontë, small and with a neatness about her dress and person that enhanced them both, what was taking place within her. As a teacher she was particular and painstaking, but too withdrawn to fire her pupils with her enthusiasms. No one thought Miss Brontë, with her Quaker-like exterior, had enthusiasms, ardours, dreams; that she housed not only passions but the passion of the artist.

There were of course good moments even at Roe Head. Watching at the dining-room window to see George Nussey, as he drove past in his gig, whirl a packet over the garden wall, the delight of running out to find letters from Ellen inside. And companionable evenings sitting with Miss Wooler; they were equals then, not even headmistress with her under-teacher. Miss Wooler obviously considered that what the over-conscientious Charlotte needed when released from her duties was company, and when she could she arranged with Mary Taylor or Ellen Nussey for her to stay with them at week-ends. But these visits were not altogether respites to Charlotte in her increasingly neurotic state. For one thing, they served to make the return to bondage worse by comparison; for another, they deprived her of the little solitude she had; and for a third, owing to the incessant tug-of-war going on inside her, she had begun to feel guilt over even the most innocent pleasures.

And there were the holidays at home when they were all

together again and the world swung to rights. Health always returned to Charlotte the moment she crossed the threshold of home where she could be herself. Haworth and home—they awoke sensations which lay dormant everywhere else. Ellen came to stay with her, and the days were bright with companionship as though high summer would last forever.

But back at school it was back to teach, teach, teach. In this woman's world, without the stimulation and interest of masculine contact, she was never alone. Long weary walks with her pupils—if those girls only knew how she loathed their company. Sitting in the schoolroom by herself she heard the bells of Huddersfield parish church and felt she could have written gloriously. At that moment a dolt came in with her lesson to be corrected, and she wanted to vomit. Branwell sent her what he had been writing lately—a letter from Northangerland to his daughter; she lived on that for days. The moments when she could think her own thoughts were all stolen, delicious as forbidden fruit. Then her mind would relax from the stretch it had been on all day, and she could return to the ark which for her floated alone, alone, alone, on a desolate boundless sea. Then she could people her world with her own characters, shining in gay circles, their faces looking up at her, their eyes smiling, beckoning, coming and going in throngs and crowds, speaking audibly to her. But her ideas were too shattered to form any definite picture as they would have done at home. She could not write of them except in total solitude; she hardly dare think of them.

Life was racing on, she was nearly twenty-one, and what had she achieved, what was she achieving, slaving at teaching day in, day out? After clothing herself and Anne she had nothing left, and she had hoped she would be able to save something, however small. She had forgotten only the other day to return Ellen's work-bag to her—that warned her she was getting past her prime. What if Aunt's ghastly Calvinistic doctrines were true? If they were, she was already the outcast she felt. That wind she was listening to this evening—she had heard it at home as it stormed over the parsonage, down the graveyard and round the church. Perhaps Branwell and Emily were listening to it at this very moment and thinking of her and Anne.

No private journal or letters such as Charlotte's to Ellen Nussey remain to reveal Anne's thoughts at this time. It is unlikely they were ever penned. She would not write to Emily of her unhappiness when she had taken Emily's place at school. Also she was by nature more reticent than Charlotte. Charlotte could bemoan and dramatize the happenings of the day, Anne suffered them in silence. But she had one outlet, her poetry.

Verses by Lady Griselda and other Gondal characters were written by Anne, parted from Emily and home. Amongst the green lush beauty of her new surroundings, the north wind Charlotte heard spoke to her too of the countryside she remembered—lonely, wild, majestic, bleak and dreary, stern and lovely as it used to be. And already, aged sixteen, the schoolgirl Anne was looking back to past happiness that would never come again. The theme of imprisonment was dominant in both hers and Emily's poetry, but with this difference. Anne's characters remained in prison, having done with life and all the bustling world above. Emily's had visitations so tremendous in their impact that the prisoner did not ask for freedom.

At home she also was writing poems:

> *High waving heather, 'neath stormy blasts bending,*
> *Midnight and moonlight and bright shining stars:*
> *Darkness and glory rejoicingly blending,*
> *Earth rising to heaven and heaven descending.*

That moment of consummation when earth met heaven and heaven transformed earth globed eternity.

The secret of contentment is fulfilment, but Emily was not fulfilled, although she was breathing once more the air of home. She was conscious of a sense of failure at being unable to endure exile, to bear what Anne was bearing, to have forced Anne to take her place. She brooded over her weakness as she helped Tabby about the house and tramped the moors with Branwell or by herself and Jasper until she felt she could live with it no longer. The determination formed that she would take a governess's post to prove to herself she could stand anything.

Branwell was occupied with various ploys. He was made a Freemason although he was well under the age, but both his father's sexton and parish clerk pulled the necessary strings. The Lodge of the Three Graces held their annual dinner at the Black Bull and their regular meetings in a private house in a little street which came to be known as Lodge Street. It was on occasions such as these that Branwell was at his best, accepted as the life and soul of the party by his elders, playing the piano for their songs and leading the toasts. At the same time he became the secretary of the Haworth Temperance Society and he taught in the Sunday School.

Like Charlotte, he was not cut out to be a teacher, but he had none of her control. He fairly crackled with impatience as his yokel scholars read out in their slow plodding voices. 'Get on! Get on!' he screamed at one, 'or I'll turn you out of the class.' 'Tha willn't, tha old Irish——' replied his pupil, rising from his desk to thud from the room under his own steam.

When Charlotte was home for the Christmas holidays their writing became the chief topic of discussion. If only someone on whose judgment they could absolutely rely would read something they wrote and pronounce whether or not they should continue: someone like Southey, the Poet Laureate, for instance, or the divine Wordsworth.

With the intrepidity of the shy, Charlotte wrote to Southey, Branwell to Wordsworth. This meant so much to her she would have dared anything. Southey was better known as a poet and she enclosed poems for his criticism. She, who was to become one of the greatest novelists writing in the English language, wrote poetry that had none of the limpid quality of Anne's, or the drama and power of Emily's. Even Branwell at his unsteady best was a better poet than she.

After the dispatch of their letters came the long tedium of waiting. Would they receive replies or would they not? Perhaps one would come today. Two, three months passed, and Charlotte was back at Roe Head. She would never hear now. But she did. Southey, the Poet Laureate, wrote to her explaining he had been from home, which was why she had not heard from him sooner.

Her letter to him has not survived, but the poet thought it flighty. His reply is kindly enough but couched in the language of one whose fires of youth have now not even the glow of embers.

He was a voluminous letter writer and his to her was lengthy. He replied that she obviously possessed, and in no inconsiderable degree, what Wordsworth called the faculty of verse—he was not depreciating it when he said that in these times this was not rare. He warned her that the day-dreams in which she indulged were likely to induce a distempered state of mind and that literature could not and ought not to be the business of a woman's life. The more she was engaged in her proper duties, the less leisure would she have for it, even as an accomplishment and a recreation. She could of course write poetry for its own sake—the less she aimed at, the more likely she was to deserve and finally obtain it.

Charlotte's measure can be gauged by the spirit with which she accepted this advice. She had aimed at the sun and caught a crow, but her eyes were still blinded with light. Southey, the Poet Laureate, had written to her. She thanked him for his kind and wise advice and told him his letter was consecrated. 'I trust I shall never more feel ambitious to see my name in print; if the wish should arise, I'll look at Southey's letter and suppress it. It is honour enough for me that I have written to him, and received an answer.'

Southey was so touched by her letter that he wrote to tell

her so, inviting her to come to see him if she ever visited the Lakes. She penned on his letter: 'Southey's advice to be kept for ever. My twenty-first birthday, Roe Head, April 21, 1837.' If she lived to be an old woman, thirty years hence, she would remember her longing for a writing career as a bright dream.

Branwell, who had no judgment either of his own or other's work, did not enclose examples of his best poetry to Wordsworth but some infantile verses. His letter had none of the excesses of those he sent to *Blackwood's*. One sentence alone struck an unfortunate note, but it was short and did not falsify the tenor of the whole, written by one desperately craving for guidance. 'As you would hold a light to one in utter darkness—as you value your own kindheartedness—*return* me an *answer*, if but one word, telling me whether I should write on, or write no more. Forgive undue warmth, because my feelings in this matter cannot be cool; and believe me, sir, with deep respect, your really humble servant. P. B. Brontë.' The very contraction of his full name into initials betokened an unconscious shifting of emphasis for the better.

This letter to Wordsworth alone survives, but there must have been at least one other, for we know that the poet, who did not reply, told Southey it disgusted him, containing as it did gross flattery of Wordsworth and plenty of abuse of other poets, including Southey.

Neither Charlotte nor Branwell knew it, but they had parted company. They, who had done everything together, no longer were going the same way. Charlotte through her own sustained efforts was on the road uphill, Branwell on the way down.

It was necessary for conveyances descending Haworth's precipitate village street to have good brakes, which was what Branwell's vehicle lacked. For a time the flagstones set edgeways to retard wheels and give horses a surer grip kept him on the road, but it was only for a time.

2

I'm happiest now when most away
I can tear my soul from its mould of clay,
On a windy night when the moon is bright,
And my eye can wander through worlds of light—
When I am not, and none beside—
Nor earth, nor sea, nor cloudless sky—
But only spirit wandering wide
Through infinite immensity—

Emily Brontë

HAWORTH CHURCH was a moorland church, its square tower like a keep, its stout stone weathered black. It was old and its interior as unembellished as its exterior, the high box pews large enough to house whole families. The focus was the big three-decker pulpit with its sounding-board and inscription: 'I determined not to know any thing among you, save Jesus Christ, and Him crucified.'

The first thing Mr Brontë did when he entered it on Sunday was to place his watch on the cushion of the desk to time his sermon. He preached with nothing in his hands, which meant he preached extempore. His congregation would have thought very little of him had he done otherwise. They sat stolid and apathetic under him until he began his sermon, then they fixed him with their gaze, measuring him and what he was telling them, their expressions combative and considering. He never preached above their heads but to them, and he never left the pulpit until he had made parable or text clear, concluding with the words: 'Through our adorable Lord and Saviour, Jesus Christ.'

He was still as straight as he had ever been, but his hair now was the fine silver which red hair becomes with age, and his sight was beginning to fail him. Well, time stayed for none, in pulpit or in pew. Because his eyes were no longer strong he had to have a curate to assist him for a time, yon Mr Hodgson who had stayed in West Lane. Mr Hodgson had thought the world of his vicar but found him nervous, sending at the last moment for him to officiate as he was too unwell to do so himself as arranged.

The vicarage pew was the roomy one near the pulpit. The vicar's Pat did not share it with the family, but accompanied his Sunday School class to another one. Mighty little he ever heard of his father's sermon, sitting there in the corner to catch the light from the window on the book he was reading. Nor would he brook any interruption from any of his scholars, but would go behind the culprit and, twisting a lock of his hair round his finger, corkscrew him to his feet.

The only time they ever saw Miss Branwell was in church. They always said she was a bit of a tyke from the look of her, and so it proved when Tabby fell on the icy main street the winter before and broke her leg, for Miss Branwell was all for packing her off to her sister's for good. Sensible enough when you came to think of it—Tabitha Aykroyd must be nearer seventy than sixty and past her working days. But the parson's lasses would have none of that. Tabby had tended them when they were wee and helpless and they would tend her when she was old and stricken. Not a mouthful of food would they swallow until the old tyke came round to their way of thinking.

Miss Brontë always tried to hide herself from observation, making herself even smaller than she was, but the Emily one sat straight as her father, her back to the pulpit. On the whole they thought they liked her better than Miss Brontë. Not that they ever came in contact with her; she did not teach in the Sunday School like the other three, but the girls from the village who went to help at the parsonage said she was real jovial and hearty with them. A deal of folk thought her the cleverest of them all, but she was so timid she could not frame to let it out. They were all timid, the vicar's lasses, but she was the timidest of the three, turning tail like a wild thing if any boy or man from the village happened in the parsonage.

As for the youngest, Miss Anne—they had always noticed folk with a skin like hers that flushed as you looked at her were not long for this world. The wonder was she had lasted till now, having to be dosed and given inhalations since she was small, but there she was taller than Miss Brontë—her and the Emily one growing fast, taller than most young ladies you saw.

Anne sat next to Aunt in the family pew where she always sat. Soon she would be returning to school with Charlotte. She had received a prize for good conduct just as Charlotte had when she was a pupil. Anne's book was Watt's *On the Improvement of the Mind*, and Miss Wooler had written on it that it was with her kind love. Miss Wooler was indeed very kind, but kindness did not make a bridge across from her to you. Only with your very own, only with Emily, was there no need of a bridge.

She and Emily had written their new diary paper on Monday, which was Branwell's twentieth birthday. Emily had illustrated it with a picture of herself and Anne sitting at the table in the drawing-room wondering what they should put in. Emily guessed that in four years' time, when they came to write their new diary papers, they would all be right and tight as they were now, comfortable at home. Anne hoped they would still be comfortable, but guessed they would all be somewhere else. She found herself wondering where they could all possibly be. So much had happened since she and Emily had written their last diary papers less than three years before—it had been winter then, now it was summer. Emily had gone to school and come home, she had started and was still at school, Branwell had gone to London and returned home. Charlotte was still teaching at Roe Head. Next term the school was moving to Dewsbury Moor, a distance of some two miles from Roe Head. She and Emily knew where the snow lay deepest.

Papa was beginning his sermon. Anne heard him ask why true believers, having the promise of life to come, should create for themselves artificial sorrows, and thus disfigure the garment of gospel peace with the garb of sighing and sorrowing? But how could you be a true believer when your sin separated you from your Redeemer? Every time you had an asthmatic attack you came face to face with death and what lay in store for you because you fell so far short. That was God warning you, as Aunt had warned you, of your unpreparedness to meet Him, but no matter how often you were warned you were still ill-equipped for your Judgment Day.

Heald's House might be only a distance of two miles from Roe Head, but when she and Charlotte returned to school it was to a complete change of surroundings. Miss Wooler was talking of her retirement and Heald's House was smaller than imposing Roe Head. It stood in a garden, not grounds, and was much older, as the date 1569 on the corner-stone testified, with unexpected flights of stairs leading to hidden rooms, sloping floors and out-of-the-way windows. Like most dwellings of its period it had a text inscribed on its lintel to bless or warn those who passed in and out below—that on Heald's House was 'Say God be Here'.

During this, the winter term, Anne caught a cold she was unable to throw off. Charlotte, immersed in her own miseries, suddenly woke up to the fact that her un-complaining sister was ill. Her short hack of a cough, her difficulty and pain in breathing, brought back to the older sister what had happened to Maria and Elizabeth. Perhaps her anxiety exaggerated the delicate Anne's symptoms. Miss Wooler, on the other hand, as probably minimized them—everyone had coughs or colds or both, which were only natural to the season of the year. Anne's would just have to run its course.

The headmistress had come to depend more and more on

her responsible teacher whom she hoped to groom to take over from her on her retirement. But Charlotte did not fit readily into plans made for her. Also she had to remove from her doorstep the unwanted load of the knowledge that Anne had reached such a pass through neglect. A scene flared up between the two women, with Charlotte taking the offensive, ostensibly over Miss Wooler's indifference to Anne's health.

Very wisely, Miss Wooler wrote to Mr Brontë to tell him how she had been taken to task, and reproached most bitterly. Papa tactfully replied that Charlotte's apprehensions had caused her undue warmth and, as it was nearing the Christmas holidays, told his daughters to come home. Anne did not return to school; through Miss Wooler's kindness she had remained a year longer than was intended, a total of two years and three months.

Both she and Charlotte passed through a religious crisis while one was a pupil and the other a teacher. Anne received much solace from a Moravian bishop who visited her while she was ill and was able to lead her beyond arid Mount Sinai to a green place of hope and trust. But although she could reject for others her aunt's doctrine of damnation, she with her too tender conscience was never to free herself entirely from the sense of her own unworthiness. Like the path of the pilgrim Bunyan, every step of her way had to be fought for and was hard-won.

Mary Taylor put her finger unerringly on the mark with her comment that Charlotte was free from religious melancholy when she was tolerably well. Writing was her health, and without that stimulus she was a prey to self-examination, doubts and gloom. Her despondency was more active than Anne's and took the form of actual hypochondria, when her nights were tormented with hideous dreams and her days made joyless with depression.

On her return alone to Heald's House her nerves became such that she, normally so self-controlled, would scream at a sudden noise. Miss Wooler prevailed on her to see a doctor, who advised her, as she valued her life—to quote Charlotte's dramatic description to Ellen—to return home. She left Dewsbury Moor, which had become a poisoned place to her, for good in the spring.

That her state of mind blackened everything, and in certain cases everyone she looked upon, she was well aware. When she looked back upon these days she could write to Miss Wooler that she could have been no better companion for her than a stalking ghost. 'I remember I felt my in-compacity to *impart* pleasure fully as much as my powerless-ness to *receive* it.' By this time she knew that her headmistress, like good wine, improved with the keeping.

Emily had taken the post as teacher at Miss Patchett's school some four miles out of Halifax. Law Hill was a square, three-storeyed building which gave a curious impression not so much of emptiness but of being only a façade with nothing behind it. Approached by an in-credibly steep path, its sightless-looking windows were seen at a far distance. A farm was attached and, across the yard, a building which served as schoolroom. There were some forty pupils and the school had an excellent reputation, as did its headmistress, a handsome woman in her mid-forties who was a redoubtable horsewoman.

One of Emily's pupils remembered her fondness for the school dog which, she once characteristically told her class of small girls, was dearer to her than they were, but she was not unpopular. Charlotte wrote to Ellen that she feared Emily would never stand it—hard labour from six o'clock in the morning until nearly eleven at night, with only one half-hour off for exercise. But Emily stood it, probably for at least eighteen months.

Her safety valve was her poetry, and the fact that she was able to write so much, although fragmentary, proves that despite the hard labour she must have had some time by and to herself. All three Brontë girls were introspective. Their external existence was like the husk protecting and preserv-ing the kernel, and their temperaments acted like climate.

Anne's temperament was more despondent than her
sisters', but she was the one of the three most successful at
adapting herself to the circumstances she met outside her
habitat. Charlotte's interior life was the storehouse of her
imagination, and she needed freedom and tranquillity of
mind to quarry this richness. Both Anne and Charlotte,
despite their love of home, wanted to go out into the
world, Anne to do something useful such as earning her
living, Charlotte to go where there was life and movement.

But Emily was not a seeker; she was a seer, not in the
ordinary sense of the word, which is that of soothsayer, but
one to whom vision is granted. That moment of consummation when the visionary and his vision become one was
not denied her. She did not seek, she waited for it, and such
was its fulfilment that a lifetime seemed short to clothe its
splendour.

Even more than her sisters, away from home she was
haunted by all that was familiar and dear, the old church
tower and garden wall, the cloudy skies and long low hills
simplified as childhood. At Miss Patchett's everything was
alien. The fine views over the Calder valley circled by
heights blue with distance said nothing to her. This was not
home. A dull day reminded her of those days at Haworth
that sometimes come in summer's blaze when the earth was
motionless and the green on the hill deepened. When May
flowers opened and leaves unfolded, when bees were in
every blossom and birds on every tree, she remembered the
soft unclouded blue of a summer's day on the moors
behind the parsonage, when the earth was bright as Eden
used to be and she lay on her back amongst the long
grasses bending over her. She neither dreamed nor slept
then, she lapsed away. She was sure the soul was free to
leave its body. And she loved December as much as July's
golden gleam, the wintry light over flowerless moors, a tree
whitening in the whirl of snow, tempest in the air.

But unconsciously she was absorbing impressions, sights
and sounds, the life of a farm geared to cattle going out to

pasture and returning to be milked, the rough servants clumping in and out of the farmhouse knotted around with squat outbuildings, earth furrowed by a plough, rutted with cartwheels, a road beaten into the moss by hoof and pad. The house itself creaked with its story of the man who had built it seventy years earlier after he filched from his benefactor most of his property.

At about the same time as Emily left home to be a teacher Branwell is said to have gone to a school as an usher, but he did not survive it for longer than a term. His shock of carroty hair and small stature made him too easy a butt for both pupils and staff.

On his return home Aunt paid for him to go to Leeds and work in his master's studio. This was cheaper than Mr Robinson coming to him, but even so it entailed his spending a night away each painting lesson. When it was decided he was capable of setting up as a portrait painter himself, Bradford was settled upon. Where better, inhabited as it was by his father's old friends who could keep an eye on him, and a thriving community amongst whom he could surely build up a clientele?

Again his family rallied and a studio was rented for him in Fountain Street. Now he would fulfil himself, he was on his own, his circle fellow artists like himself, poets, mezzotint engravers, some not setting out as he was on the road to fame but had already arrived. He met the spectacular Halifax sculptor Joseph Leyland and his brother Francis, bookseller and painter. It was a circle of kindred spirits in which he could take his place, expand, reach his full stature, meet them on their own ground, their clubs the Bull's Head and the George Hotel, the New Inn and the Talbot.

His landlady's family, the Kirbys, thought him a steady, industrious and self-respecting young gentleman. He liked their little daughter to dine with him sometimes because she was so pretty, always smiling, and her cheerful prattle charmed him. Francis Leyland remembered him as of gentlemanlike appearance, a little below middle height, with a voice of ringing sweetness, whose utterance and use of English were perfect. Small boys enjoyed meeting him in Bradford's streets not only because he handed them out pennies but because he joked with them.

Uncle Morgan, his father's oldest friend who had been Maria's godfather, found him lodgings and was his first client. He brought him another, even more important than himself, the vicar of Bradford. Mr and Mrs Kirby commissioned him to paint their pictures, and that of their little daughter. He executed self-portraits to keep his hand in while he waited for other commissions to come his way. He would have painted Nancy Garrs, their old nurse who now lived in Bradford, but she laughed him off with the excuse that she was not good-looking enough, and was photographed instead. No sitters made their way to Fountain Street. Bradford's prosperity was derived from the woollen trade: it had little interest in the arts and a glut of better-known artists to supply the little it had.

A fellow artist, looking at Branwell's work in later years, conceded he could catch a likeness, was a fine draughtsman and knew how to place his work, all necessary attributes for a portrait painter. But he came to the conclusion that he had never been instructed in the right mode of mixing colours, for the pigments he used, the vital flesh tints, had all but vanished, leaving little but boiled oil.

But Branwell had worked under a fine master whose other pupils did not reveal this failing. The likelihood is that it was not lack of instruction but a failure to carry out what he had been taught that was responsible for his falling short. Nor had he ever studied anatomy or the antique. After he left Bradford his landlady complained to a fellow artist he had not completed his pictures of them. 'How can I come paddling to Bradford with my wallet on my back in order to varnish her portraits?' Branwell demanded, warm with indignation, from Haworth. To silence her chattering he paid his fellow artist, who had also been one of Mr

Robinson's pupils, to complete them for him. Of all Branwell's portraits, those of his landlord and landlady are the most finished, the two in which another man had a hand.

He and Emily were at home on holiday in June 1838 when Mary and Martha Taylor came on a visit. To Charlotte the society of the Taylors was one of the most rousing pleasures she knew, and never had the parsonage been gayer than during their visit.

The Taylor family were as unconventional as the Nusseys were conventional. The two girls had voiced their dominant father's views since the days when they had worn muslin dresses and sashes. They were furious Radicals, stout Republicans, intolerant Dissenters and ardent feminists. Who said women were inferior to men, unless it was men, and why should sisters not have the same opportunities as their brothers? When Mary was asked what her religion was she had replied that was between God and herself. 'That's right', said Emily from where she lay on the hearthrug. Mary was determined her life would be life, not a black trance like a toad's buried in marble. Better to try all things and find them empty than to try nothing and leave your mind a blank. That was what the parable in the Bible really meant about the man who buried his talent in a napkin, the despicable sluggard.

Mary saw the parsonage inhabitants quite differently from Ellen Nussey. Miss Branwell, for instance, who kept the three Brontë girls sewing charity clothing not for the good of the recipients but of those who sewed. And Charlotte with her first-class brain accepted such treatment as natural. 'Aunt' corrected Mary for using the coarse word 'spitting'. She was very odd in appearance in her antediluvian clothes, very precise. As for 'Papa', he struck Mary as the soul of selfishness who seemed to be under the impression that his children, particularly Charlotte, existed solely to minister to his comfort. That outrageous cravat he wore; every time he had a sore throat, or thought he was going to have one, he gave it another turn round his neck. He used white silk lute-string to cover it too—Charlotte said it was his one extravagance. They helped her to wind the white sewing-silk for him in the evening.

Charlotte wrote to Ellen that there was such a noise about her she could not write any more—Mary playing the piano, Martha chattering as fast as her little tongue could run and Branwell standing beside her, laughing at her vivacity. But as always Charlotte could not trust happiness. When she saw Mary's fey spirits she remembered how Miss Wooler used to say she was too pretty to live. She imagined Mary's bright colour was hectic, as Maria's and Elizabeth's had been; she even believed that Mary's breath came short as theirs had done.

But she was wrong about the cause of what she took to be symptoms. Mary's radiance and happiness were because she was falling in love with Branwell.

3

A Roland for your Oliver
We think you've justly earned;
You sent us such a valentine,
Your gift is now returned.
We cannot write or talk like you;
We're plain folks every one;
You've played a clever jest on us,
We thank you for the fun.
Believe us when we frankly say
(Our words, though blunt, are true,)
At home, abroad, by night or day,
We all wish well to you—

Charlotte Brontë

CHARLOTTE had not to think twice before refusing her first offer of marriage. It came, by letter, from Henry Nussey, one of Ellen's numerous brothers, who was a curate. Charlotte knew what manner of woman would suit him. 'The character should not be too marked, ardent, and original, her temper should be mild, her piety undoubted, her spirits even and cheerful, and her *personal attractions* [the writer underlined these two words] sufficient to please your eyes and gratify your just pride. As for me, you do not know me; I am not the serious, grave, cool-headed individual you suppose; you would think me romantic and eccentric; you would say I was satirical and severe.'

Henry Nussey had written to her on his twenty-seventh birthday, on the same day that he had received a decisive no from his one-time vicar whose daughter he had asked in marriage. Ten days later he recorded in his diary: 'Received an unfavourable report from C.B. The will of the Lord be done.'

77

Charlotte's second proposal came a month or two after her first, and from another clergyman. But this young Irishman, fresh from Dublin University, was totally different from grave, temperate Henry Nussey. He was witty, ardent and clever, and Charlotte met him only once.

A wife was a very necessary adjunct for a clergyman and the ground must be well prospected for a suitable partner. Mr Hodgson, Papa's recent curate, now a vicar, brought his curate to Haworth parsonage with its three marriageable daughters one afternoon in May. David Bryce at once hit it off with Charlotte who, always at ease at home, laughed at his jests and matched his conversational acrobatics with her own liveliness. The Irish might lack the dignity and discretion of the English, but there was no ice to break with them. Certainly towards the end of the visit young Mr Bryce's nosegays of compliments had become bouquets, and Charlotte, who looked upon compliments as flattery, cooled somewhat.

A few days later she received a letter she turned over and over before opening, for it was from neither Ellen nor Mary, her only correspondents. It was from the irrepressible young Irishman who asked her to marry him in terms as warm and fond as Henry Nussey's had been formal and tepid.

Charlotte refused him. Haworth, to whom their parson's family was an absorbing topic of interest and who, in the manner of all villages, knew everything about everybody, were well aware of the mission of Mr Hodgson's companion when they watched the two men climb the brae together to the parsonage. They concluded that the reason why no engagement was announced was that Mr Bryce was delicate. Mr Brontë had enough sense not to allow any daughter of his to marry a consumptive man who could not last long. Everybody was of course proved right when within a matter of six months the Reverend David Bryce died.

The four Brontë children were like people born with a

skin short; they were affected acutely by circumstances
which would be trying to ordinary individuals. This was
particularly true of Charlotte who, in her different posts as
governess, found herself, a highly superior person, in an
inferior position against which she reacted strongly
enough to be unreasonable. She knew she was prone to
exaggeration and to scorn those who were better off than
herself. 'Proud as peacocks and wealthy as Jews,' she
described the Sidgwick family in her first situation. Within
a month of taking up her second she asked leave to spend
a week-end with Ellen—surely her mistress could not
refuse when she worked so hard for her.

One of her first letters home from the Sidgwicks contains
an unconsciously revealing sentence: 'The children are
constantly with me.' The first essential for a good teacher is
to like those she teaches, and children in Charlotte's eyes
were horrid. It was unfortunate that her charges did
nothing to mitigate this impression of them.

'More riotous, perverse, unmanageable cubs never grew',
she wrote to Emily, whom she addressed as 'Dearest
Lavinia'. In another letter she called her 'Mine bonnie
love'. Emily had taken Branwell's place as the correspondent to whom she had most to say. Her mistress (Charlotte
in her several posts always preferred the master to the
mistress) expected her to do things she could not do, such
as love her children and be entirely devoted to them. Mrs
Sidgwick does not sound a too unnatural mother. Her
governess conceded that she was universally considered an
amiable woman, and her manners were fussily affable, but
she talked a great deal and not to much purpose. Now, Mr
Sidgwick was a hundred times better and had a far kinder
heart. Granted he very seldom spoke to the governess, but
when he did she always felt happier and more settled for
some minutes after. He never asked her to wipe his
children's smutty noses or tie their shoes or fetch their
pinafores or set them a chair. Whereas Mrs Sidgwick overwhelmed her with oceans of needlework, yards of cambric

to hem, muslin nightcaps to make and, humiliation to crown all, dolls to dress.

Charlotte was correct when she wrote that a private governess as far as her employers were concerned had no existence, and was not considered as a living and rational being except as connected with the wearisome duties she had to fulfil. When one of the children, grateful to her for not betraying who had cut her temple, declared, 'I love you, Miss Brontë!' his mother expostulated, 'Love the *governess*, my dear!' From their point of view, Miss Brontë was remembered by the Sidgwick family as touchy. When invited to walk to church with them, she thought she was being ordered about like a slave; if not invited, she felt slighted.

Anne took her first post as private governess before Charlotte set out on hers. Papa was amused at the thought of his little Anne on her own; Aunt Branwell did not consider she had learnt to look after herself yet, and Charlotte was dubious. Anne stammered when nervous: what if her mistress thought she had a natural impediment in her speech? But Anne persisted until she had her way. She wanted to go out into the world, enter upon a new life, act for herself, use her unused faculties, her unknown powers. Of the three sisters she was the only one fond of children, and she looked forward to teaching the very little ones, for with her lack of confidence she did not consider herself fitted for the older members of the family. Yet by the time she left Miss Wooler's she had more accomplishments than either of her sisters.

If Charlotte's wards were unmanageable cubs, Anne's were young fiends. There were five in the family when she arrived at Blake Hall and she had charge of the two eldest, a boy of six and a girl of five. She had not known such children existed whose better nature could not be appealed to because to all appearances they had none. They thought nothing of torturing animals and birds, and their governess's horror only served to sharpen their enjoyment. When they found a nest they gloatingly told her what they were going to do to its occupants—tear their wings off. Anne killed the fledglings outright by dropping a stone on top of the nest. At five and six any Brontë could read and write; her charges could do neither, and made it clear they had no intention of learning, pretending they did not know even the alphabet. They had to be carried or dragged to the table to be taught, and held down by force until the lesson was done.

After eight months of this endurance test Anne believed her charges were at last becoming more humanized, a pious hope, for she reflected that a child of nine or ten as frantic as these two at five and six would be maniac. Then the bolt fell—she was told not to return after her Christmas holidays as her services were no longer required. Her mistress when she was a grandmother remembered a very unsuitable governess she had once employed called Miss Brontë who had tied two of her children to a table leg in order to get on with her own writing.

Anne had left home in spring, full of bright hopes and ardent expectations. Now she was returning in winter, dismissed. All her protestations about how well she would manage had ended in ignominy. Papa, Aunt, Charlotte, would be too kind to say I told you so, but they would be unwilling for her to try again, and she wanted to try again. All parents were not like Mr and Mrs Ingham, all children were not a Joshua or a Mary. The next family would be better—it could not be worse.

There were changes at the parsonage on her return. Emily had left Law Hill, probably on the marriage of Miss Patchett, and was at home now for good—those glorious two words where she was concerned. Her happiness and a sense of completion in the daily round sometimes made her feel guilty—she should be earning her living instead of enjoying this beatitude. But 'the parsonage could not have done without her at that time, for Tabby, whose broken leg had not mended properly, was so crippled she could not manage the work. The girls said she would be back, her absence was only temporary, and would not let Aunt fill her place.

Anne found Emily in command of the kitchen, doing all the cooking and baking for the household, her fire-flushed face smiling with triumph when she drew her bread from the oven. Charlotte's daily tasks were household duties, making the beds and turning out rooms, and ironing. She had never ironed in her life before and upset Aunt by scorching the first batch of washing she attempted.

And there was a newcomer to the close-knit parsonage circle—Papa's new curate, a Mr William Weightman. Papa had had a curate before him and was to have several after him, but none belonged as he did, the only one the parishioners would see walking over the moors with all the vicar's lasses.

He entered a room like a breeze, and his ruddy good looks imparted health as though the sun were always shining full upon him. There was no one in the parsonage to whom his coming did not make a difference. It was a long time since Miss Branwell had had the enjoyment of being teased. As for Mr Brontë, he would have suffered with little comfort a curate who preached the appalling doctrines of personal election and reprobation, so derogatory in Papa's opinion to the attributes of God. Yet Mr Weightman's sermons were his vicar's one cause for anxiety. A brilliant classical scholar, he could not help preaching above the heads of the Haworth congregation, although every time he went into the pulpit Mr Brontë reminded him to speak plain.

He became so part and parcel of the parsonage that it was difficult to remember it without him, yet his every visit was an advent. He was cavalier, escort, entertainer-in-chief. Never had the Brontë sisters, who were now all at home, had so light-hearted a year. They experienced the excitement of receiving Valentines for the first time in their lives, each with different verses—'Away, fond love' and 'Soul divine'—composed by the curate, who walked ten miles to post them so that Papa would not guess the sender.

So many visits up the steep main street to confide in Charlotte about the love of his life he had left in Appleby. His vicar's eldest daughter was all interest, sympathy, wise counsel, until it was borne in upon her that the loves of Mr Weightman's life took diverse forms and were not located only in Appleby. There was not a household with an unmarried daughter that he entered in Papa's parish which he did not leave agog, and when Ellen paid a visit to the parsonage a new star swam into the impressionable Willy Weightman's orbit to dazzle and charm him. A fourth Valentine was written, 'Fair Ellen, Fair Ellen'.

Charlotte was fearful lest her friend would be numbered amongst his conquests, like Sarah Sugden and Caroline Dury, and when his reverence would have squired the parsonage guest on a moorland walk Emily accompanied them to play gooseberry. Laughingly he called her 'The Major' after that. He had become so one of them that Emily ran and danced on the moors when he was with them as she did when they were by themselves.

Something happened to sour Charlotte's relationship with her father's curate in the short period before the 'sister' who listened to his confidences became his severest critic. Looking back on these early days of their acquaintanceship she saw herself as she imagined he had seen her—a cheerful chatty kind of body who had lent him an attentive ear when he felt lonely in new surroundings. Now that he had plenty of acquaintances to cheer and amuse him she did not care—and neither did he.

When she congratulated Ellen on remaining heart-whole where he was concerned she was congratulating herself on exactly the same count. When she told Ellen she was convinced he was a thorough male flirt, enumerated those who were smitten by his charms, mentioned he had been back to Appleby to his first lady love and stayed for up-wards of a month, she was reminding herself of all these undisputed facts. When she wrote to Ellen, 'Don't think about him—I am not afraid you will break your heart—but don't think about him', she might be writing to Ellen, but she was also counselling herself.

He was two years older than Charlotte, but now she seldom mentioned 'our reverend friend' without stressing his youth, although she always had to admit he was a *clever* lad. And she began to refer to him as 'she' and 'her', 'our friend Miss Celia-Amelia'. 'He pleases so easily that he soon gets weary of pleasing at all. He ought not to have been a parson. Certainly he ought not.' But in the same letter she related how she discovered by chance that he had sent a dying girl a bottle of wine and delicacies recommended by her doctor, and how the girl's mother had told Charlotte her father's curate was always good to poor folk like them.

When Anne returned from Blake Hall before Christmas it was to find Papa's new curate one of the family. It was predictable that she should fall in love with him. The very resilience of his good health had its tonic effect on one who had always been delicate; he was sanguine and gay, she inclined to dejection.

He was like the sun, shedding its effulgence by its very nature to shine. He did not single her out, but she did not think of him as a flirt as Charlotte did. Her opinion of him was Papa's opinion, that his character wore well—what he gained at first with his prepossessing manners he did not lose afterwards. His was the lightest heart Anne had ever known, the kindest she would ever know.

She was in love with him, but no one knew of her love, not Willy Weightman himself, or Charlotte, or even Emily. When they sat round the fire in the evening, the best hour of the day, talking and laughing, and she heard him enter the house, no one but she knew how her heart leapt within her. No one but she felt the ache strong as anguish when he did not join them and she heard Papa bidding him good night.

Branwell found a good friend in his father's new curate, probably the best he was ever to have, for his friendships tended to be lop-sided. His Haworth associates were older, and none was his social or academic equal. John Brown, his father's sexton, was nearly double his age, a handsome man who was a stone-mason by trade. The Brontës had visited the Browns in their small neat cottage since they had been children. Mr Brown in his stone-cutter's yard at the parsonage gate was as familiar to them as a landmark. each of the six Brown daughters as they grew up came to the parsonage to help Tabby or take her place when she was ill. Papa thought a lot of John Brown, who had educated himself, and when his vicar composed the epitaph for a fellow clergyman's tombstone John Brown could ask him to make it lengthy as he would have it to cut.

With his social equals Branwell, who seldom raised his gaze from the ground, could be subservient, and he liked to impress his inferiors with his virtuosity. Now, at twenty-three, he needed the stimulus of drink to fire and excite him, for the older he grew the more quickly did his enthusiasms consume themselves until he was left only with a morbid hunger. He had begun to take opium, which could be had for the asking at any druggist's; it was cheaper than ale or spirits and without their aftermath. It produced exaltation, a sensation not so much of being poised on a pinnacle of ecstasy but of being poise itself, generating harmony, making him conscious of neither hunger nor satiation but of perfection.

Branwell needed a friend at this period in his life, for his venture to set up as portrait painter in Bradford had petered out, leaving a backwash of petty debts and irritations. His relationship with his family had deteriorated since his return from London some four years before, for he could not take criticism. Their hope and what was to have become their stay was now more like the Prodigal Son without the penitence; even the far country was unreal.

Willy Weightman was Branwell's contemporary and his equal. As he was like a son to his vicar so he was like a brother to the son. The stability of his cheerful temperament and the strong religious beliefs of his calling provided Branwell with a companionship he had not known before. They could discuss Horace's *Odes*, which Branwell had begun to translate. The young curate might be the young Lochinvar of Charlotte's descriptions, but his relationships were normal. He could write to Branwell from Ripon, where he had gone to pass his final ordination examination, that he had been at several balls and twice head over ears desperately in love. Branwell, who had been writing of love, lust and passion since he had been a boy, had probably at the age of twenty-three never flirted with a girl, and shied from even the pressure of a hand.

He procured the post of tutor to a magistrate's family in Broughton-in-Furness and left home full of hope and resolution on the first day of the new year. Charlotte was not sanguine that he would settle down in his new post; she knew his variable nature, his strong turn for active life. Unconsciously she used the past tense when she wrote to tell Ellen about this new project, 'Branwell who used to enliven us ...'

But Branwell himself had no doubts. He was moving into the magical romantic landscape of the Lakes, the domain of his gods Wordsworth, Hartley, Coleridge, Southey, de Quincey. His pupils were two fine, spirited lads, his employer a retired county magistrate of a right hearty and generous disposition, the wife an amiable woman. He had time on his hands and freedom to enjoy it, for he did not live with the family but lodged with the local surgeon, who had an attractive daughter.

'His wife is a bustling, chattering, kind-hearted soul', he wrote to his crony John Brown in Haworth some weeks after his arrival; 'and his daughter!—oh! death and damnation! Well, what am I? That is, what do they think I am? A most calm, sedate, sober, abstemious, patient, mild-hearted, virtuous, gentlemanly philosopher—the picture of good works, and the treasure-house of righteous thoughts.' Very like, making allowances for Branwell's

over-statements, what the Kirbys at Bradford had thought
of him when he first went to lodge with them. 'Every
lady says, "What a good young gentleman is the
Postlethwaites' tutor!".'

The letter was a very long one which began, 'Old Knave
of Trumps, Don't think that I have forgotten you,' and was
handed round each and every Brother of the Lodge for
whom the writer had a message either individually or
collectively. 'Keep to thy teetotalism, old squire, till I
return', the Worshipful Master of the Lodge was enjoined.
After describing a night of drinking he had spent with
strangers on his way to his new post, he told Brown he had
tasted nothing stronger than milk and water, nor, he hoped,
would he until he returned at midsummer when he would
see about it. Meanwhile he was getting as fat as Prince
William at Springhead. He rode to the banker's at Ulverston
with Mr Postlethwaite, where he sat drinking tea and talking
with old ladies. 'As to the young ones! I have one sitting
by me just now—fair-faced, blue-eyed, dark-haired, sweet
eighteen—she little thinks the devil is so near her!'

The point that must be made is that Branwell really
thought he was the devil. Unlike his father, who had a lot
of the puritan in him but who was not puritanical, he had
no stability. A friend in his old age recalled that Branwell
was ever in extremes, either gloriously great or ingloriously
small. Seesawing between two extremes does not make for
equilibrium. The life and soul of the party comes to a dead
halt when the toasts are all drunk, the room no longer spins
round and the candles that had danced in their eyes have
guttered out. Another friend considered he magnified the
common pleasures and enjoyments of his leisure hours into
crimes and omissions of duty. Charlotte had written herself
free of Angria some years before, shedding it as a lizard sheds
its skin. Branwell was so enmeshed in his world of make-
believe that he was ridden with a guilt that his paper
character, the satiated, cynical, rebellious *roué* of a Percy,
never felt for all his profligacy. The creator had substituted

the dream for reality, and when the dream shrivelled in the light of day he was left in an uninhabitable no man's land.

But meanwhile his life had a certain rhythm that was beneficial as long as he could sustain it. His surroundings were attractive, his duties pleasant and anything but onerous, and he had both time and freedom to pursue his literary work.

Translation was the best discipline Branwell's art could undergo, for he had to prune the verbiage, and he could have chosen no more felicitous an author than the Roman poet with his perfection of form and urbane common sense. Branwell's translations of Horace's *Odes* are an achievement, and his work on them is probably the most rewarding he was ever to know. He sent two to Hartley Coleridge with a humble letter asking him to pass judgment on them. Hartley Coleridge not only answered but invited the young man to visit him.

Thus on the first day of May 1840 Branwell came into personal contact with a literary giant and a famous man. Eldest son of an illustrious father, his host had been an infant prodigy. Now that he was growing old, his hair prematurely silver-white years before, something of the prodigy and infant still clung to him. Short and stout, with a smiling broad face, he did not seem to inhabit this world but some other element, to float rather than walk, using his arms like wings.

In a cottage room where the green summer sunshine filtered through the drawn blind, suffusing it with a light too bright for dusk and too glimmering for dawn, Branwell heard this man of genius tell him to make literature the object of his life. He saw the books stored in what looked like pigeon-boxes, the cocked hat and feather and sword above the fireplace with its hobs and cave-like recesses, dusty papers piled on the floor, the table and window-seat—home of a man whose life was dedicated to his calling. And, sitting in the grotesque old-fashioned chair opposite, the poet-philosopher advised him to finish the first book of the

Odes and send it to him: he would use his influence to try to find a publisher for it.

Late that night Branwell returned to Broughton-in-Furness, his head bumping amongst the stars, trailing clouds of glory, and drunk as a lord. Mr Postlethwaite heard of his condition probably from the surgeon land-lord, and concluded that the sort of poet chap with whom his employee had spent the whole day was obviously no go. He determined to keep a closer eye on his sons' tutor.

Literature, not teaching, was now Branwell's aim. Encouragement such as he had received went to his head like wine. His lessons began to consist of sketching for his young pupils and making up stories for them round his sketches. In his free time he roamed the romantic Lake countryside and dreamed in wayside inns. He wrote to his father and asked him to request Mr Postlethwaite that he be sent home, for he had to finish his translations. Mr Brontë's letter more or less coincided with Branwell's dismissal when he did not turn up at lesson time and was discovered incoherent with drink, after carousing with a Leeds friend at a chance meeting.

He returned to Haworth to finish his translations and found Charlotte had a visitor—Mary Taylor. His sister had engineered the visit, for she knew her brother was attracted to Mary and that Mary was in love with Branwell. It was the attraction of opposites: Mary was purposeful as Bran-well was ineffectual, intellectual and down to earth as he was romantic and in the clouds, practical as he was emotional.

The pretty fair-haired Mary, generous to a fault, saw no reason to hide her love, and the feeling Charlotte's brother had once felt for her turned to contempt. She was too real, and he was afraid of reality because he could not cope with it. His dream must remain unattainable, never be translated into flesh and blood with a life of its own to make un-manageable demands.

As a boy he had once dreamed that he saw Angria

devouring Percy. That was what was happening to him; the leech Angria from which he could not detach himself was sucking dry his life's thin blood.

4

. . . sat amid
The bustle of a Town-like room
'Neath skies, with smoke-stain'd vapours hid—
By windows, made to show their gloom.
The desk that held my ledger book
Beneath the thundering rattle shook
     Of engines passing by;
The bustle of the approaching train
Was all I hoped to rouse the brain
     Of stealthy apathy—

Branwell Brontë

SHORTLY after he returned home Branwell sent his translation of the first book of Horace's *Odes* to Hartley Coleridge. 'Great corrections I feel it wants,' he wrote, 'but till I feel that the work might benefit me, I have no heart to make them; yet if your judgment prove in any way favourable, I will rewrite the whole, without sparing labour to reach perfection.'

It was the mistake of a tyro to dismiss the goodly company of former translators by saying that he had dared to attempt Horace only because he saw the utter worthlessness of all previous translations, and to mention that any remuneration he received he would share with his correspondent through whom alone he could hope to obtain a hearing with that formidable personage, a London bookseller. But the gentle Hartley Coleridge was likely only to notice the youthful author's PS.: 'If anything in this note should displease you, lay it, sir, to the account of inexperience and *not* impudence.'

Now there was nothing to do but wait at home throughout the summer months until he heard from Mr Coleridge the fate of his *Odes*. All his sisters were at home; this was 1840, their blithe year, with their father's curate to squire them. Branwell relations from Cornwall visited them, a mother, father and daughter. It was a pity Willy Weightman was absent at the time, for he would have been a support to the Brontës in dealing with their worldly southern guests, who had a very high opinion of themselves and a patronizing one of their hosts. Branwell's cousin was a handsome big girl who managed, although bouncing with good health, to affect a fashionable languishing air and who talked soulfully of her conversion. The parsonage settled back into itself after this alien intrusion; the clock on the stairs took over again, a fly could be heard buzzing on the window-pane and the twang of some insect outside became audible. Nothing could be so quiet as the parsonage to Branwell, every sound encircled by its own stillness.

Like Branwell, Charlotte was desperate for advice and guidance; she sent Wordsworth the opening of a new book in the hope of receiving both. Wordsworth dismissed the story as an imitation of Richardson; he was puzzled by its author, who signed the accompanying letter with initials so that he could not tell whether it was an attorney's clerk or a novel-reading dressmaker who was writing to him. Charlotte's reply thanking him was facetious; nor did she gratify his curiosity as to her sex, advising him not to be misled by her feminine handwriting or the ladylike touches in her style and imagery—she might employ an amanuensis.

She could agree that her new story, had she gone on with it—and she had materials in her head for half a dozen novels on the same theme—would have worked out on Richardsonian lines. What she did not know was that it was the product of a transition period, and so was bound to be imitative. She had disentangled herself from the fantasy and make-believe of Angria, and was now unconsciously preparing her tools to handle 'real' characters who would b' strong enough to make their own plot.

She was reading through a batch of some forty French novels Mary's father had lent her, disgusted by their lack of morality but fascinated in spite of herself by their development of character. It was an unsatisfactory hiatus for her when she put aside her writing, and her letters to Ellen began to prick at Willy Weightman.

Nothing came of the publication of Branwell's translations. The most likely explanation is that Hartley Coleridge was unable to place the manuscript. Charlotte wrote to Ellen at the end of September that her brother had set off to seek his fortune in the wild, wandering, adventurous, romantic, knight-errant-like capacity of clerk on the Leeds and Manchester Railroad, where he took up the position of assistant clerk in charge at Sowerby Bridge station.

Railways had begun to criss-cross the countryside, linking north with south, east with west. They were the precursors of the new age. Nothing stopped them or proved insuperable. Incredible feats of engineering were performed, tunnels hollowed through mountains, hills flattened, shafts sunk, bridges reared—monuments of their architects' skill, the treacherous enemy of water at last overcome by pumps and floating roads.

Branwell's salary was £75 a year, to be increased by £10 annually until it reached £105. He put forward his father and the landlord of Haworth's Black Bull as the two necessary guarantors to stand security for him; his father was accepted but not the landlord. Aunt Branwell had once again to come to her nephew's aid.

This was a new world he was entering, raw with novelty and active with change. The only thing completed at the station when the chief clerk and his assistant arrived to take charge was the railway line, and they shared the excitement with the huge concourse of sightseers a few days later as the first train came pounding through the rocky valley. Everything clanged here or raised its own echo. Their temporary offices smelled of green wood after rain which rat-tatted on the corrugated roof like rifle-shot.

Branwell lodged in an old house with wooden shutters and an arched doorway overlooking the station. It sold beer, but there were at least six other more important inns or ale-houses in the village, each with its distinctive clientele. The young railway clerk with his uprush of red hair, Roman nose and small mouth buttoning his face, was soon at home in each. It was a hard-drinking age. His superior was reported to drink ten pints of beer one after the other before starting work in the morning.

The chief attraction of Sowerby Bridge for Branwell was that, at the end of an uphill two and a half miles, Halifax was reached, for there he met again artists and men of letters who had gravitated from Bradford, notably Joseph Leyland. The sculptor had returned to his childhood home and now lived with his widowed mother and antiquarian brother above the family printing works. His two gifted sons were contemporaries of Branwell who liked to watch the great man their father work in his studio with his big hands. Together they would go to the Old Cock or the Talbot, to the welcome of warmth and the conviviality of friends, the heat of discussion, the strong smells of malt and spirits, all building a security that made one forget the winter night banked outside waiting for one to zigzag downhill on a frost-bound road hard as iron.

All the Brontës were now away from home earning their livelihood except Emily, and she could not be spared, for Tabby's place had been taken by the sexton's thirteen-year-old Martha. 'Emily is as busy as any of us,' Anne wrote loyally in her regularity paper that summer, 'and in reality earns her food and raiment as much as we do.'

At the same time as Anne was penning this in her new employment, Emily was writing her diary note at home before folding it small to fit into the tiny pin-box. It was her birthday, 30th July 1841, a wild wet Friday evening, nearly nine o'clock. She had tidied out her own and Anne's desk-boxes before she settled down to write with schoolgirl spelling. She was twenty-three today.

It had been a day very like any other. Aunt had read from *Blackwood's Magazine* to Papa and was now upstairs in her room. Papa was in the parlour, the name the Brontës used for his study. They, with the geese Victoria and Adelaide, and Hero the hawk, and Keeper who was in the kitchen, were all stout and hearty, which Emily hoped was the case with Charlotte, Branwell and Anne.

'We are thinking of setting up a school of our own,' she wrote, 'but nothing is settled about it yet, and we do not know whether we shall be able to or not. I hope we shall.' Perhaps in four years, at the time appointed for the opening of this paper, they—Charlotte, Anne and she—would all be merrily seated in their own sitting-room in some pleasant and flourishing seminary. Their debts would be paid off and they would have cash in hand to a considerable amount. Anne and she would perhaps slip out into the garden for a few minutes to peruse (Emily spelled it 'piruse') their papers. Emily hoped either this or something better would be the case in four years' time.

'Papa, Aunt and Branwell will either have been, or be coming—to visit us', she wrote. 'It will be a fine warm summer evening, very different from this bleak look-out.'

She had written a whole poem only a day or two before which began, 'I see around me tombstones grey/Stretching their shadows far away'. Much of her work was fragmentary, like the stone chippings the sexton's chisel struck off, but not all, and her poetry dealt like his epitaphs with the fundamentals.

Emily's interior life was as spacious as the landscape that met the gaze from the field path behind the parsonage, and against so ultimate a background everything was simplified. Now as her thoughts worked on the unhewn material of her mind they released poems singularly personal, so that each was like a part of herself. She was unaware there was anything unusual about them or her; she accepted herself as she accepted others, without question. The apartness that was to isolate her even from her own family did not encircle her now. It has been said that the secret of contentment is fulfilment, for the contented being is the being who is able to realize its own nature and does not feel anywhere frustrated;[1] and that a happy life must be to a great extent a quiet life, for it is only in an atmosphere of quiet that true joy can live.[2] Emily's life at this period fulfilled such conditions. Her horizon knew no bounds, she ranged in regions where the world was an intruder, the world to which her sisters were pinioned by their more human nature.

Anne was more 'human' than Emily in that she had the natural longings to be a wife and mother. After over a year at home she had taken up work again, but she was not happy in her new post. 'I dislike the situation and wish to change it for another,' she wrote in her diary paper after some months at Thorp Green Hall, the property of her new employer, the Reverend Edward Robinson.

If she, child of a parsonage, expected to enter a household with a similar climate to that of home, she was disillusioned almost on arrival. Her employer, of whom she saw little, was a clergyman only in name and had never taken up a living. His parish was the hunting-field, his language liberal with oaths. He was forty-one, a year older than his wife, a handsome dashing woman who certainly required neither rouge nor padding to add to her charms. It was a worldly careless household. The mother's interest in her daughters' education was purely social, that they should acquire the polish of accomplishments. The children not unnaturally reflected the parents' standards of conduct, and Anne discovered to her horror that they had never been taught a proper distinction between right and wrong.

There were three girls, the eldest fifteen, and one boy, the youngest of the family, aged nine. The only contact the governess had was with her pupils. All her meals were taken in the schoolroom. There was not even a village shop where she could exchange the time of day with fellow customer or

[1] J. B. Priestley.   [2] Bertrand Russell.

proprietor, and she might not have been present for all the notice her pupils' friends took of her.

She wrote her diary paper at Scarborough, where she had accompanied the Robinson family and where she saw the sea for the first time. It had the same effect on her that it had had on Charlotte, one of liberation. She wrote in her autobiographic first novel *Agnes Grey* how she felt as she followed her pupils along the sands: 'Refreshed, delighted, invigorated, I walked along, forgetting all my cares, feeling as if I had wings on my feet, and could go at least forty miles without fatigue, and experiencing a sense of exhilaration to which I had been an entire stranger since the days of early youth.' But back at Thorp Green the fashionable shallow atmosphere closed round her again like a malaise.

Poetry was her one release. It came to her as a natural outlet to put into verse her sorrows or anxieties, feelings so painful they had to be kept to herself but which she could not wholly crush. She was to write that these poems, relics of past sufferings and experiences, were like pillars of witness set up in travelling to mark particular occurrences. Time would obliterate footsteps, the face of the country might change, but the landmark of a poem remained to remind her how she had felt when it had been set up. Shortly after returning from Scarborough to Thorp Green she wrote three simple verses, two of which run:

> *My life is very lonely,*
> *My days pass heavily,*
> *I'm weary of repining,*
> *Wilt thou not come to me?*
>
> *Oh, didst thou know my longings*
> *For thee, from day to day,*
> *My hopes, so often blighted,*
> *Thou wouldst not thus delay!*

Both Anne and Emily in their regularity papers wrote of their school scheme. Charlotte, who had the driving power to set their compasses, described the project as their pole star, and once it appeared over the horizon never allowed herself, or the others, to lose sight of it.

Would Ellen ask her sister Anna if she thought it would be possible to establish a respectable but not a showy school with a capital of £150? Aunt had intimated she might give a loan if a suitable place and pupils were found, and Charlotte did not think she would like to risk more than £150 on such a venture. Charlotte had thought of Burlington, or rather the neighbourhood of Burlington—could Ellen remember if there was any other school there besides Miss J.'s? Charlotte imagined the ground in the East Riding was less populated with schools than the West— that would mean of course going farther from home into a district where they had neither connections nor acquaintances.

Miss Wooler, when she heard of the idea, suggested her establishment at Dewsbury Moor,complete with the loan of furniture. It had begun to lose ground since her retirement, for none of her sisters, two of whom were married, had her interest in it or her talent for teaching and direction. Charlotte, now in a new situation, leapt at this offer from her old headmistress.

Then she received Mary's letter. The two Taylor girls, who had lost their father at the beginning of the year, had gone abroad, Martha to be finished at a school in Brussels, Mary to be with her and tour the Continent.

Charlotte hardly knew what swelled in her throat as she read of the places, the pictures and cathedrals Mary had seen. Something seemed to expand boldly within her as though for that moment her spirit took strong wings. She longed to see, to know, to learn. Where were restraint and steady work getting her or any of them? She wanted them *all* to get on. She knew they had talents, and talents should be turned to account.

Every word the practical Mary wrote struck an answering chord in Charlotte. Schools in England were so numerous, competition so great, that unless the Brontë sisters had something superior to offer their hard struggle might well end in failure. The whole project should be postponed for six months and Charlotte should contrive, by hook or by crook, to spend that period in some establishment on the Continent acquiring a thorough familiarity with French. Mary, from her first-hand knowledge, advised Belgium not France, Brussels not Paris. The fare to Belgium cost no more than £5, living was half as dear as in England, and the facilities of education equal or superior to any other place in Europe.

With such unlimited vistas and widening horizons opening dazedly before her, Dewsbury Moor struck Charlotte as an obscure and dreary place, really not adapted for a school. If she went to Belgium she would not only perfect her French but improve her Italian and even get a dash of German. Belgium it must be, and Brussels, where Mary's cousins would introduce her to connections infinitely more improving, polished and cultivated than any she had yet known.

At the end of September, Charlotte wrote to Aunt Branwell from Upperwood House, where she was employed as governess. She knew her aunt was not fond of making shabby purchases, that when she conferred a favour it was often done in style. She could depend upon it that her £50 or £100 thus laid out would be well employed. Charlotte knew of no other friend in the world to whom she could apply except her aunt. If Emily would share these advantages with her (always there is some trepidation when Charlotte speaks of Emily and she hastened to add 'only for a single half-year') they could take a footing in the world on their return which they could never do now. Emily was suggested instead of Anne, for Anne's turn might come at a later period once their school was started. Charlotte felt an absolute conviction that, if they were allowed this advantage, it would be the making of them for life. Papa would perhaps think of it as a wild ambitious scheme, but who ever rose in the world without ambition? When he left

Ireland to go to Cambridge University he was as ambitious as Charlotte was now.

Aunt Branwell, whose eyes had been opened to the fickleness of her favourite Branwell, said yes.

From that moment Charlotte began to plan, to act, to write. One day everything seemed to be fitting in, working out, moving; the next to be stagnant. Belgium was a long way off, and it was difficult from her base in Upperwood House to spur people to·the proper speed. Mary wrote that they could scarcely expect to leave before January—Mary's price was above rubies to Charlotte, heartening her. Papa must write a letter to the English Episcopal clergyman in Brussels, but not until Charlotte told him when, and what was best to be said. The Château de Koekelberg where Martha Taylor was resident was out of the question because of its high fees, but Charlotte wrote to a *pension* in the Rue d'Isabelle in Brussels. Her anxiety about possible extras was conveyed to the Directress Madame Heger and her husband, who realized that the Mesdemoiselles Brontë were daughters of an English pastor of moderate means, anxious to learn with a view to teaching others, and quoted a specific sum which included all expenses. Things reached the stage of making arrangements for the journey. Papa would accompany them, and Mary was returning to Brussels with her brother Joe, so they could all travel in the one party.

And there were fears at home to be allayed. Charlotte was so sure this was the best course to take that her very energy made it so; Emily was not. Why go to Brussels when there was Dewsbury Moor? And what about Anne, who was being left out of everything? Charlotte exhorted everyone to hope. Emily must not grieve over Dewsbury Moor—Miss Wooler had made it clear she had wanted neither her nor Anne, only Charlotte, for the first half-year. Anne might seem omitted from the present plan, but if all went well Charlotte trusted she would derive her full share of the benefit from it in the end. So carried away was the

eldest sister that the apologetic 'only for a single half-year'
Emily was to endure in Brussels was now extended considerably. Emily was told that before their six months
abroad were completed, they would have to seek employment in Brussels—Charlotte had no intention of returning
home for at least twelve months, provided of course that
they and those at home retained good health. Her letter
concluded:

'I shall probably take my leave of Upperwood about the
15th or 17th December. When does Anne talk of returning?
How is she? What does William Weightman say of these
matters? How are Papa and Aunt, do they flag? How will
Anne get on with Martha?' An anxious point, for Anne
would now have to take Emily's place at home—some
comfort that she would be able to leave her distasteful
employment. 'Has William Weightman been seen or heard
of lately? Love to all. Write quickly. Good bye. C. Brontë.
I am well.'

Of course she was well. For the first time she was riding
the crest, entering into her own.

Branwell was expected home at Christmas, but he did not
come. Instead he turned up for a week-end in the middle of
January shortly before his two sisters left. He was no longer
at Sowerby Bridge because in the autumn he had been
promoted to clerk in charge at Luddenden Foot station,
with a clerk, what would be called a porter now, under him.

Luddenden was linked to Sowerby Bridge by a long
tunnel. Even when the open was reached, the shadow of an
excavated pit lay upon the new station which had shouldered
itself out through rock. As at Sowerby Bridge, the only
completed thing about it was the permanent way, and the
railway company had not even begun to build offices for its
staff. Branwell lodged in a cottage farther up the hill, and
during the day sat in a room in the station overlooking
the double rails. The shuddering rattle of passing engines
shook everything in it, making the very ledger jump in his
closed desk. The din and smoke that grimed the windows

gave him the sinister impression that this room was in a
town instead of being in the country. Between the trains,
mostly goods and through traffic, with their deafening
noise, was silence, and Branwell was frightened of silence as
much as he was intimidated by noise. The village of
Luddenden, a mile or so uphill from the station, was like
release, and it became a necessity to reach the Lord Nelson
Inn which stood in a square at the top beside the church.

Although Sowerby Bridge was only two miles away, he
had not the same contacts with his friends while he was at
Luddenden. New ones had to be made: Grundy, the young
railway engineer, a clergyman's son like himself, and, in that
wool-producing district, mill-owners and merchants; and
the wild thirsty Irish labourers who lived like a pack in the
huts near the canal at the station.

The notebook he kept at this period is like the memoranda of his mind: unfinished drawings of his colleagues
beside some of the finest and some of the worst poems he
ever wrote, jottings referring to the coal and wool traffic
passing through the station, disbursements, data about
letters he was writing for the village youths to whom he
acted as scribe, the address of a warehouse in Manchester,
the advertisement of a book dealing with the causes of the
premature decline of manhood, a list of fourteen famous
men about whose lives he intended to write.

On the first page of the notebook is an entry important
enough to be dated and initialled: 'At R. Col last night with
G. Thompson, and Titterington, R. Col, H. Killiner and
another. Quarrelled with J.T. about going but after a
wrestle met him on the road and became friends. Quarrelled
on the subject with G. Thompson. Will have no more of it.
August 18th, 1841. P.B.B.' After the note are the words
'Jesu—Jesu—Jesu'. 'Jesus Rex', 'Jesus Salvator', 'Holy
Jesus' divide the memoranda and entries, the data, sketches
and poems.

A year later Branwell was to write from Haworth to
Grundy: 'I would rather give my hand than undergo

again the grovelling carelessness, the malignant yet cold debauchery, the determination to find how far mind could carry body without both being chukked into hell, which too often marked my conduct when there, lost as I was to all I really liked, and seeking relief in the indulgence of feelings which form the black spot of my character.'

In a dual personality such as conscience-stricken, guilt-ridden Branwell Brontë's, the line between temptation and yielding is indistinct. Also in his day the classes had the immutability of the caste system, the strata did not mix; into the bargain the Irish with whom he consorted were all Roman Catholic.

The Irish! His roots clawed back to Ireland, and his grandmother had been a Roman Catholic until she married his grandfather. His Protestant forebears believed that Catholicism was the Scarlet Woman and the Whore of Babylon. Branwell, son of a Methodist clergyman, believed that too, and yet—and yet—*Salvator Jesus*.

It was unlikely that his family when they saw him in January received any indication of the crisis he was passing through. Nearly forty years later Grundy recalled that he had once or twice accompanied Branwell to Haworth parsonage, driving the twelve miles in a hired gig, and that in his own home Branwell was at his best, eloquent and amusing, although on the journey back he would burst into tears and swear he meant to amend.

The brother would be glad for her sake that Charlotte was escaping to Brussels as he had been glad, a few years before, when Ellen Nussey, learning that Papa and Aunt were not sure it was quite proper for two young ladies to visit the seaside by themselves, descended on the parsonage in a carriage and in the joyous surprise swept her friend and luggage away with her. A brave defeat, Branwell had grandiloquently dubbed it, the doubters fairly taken aback. 'You have only to *will* a thing to *get* it', he had declared. What a heartbreak that word 'only' contains in such a sentence.

Now that the restricted scene of Haworth parsonage was about to extend into a foreign *pension* and enthralling new characters waited in the wings to fill her stage, the tenuous feeling Charlotte had once had for Willy Weightman was finally exorcised. Ellen, invited to spend a few days with them before she and Emily left for Brussels, was told that Charlotte was most curious to see a meeting between her and his young Reverence—Charlotte was convinced he would again be desperately in love. 'He sits opposite to Anne at church, sighing softly, and looking out of the corners of his eyes to win her attention,' she wrote, 'and Anne is so quiet, her look so downcast, they are a picture.' Thus lightly Charlotte dismissed Willy Weightman out of Anne's life—if his amorous glances were not directed at her younger sister, they would be at someone else. 'He would be the better of a comfortable wife like you to settle him,' her letter to Ellen continued; 'you would settle him I believe—no one else would.'

Charlotte, like everyone else in the household including Anne, had believed that the youngest sister would remain at home now, and she was glad to give in her notice when she left for the Christmas holidays. Yet Anne went back to Thorp Green just before Emily and Charlotte set out for Brussels. Certainly the Robinsons were anxious for her to return to them, and it was arranged that she should go—if the parsonage could find a good servant to do Emily's work.

She left when the sexton's ten-year-old Hannah was engaged to help her thirteen-year-old sister. In the book she began to write on her return to Thorp Green, Anne spoke through the narrator of the passion of grief Agnes Grey endured when she had to mask the secret changes of her soul and behave as though she felt nothing.

'I was a close and resolute dissembler', she wrote, 'in this one case at least. My prayers, my tears, my wishes, fears and lamentations, were witnessed by myself and Heaven alone.' It was safer to think of Willy Weightman at Thorp

Green than to remain at the parsonage within his orbit. 'Yes, at least, they could not deprive me of that. I could think of him day and night; and I could feel that he was worthy to be thought of. Nobody knew him as I did; nobody could appreciate him as I did; nobody could love him as I—could, if I might: but there was the evil. What business had I to think so much of one that never thought of me? Was it not foolish? was it not wrong? Yet, if I found such deep delight in thinking of him, and if I kept these thoughts to myself, and troubled no one else with them, where was the harm of it?'

At the beginning of February Charlotte and Emily left home with Papa, bound for Brussels. This was Charlotte's hour, she had waited nearly twenty-six years for it.

In the emptied house, against which the harsh winds thudded and sawed, Aunt Branwell was left alone. The place, unsettled with the preparations and subsequent departures, took some time to subside. She felt irritable in consequence. The older she grew, the more attenuated became her contacts, and the two girls struck her as inconsequential as bubbles.

Keeper, Emily's dog, was kept in the kitchen, out of her way. She had never held with the children's pets—they would always remain children to her, at the other end of the attenuating cord, feeding their dogs and cats with their own porridge and milk. She had been glad when Anne's cat had not returned the other month, and when their wild goose had flown away. Those creatures in the peat-house with their beady eyes, hooked beaks and stretching necks! They got that from their father of course —this caring for dumb beasts and stray birds. Whoever heard of anyone keeping a hawk except a Brontë? She would see they were rid of Emily's Hero before she came home.

It was her brother-in-law she missed, her contemporary. No length of cord separated them, they were both at the same end. You missed those you made a difference to—he was losing his sight, and she read to him.

He did not hurry home; after seeing his daughters into the school he went to Waterloo to study the battleground. But he would be back any day now, and things would be the same again, hearing him enter the house and going out, and his man's step on the stair.

5

Life seems more sweet that thou didst live,
And men more true that thou wert one;
Nothing is lost that thou didst give,
Nothing destroyed that thou hast done—

Anne Brontë

THE first night she was in London Charlotte lay in the dark, narrow room of the Chapter Coffee House and heard the knell of a bell proclaim midnight. Each stroke delivered its own deep, deliberate note so charged with force that after the twelfth the air still hummed. In the suddenly silent room she said to herself: 'I lie in the shadow of St Paul's.'

The first thing she did when she woke in the morning was to part the curtains at the long narrow window and see the February sunrise struggling through the London fog. Her gaze was drawn upwards as though by a magnet to the solemn, orbed dome of St Paul's, dark blue and dim in that early morning half-light.

She felt her inner self move. Only then did she realize that all her life she had been fettered, and in that moment she shook her wings half free. She had a sudden feeling that she, who had never yet truly lived, was about to taste life. In that moment her soul grew as fast as Jonah's gourd.

The three Brontës had travelled to London with Mary and Joe Taylor. Mr Brontë took them to the Chapter Coffee House, an old-fashioned tavern where he had stayed in the past when passing through London. The building itself was so old, with its low ceilings, small dark sunk rooms, wainscotted walls and heavy beams, that it gave the impression it had been rooted there before there was a Paternoster Row. Its clientele was no longer London men of letters of the calibre of Johnson and Goldsmith using it as a meeting place, but visitors from the provinces, mostly clergy. None of the Brontës realized that it was not suitable for women as all the servants except one were men.

Charlotte and Emily wanted to utilize every moment they had in London sight-seeing. The more urbane, travelled Taylors were organized by Charlotte, who could tell them where everything they wanted to view was situated and all about the various artists. The pictures and statues they must see struck Mary as dauntingly many. And of course St Paul's. Everything that was viewed was discussed at length; Emily might not speak as much as her elder sister, but she was emphatic with her own opinion.

Charlotte could have wished she had more than two eyes once they arrived on foreign soil. The grey, dead sky above them, the wet road they travelled in the diligence, the wet fertile fields on either side cultivated in patches that made them look like magnified kitchen-gardens, the wet house-tops they looked down upon, the painted farm houses, the canals like half-torpid green snakes—all were beautiful because they were unfamiliar. And the room she saw that first morning when she threw back the curtains of her bed sparkled with strangeness. It was lofty and wide as the one in the Chapter Coffee House had been narrow and dingy; everything shone, from the floor glossy with paint to the large windows of such clear glass they reflected light, as did the great looking-glass on the dressing-table and the ornate mirror glittering above the mantelpiece.

In Brussels they said goodbye to Mary, who was joining Martha as a parlour-boarder in an establishment just outside the town. The Brontës called on Mr Jenkins, the English chaplain at the Embassy, who accompanied them to their new school in the Rue d'Isabelle. On the morrow Papa left to make his way home, and they were alone—by them-selves—in a foreign *pension* with nearly ninety pupils talking a foreign language, and all girls of course. Charlotte was twenty-six, Emily twenty-four.

They slept in two beds at the end of a dormitory. Every bed had its white curtains, a long drawer which served as wardrobe and, between the beds, a stand for ewer, basin and looking-glass.

Dressing in the morning, undressing at night, pacing the gravelled walks together in the exercise hour, sitting beside each other at one of the long tables in the refectory eating the foreign food, Charlotte realized that what had happened to Emily at Roe Head was happening to her in the *pension*. Divorced from home, from all that was natural to her, finding herself amongst aliens all professing the same insinuating lush religion, she began to pine. What if Emily could not stand it, what if she had to return home? But life was more important than education; to Charlotte Emily always came first.

The only time she was freed from anxiety was when they sat side by side in the back row of the largest classroom engrossed in their studies. No fewer than seven visiting masters and three resident women teachers comprised the staff. Into the bargain M. Heger, husband of the Directress, was professor of rhetoric, and as time passed he outweighed everyone and everything else in the establishment as far as Charlotte was concerned.

He watched his two new pupils for some time before he actually spoke to them, merely correcting their exercises. Charlotte was more proficient at French than Emily, but as far as their master was concerned neither knew anything of the language. By this time Charlotte realized Emily's resolution was going to carry her through her exile. She alone knew the remorse and shame her sister had felt at her Roe Head failure; she alone knew the effort it caused her now to rally and face the facts. Her relief made her attitude to her younger sister placatory, protective, as though to make up to her for something for which she felt responsible. Emily had the stronger personality of the two, and Charlotte was nervous of her reactions. Monsieur Heger considered that the younger sister tyrannized over the elder, and Laetitia Wheelwright, an English pupil at the *pension* with a clutch of younger sisters, noticing Charlotte's devotion, came to the same conclusion.

Charlotte was first attracted to Laetitia when she saw her standing on a stool in the classroom, scornfully viewing some Belgian pupils who as usual were behaving badly. Charlotte thought her expression so English, and to find that Laetitia shared her opinion of their schoolfellows created a bond. The adolescents, with their full-blown figures, insolent eyes and strongly marked brows, were the worst.

The two sisters struck even their fellow English as odd. Their Irish-Yorkshire voices for instance sounded strangely on ears attuned like Laetitia's to the clipped, well-bred accents of Londoners. As to their clothes—if unsophisticated Haworth considered them dated and dowdy, amongst their wealthy, fashionable co-pupils they stood out like anachronisms, particularly Emily's. Charlotte at least was *petite* and always trim, whereas there was much more of Emily to be untidy. She did not care what others thought of her ridiculous leg-of-mutton sleeves which had gone out of fashion in her aunt's youth, or her skirts which fell lankily between her long legs when everyone else's were bouffant with stiffening and petticoats. She gloried in being different. When teased about her appearance, she replied with warmth: 'I wish to be as God made me.'

Her lack of conformity and her taciturnity were taken for unfriendliness. There is something disconcerting about a guest who seldom speaks and who, when she has to make a remark, utters it in monosyllables. The sisters' palpable lack of enjoyment as visitors caused the Jenkinses to stop inviting them, to the relief of the sons of the house who had to escort two silent Brontës to and from their home.

Laetitia Wheelwright did not take to Emily; but, despite the difference in their ages, she remained a friend of Charlotte's until the older woman's death. On the other hand a

Belgian, recalling the days when she was a girl at the *pension*, vouched for herself and others that Emily was the favourite, that she was sympathetic, kinder and more approachable than Charlotte, and much better looking despite her pallor and thinness. Before she left, Emily gave the Belgian girl a sketch she had made of a tree, every twig, every branch, every scroll of its trunk meticulously drawn.

To Charlotte her birthday was not so much an occasion for celebration as the painful reminder of still another milestone. At home she had looked at her face in the mirror and seen old age begin to stamp it, but her twenty-sixth birthday which fell in April while she was at the *pension* found her almost jocund. She was a schoolgirl again, not a shy over-anxious pupil at Roe Head but an adult with every inducement to learn, learn, learn. She and Emily might be isolated in the midst of numbers because of the difference in their religion and language, but Charlotte found her present life delightful and congenial compared to her former one of governess. It was joy for her to submit to authority instead of exercising it, to obey orders instead of giving them. Happily she wrote to Ellen that she returned to this state of affairs with the same avidity as a cow, long kept on dry hay, returning to fresh grass.

No one could wish for a finer teacher than M. Heger. He was professor at the boys' academy near by but taught literature at his wife's seminary, a small vigorous man of thirty-three. Everything about him was sudden, even the very way his bountiful black hair sprang from his head. As it whitened with age his kindliness of heart sweetened into geniality, but in the Brontës' day he fairly danced with vitality and foreign excitability.

The French believe that what matters in learning is not to be taught but to wake up, and Charlotte, for the first time in contact with an outstanding intellect, was awake as she had never been before. She responded to his tuition as the flint responds to the friction that causes ignition, revelling in her difficulties when he forbade her to use either dictionary or grammar. His explosions when he came across an English word in her French composition made her weep, much to his surprise. But that set things to rights once more between them, and the fascinating relationship, unpredictable as fireworks, began all over again. What Charlotte did not realize in her new-found happiness and fulfilment was the dependence of the pupil on the master for that happiness and fulfilment.

Emily did not weep when their teacher corrected her work. Charlotte was nervous about her and M. Heger, for they did not get on well together. For instance, when he told them he proposed to analyse some French masterpiece for them, pointing out its excellencies and weaknesses, after which they were to write an essay in the style of the author analysed, Emily said flatly she did not approve—by such a method they would lose all originality of thought and expression. She was prepared to argue her point, but Monsieur Heger had not the time to listen. Charlotte also was dubious of the wisdom of such a scheme, but said she was bound to obey him as long as she was his pupil. Monsieur Heger could be said to have won.

He was too good a teacher not to realize that the English-women were unusual not only in their diligence and capacity to learn but in the power of their minds, and Emily he rated higher than Charlotte. He gave them some private lessons at the beginning which excited much jealousy and spite in the school. The Belgians disliked the dedicated, hard-working English, and Charlotte's opinion of her Belgian fellow pupils was that they were cold, selfish, animal and inferior, whose principles were rotten to the core.

Proud of his new scholars' progress, Monsieur Heger had their compositions read out in class. He marked their essays very fully, pointing out to Charlotte the danger of her theory that genius was a gift from God and its possessor had nothing to do with it, and telling Emily that her letter in French, purporting to be written to her parents in England, showed no affection and so was of little value.

It was Madame Heger who made all the arrangements regarding the English sisters, proposing both should stay on for a further half-year, Charlotte as English teacher and Emily to take young pupils for music. This would allow both to continue their studies and have board in lieu of salaries. So resolved was Charlotte to stay on in Belgium and at the *pension* that she refused a remunerative post she was offered in England.

Emily, whom Charlotte described as working like a horse, was making rapid progress in French, German, music and drawing. She liked to give her music lessons in the play hour so that she would not use up any of her own working time teaching, to the distress of her small pupils who sometimes left her class in tears. Charlotte was not so apprehensive for Emily now; she wrote to Ellen that Monsieur and Madame Heger had begun to recognize the valuable parts of her character under her singularities. It had taken Brussels to reveal to Charlotte how unlike other people Emily was. Yet there had been the occasion at home when she had given a drink to a strange dog which had snapped at her, and she had gone into the kitchen, taken up one of Tabby's red-hot irons and cauterized the wound without saying a word to anyone.

Madame Heger struck Charlotte as somewhat similar to one of Miss Wooler's younger sisters except that, being married, she was softer, whereas the disappointed Miss Catherine was soured. She was small with a motherly figure, very blue eyes and a smooth, fondant pink complexion. Despite her slight portliness, she moved gracefully as though she were gliding. Charlotte never saw her ruffled or heard her unpleasant, an ideal Directress for such an establishment. She was Constantin Heger's second wife, the mother of his children; his first wife, whom he had married when he was a very young man, died tragically soon after their marriage. He was five years younger than his second wife and seven years older than Charlotte.

Altogether Charlotte did not think she was ever unhappy.

Teaching, whatever the initial effort it entailed, benefited both Brontës. Monsieur Heger watched Emily lose whatever remained of ignorance and, what was worse to him than ignorance, her timidity, and Charlotte gain the assurance, the aplomb so necessary to a teacher. Mary Taylor, who with her sister Martha saw something of their Yorkshire compatriots out of school hours, reported to Ellen that Charlotte and Emily were well; not only in health but in mind and hope, that they were content with their present position and even gay. Mary considered they did right in not returning to England after their six months.

To Anne in her uncongenial surroundings at Thorp Green, the year in which she was not to see her sisters stretched like an eternity. They seemed very far away in Brussels, which must be a beautiful city from all accounts, one of the finest in Europe, with its buildings picturesque with age, its boulevards, fountains and statues. How flat, how uninteresting, how tedious was her post as governess to the Robinson daughters and son compared to Charlotte and Emily's every day in a foreign country; yet after her return to Thorp Green Anne had a religious experience which held the sudden brightness and abiding serenity of revelation. As her favourite poet, William Cowper, with the radiance of such a restoration still upon him, wrote:

> *Sometimes a light surprises*
> *The Christian while he sings;*
> *It is the Lord who rises*
> *With healing in his wings:*
> *When comforts are declining*
> *He grants the soul again*
> *A season of clear shining*
> *To cheer it after rain.*

So Anne Brontë could write from the fullness of her heart the lovely poem to which she gave the simple title of 'In Memory of a Happy Day in February'.

She had now been at her new post for over a year, and

her influence upon her pupils had begun to show. Certainly they thought her a queer creature who did not flatter or praise them half enough. To someone who was as obliging, quiet and peaceable as she was, it was quite surprising how certain things could put her out of temper. They learnt through experience what these certain things were; she had some very tiresome opinions so it was really better to keep her in tune, for when she was in what they called a good humour she would talk to them, and she could be very agreeable, even amusing.

She arrived home for her holidays in midsummer to find Branwell there, moody and jumpy, shifty and ill at ease. He moved aimlessly from one empty room to another, went out to speak to John Brown working in his stone-mason's yard at the parsonage gate, took a turn to the village and returned almost at once or came trailing back after being away for hours.

He had been dismissed with a docked salary from his post when the railway officials examined the Luddenden Foot books. They found the assistant had been helping himself to the till during his superior's absences from the station. His friends in the Luddenden district, and Branwell always had friends, signed a petition interceding for his re-employment, but the company, who had discovered that their clerk in charge had been in the habit of remaining away from his duties for days' on end, adhered to their decision.

The only merciful thing in her brother's situation Anne found at home was Willy Weightman. He alone through his companionship was able to rouse Branwell into contact with normality. There was something so sane about his very robustness, and during these months in the parsonage Branwell felt very near to insanity, having nothing to listen to except the wind moaning among old chimneys and older ash trees. He would have done anything to escape from the quiet of home, from the heathery hills he had walked when life held all to hope for and nothing to regret. He prodded

Grundy to try to find him some other job on the railway, but had to admit he was a fool to expect anything from the company's quarter. Yet during these spring months he achieved a lifelong ambition—he saw his name in print when several of his poems appeared in the *Halifax Guardian* and *Leeds Intelligence*. He was the first of Patrick Brontë's children to have anything published.

Anne and Willy Weightman were drawn together during her stay at home that summer, and not only through Branwell. She was conscious of warmer contacts, intangible signs. In the book she was writing, with its prosaic title *Passages in the Life of an Individual*, Anne spoke through Agnes when she found herself treasuring the goodbye of the young clergyman she loved: 'Well, and what was there in that? Who ever hung his hopes upon so frail a twig?' Yet when she joined the Robinson family in their annual visit to Scarborough she could, like Agnes, remember she was twenty-two years of age, and if she could not hope at twenty-two when could she? Who could tell what this month might bring forth?

She returned with the family to Thorp Green early in September. Shortly afterwards she received a letter from home telling her that Willy Weightman had died on the sixth of the month from an attack of cholera and peritonitis. Cholera, a frequent visitor to Haworth, may have been synonymous in those days with dysentery, and peritonitis a ruptured appendix.

Branwell had nursed him through his short illness, and sat weeping in the family pew during the funeral service. His friend was buried under the cold flagstones in the church where he had served. For the first time in his twenty-year ministry at Haworth the vicar read his sermon because his parishioners had asked that it should be published. It was as though they thought a degree of immortality would pinion to the printed page their one-time curate, who had moved amongst them when he had been alive, prayed at their hearths and blessed their homes.

Anne wrote a poem to her dead love before the year was out, leaving a blank after the 'To ——'. Curiously enough, although her grief was so green, her poem makes less painful reading than those that were to follow in later years. The freshly turned earth of a new grave was warmer than the stone slab on a tomb.

6

What matters it, that all around
Danger, and guilt, and darkness lie,
If but within our bosom's bound
We hold a bright, untroubled sky,
Warm with ten thousand mingled rays
Of suns that know no winter days?—

Emily Brontë

IT WAS of Mary Taylor that Miss Wooler used to say she was too pretty to live, not Martha, the younger sister. Martha was not in the least pretty in the conventional sense of the word, but, dancing with vivacity, piquant and unexpected, she was everyone's favourite since the days she used to sing to delight her father. She never thought twice about voicing the thoughts spinning in her mind, but her outspokenness brought its own laughter and captivated rather than shocked.

Charlotte, unaware there was any danger, went to the Château de Koekelberg outside Brussels the morning after she and Emily heard Martha was unwell, only to learn that she had died during the night. Her illness had been as short and sudden as that of Willy Weightman, and she probably died from the same cause, appendicitis. She was buried almost at once, and Mary's cousins, the Dixons, took Mary to stay with them in their house in Brussels.

Charlotte, Emily and the bereaved sister together walked the three miles to visit the graveyard on the last Sunday of October. The two Brontës had been brought up amongst table and upright tombstones, but the melancholy of this place with its sea of crosses bit into Charlotte's very soul.

A howling wind whipped the ill-omened trees of cypress, yew and willow and the rain descended as though it would never stop, sopping everything from the everlasting flowers to the wet-darkened grass.

Not at home, amongst her kith and kin in their private burial-ground in Fir Dene Wood, did Martha lie, but here, in this alien place, in heretic soil. As they stood in the wet and wind the three women felt the emotion, the ache, the sorrow of a lifetime load the present moment.

They trudged the three miles back to Brussels and spent the evening with the Dixons—a pleasant evening, Mary wrote to Ellen, in presence of her uncle and Emily, one not speaking at all, the other once or twice.

A day or two later the Brontës received word that Aunt had taken seriously ill. At once they made plans to return home. The following day they heard that she had died; nevertheless they left as soon as possible, Charlotte bearing with her a letter M. Heger had written to Papa 'Au Reverend Monsieur Brontë, Pastor Evangelique'.

They arrived back to the stillness of Haworth after the turmoil of travelling. Anne had been sent for whenever Aunt Branwell fell ill, but Mrs Robinson delayed giving her governess the message, and, when she did so, told her that there was no need to be in such agitation. Realizing that Miss Brontë would return home immediately with or without her consent, she unwillingly gave it, but Aunt was dead by the time her favourite niece reached the parsonage.

Branwell had watched by the woman who had been as his mother, the guide and director of all the happy days connected with his childhood, as he had watched by the death-bed of his friend only a week or two earlier. Aunt Branwell's illness was not lingering, but the last two days of her life on earth had been agonizing. Branwell had witnessed in her suffering what he would not wish his worst enemy to endure.

Willy Weightman, Martha Taylor, Aunt—three deaths within the space of a few weeks, milestones that led him

back in a rush of memory to the moment when he had
gasped to his dead sister in her coffin to speak to him. The
years between had worn away none of the unnatural
strangeness of that day.

The cold grave had sundered him from Maria and all her
sweetness. If there was no God, no Heaven, no Hell, then
she in her grave was 'left blackening in the storm', and the
destiny of both was to become a banquet for the worms.
If Heaven was a reality,then Maria, angel bright and angel
fair, would be shining there inaccessible as a star, for Hell,
not Heaven, was his home, carrying as he did his burden of
sin.

Had Branwell been brought up in the religion of his
grandmother, perhaps he could have eased some of his
sense of guilt in the confessional. As it was, finding no
solace in his father's or aunt's beliefs, he went his unshriven
way, scoffing at church and prayer as hypocritical, his very
irreligion the trade-mark of the fear of the reality of God,
Heaven and Hell.

Now they were all at home together after the longest
period they had ever been apart. Normality began to assert
itself as his everyday settled back into what it once had
been, with companions to walk beside him on the moors
and sit round the fire in the evening. He and Anne missed
their aunt most because she had been most to them; but
because she had never been part of their inner circle, her
death made surprisingly little difference to the tenor of the
parsonage day. 'Do not fear to find us melancholy or
depressed', Charlotte wrote later that month when she
invited Ellen to visit them. 'We are all much as usual.'

For the first time in their lives the Brontë daughters had
money behind them. Aunt Branwell's orderly will be-
queathed to the three of them and a fourth niece in
Penzance in equal shares her carefully accumulated means.
Her whole estate was valued at less than £1,500, and each
probably received something between £200 and £300.
This was an appreciable sum to the Brontës, who agreed

amongst themselves not to touch it but to keep it for the future when it could be used to further their school or some other communal project.

Their aunt had made her will nine years previously, when Branwell was sixteen, and had not included him in the disposal of her money because she had taken it for granted that he, being male, would earn his own livelihood. She left him the most masculine of her possessions, her Japan dressing-box. Charlotte received her Indian workbox and Emily her workbox with a china top and her ivory fan. But it was to Anne, who had belonged to her as neither of her sisters ever had, she left most—her watch with all that belonged to it, her eye-glass and its chain, her rings, silver spoons and books.

Life began to right itself for Branwell, and hope to soar from a candle's fitful flicker into the blaze of day. He had a future now instead of only a past gnawing at him. Through Anne's good offices he was engaged as tutor for the Robinson son. Due to his youngest sister alone he was offered a post which, after the Postlethwaite *débâcle*, he could not have hoped to gain since he was unable to supply references. When she returned to Thorp Green after the holidays he was to accompany her.

Meanwhile he was taking his place in the body of the family and enjoying what excitements each day had to offer. He sent a playful message through Charlotte to Ellen after her visit demanding why, in her bread and butter letter on her return home, she had carefully excluded him in the regards she sent to every other member of the family. 'He desires to know whether and in what he has offended you, or whether it is considered improper for a young lady to mention the gentlemen of the house. We have been one walk on the moor since you left.'

Of all the Brontës that Christmastide Charlotte was the liveliest. M. Heger's letter to Papa offered to take back both sisters, or either, in the capacity of pupil-teacher with a salary; he had pointed out that a second year of instruction would be far more valuable than the first. Charlotte knew how true that was, and was the one to accept. The offer of a post in England at fifty pounds a year did not tempt her when she thought what she would be gaining in Brussels.

Aunt Branwell's death of course left the parsonage without a mistress, which made it a necessity for one of the sisters to remain at home to look after their father and the house. Anne, who was returning to Thorp Green with Branwell, was ruled out. It was really Charlotte's duty to remain, she was after all the eldest daughter and, now Papa's sight was growing dimmer, should be at his right hand, but Emily wanted to be the housekeeper and this made it so much easier for Charlotte to do what she wanted, return to Brussels. She did not know when she had desired anything so much as that, and the knowledge that Emily would look after the house much better than she ever could, that she would watch over Papa and supply his every comfort, absolved her from any feeling of guilt.

Anne's return to Thorp Green was softened by the companionship of her brother, to whom she felt nearer than she had ever felt because his predicament had brought her closer to the man she loved. She received from the Robinsons the excellent salary of fifty pounds a year, double what she had had from the Inghams, but now that the eldest daughter had outgrown the schoolroom and she was no longer teaching Edmund, ten pounds was deducted. To his governess this was nevertheless gain, for he was a nasty little boy.

Branwell's salary was eighty pounds. He did not live in the handsome Hall as Anne did but lodged in the Monk's House, a fourteenth-century building which delighted the artist in him, for he sketched it with its long chimneys, steeply pitched roof and rough bare walls scantily pierced by slits of windows. He had therefore more outside contacts than his sister, but Thorp Green had no Lord Nelson tavern within reach, no Halifax at the end of an uphill walk, no friends to hail and jostle with comradeship in clubs or inns.

But he was as resolved as he could be about anything to make a success of his new situation. Early he realized that this depended on his charge. He spared no pains to make himself amenable to the boy, and he was after all an attractive companion for a child. His success depended also on his charge's mother, for Edmund was the apple of Mrs Robinson's eye, and pleasing one served the double purpose of pleasing the other.

He saw little of the three daughters of the house. Lydia, the eldest, her mother's namesake and the one most like her, was at that most beguiling stage of life, beginning to make her entry into the world of balls and parties, to attract to herself the shining prizes of social success. Elizabeth was a strong strapping young hoyden happiest on a horse's back, and Mary, the youngest girl and Anne's particular charge, a merry little romp.

Their employers were satisfied enough with their tutor and governess to invite their father that April to visit his son and daughter at Thorp Green. Papa accepted the invitation just as earlier he had accepted the invitation to visit Charlotte in her post as governess, for unlike his daughters he enjoyed sociabilities. The tall country vicar with his long, heavy walking-stick met his children's employer, the clergyman who had never had a charge, his handsome socialite over-bright wife and his children's pupils. He was able to write to Charlotte in Brussels that Branwell was doing well and had won the approbation of his employers.

No sister-in-law when he returned to the parsonage to pour tea from her lustre pot, or read to him, or pronounce her views with the finality of the laws of the Medes and Persians. Only Emily, yet he fitted in well with his middle daughter, who was more like him than any of his children. She had his stoicism which stripped their world bare of inessentials. He called her his brave and noble girl and taught her to shoot in the garden.

Ellen Nussey declared that her Brussels sojourn had improved Emily, rubbed off some of her roughness of manner and substituted several accomplishments generally considered as ladylike. Mary Taylor did not agree. She could not imagine how the newly acquired qualities could fit the same head and heart as the old ones. She could not see Emily turning over prints or taking wine with any stupid pup and preserving her temper and patience.

Tabby was back. She did not take kindly to doing nothing except living with her sister; the parsonage was her home. She was over seventy now, a little deaf, and she hobbled on her game leg, but she was as tough as the hard and woody chestnut which carries the remains of the fruit it enclosed on the outside. She was a member of the Brontë family by this time, jealous of her prerogative of knowing everything that concerned them, in a totally different category from the young Brown sisters or the village girls who came in by the day to lend a hand.

Emily was up first thing in the morning to do the roughest part of the work before Tabby came jogging downstairs. The old servant, fitting herself back into her old place, did not realize how much was done for her, so smoothly did the work of the house go on. Emily did the ironing and most of the cooking, and made bread. Haworth had to concede her bread was the lightest and best in the district. They had always held she was the cleverest of the bunch, learning from a foreign book propped against the salt crock as she worked, with a piece of paper and a pencil handy to make a note of what came into her head.

The village girls liked working for her, although she was in the kitchen, where you saw the moors every time the door was open, more than most mistresses. They liked to hear her welcome them, for she had a low sweet voice, and to see her consider them, her head a little to one side. She had a real, glad, good-natured look about her. But it was said that Mr Smith, who had taken Mr Weightman's place (not that the likes of him would ever fill it), would beat a hasty retreat if he came across her in the parsonage.

This was the beginning of Emily's Golden Age. The very simplicity of her daily round, the even tenor of her every day, with its time-table of morning, afternoon and night, acted on her like the rules of an Order which provide for growth of the inner life. The majority of her great poems were written during this period, the half-dozen lyrics which are among the finest of her century. She began to copy them into two small books, one for her Gondal poems and the other for her personal ones. They were written in cheap little books used for entering washing-lists. Both she kept locked in her folding rosewood desk.

She has been called the sphinx of literature, but to Emily there was nothing enigmatic in what she wrote. She did not so much describe as say what she felt and saw. 'Heavy hangs the rain-drop/From the burdened spray'. Because her experience was unique, what she wrote was unique, startling with reality.

And what was her experience? Something came to her in early youth which mystics seek—direct communion with God. Emily's god was not the God of her father, she did not reach union as the Christian mystics did, through Jesus Christ, their Lord and Saviour. Her god could better be described as Being. It was with Being she was united in an experience so overwhelming that life could never be the same again.

> *Oh! dreadful is the check—intense the agony—*
> *When the ear begins to hear, and the eye begins to see;*
> *When the pulse begins to throb, the brain to think again;*
> *The soul to feel the flesh, the flesh to feel the chain.*

She longed for the return of that moment pierced with eternity, and nothing or no one could take its place or make up for its loss. 'Strange Power! I trust thy might; trust thou my constancy.' When she came to write her one novel, it was imbued with passion, the passion of man for woman and of woman for man, but her experience with the ultimate made sexual attraction unnecessary for her. The lesser was engulfed by the greater and left no margin.

She had the mystic's joy which transcends the more human happiness, dependent as it is on its syllable 'hap', which means chance. Joy is the cause of itself and produces itself. It drenched the earthly world for Emily, sky, sun, moon and stars, the very ground under her feet. 'The whole world awake and wild with joy', she wrote of a hot July day.

Feeling so intense brings its own quietude, as a brimful well is still with its own plenitude. Emily Brontë was contained, she did not overflow into ecstasies, but was rational and unhysterical. She had fallen into reveries since she had been a girl, as her sister Maria had begun to do before her death. Charlotte called them trances when later she came to remember them—the pure gift of God to His creature, the free dower of nature to her child. But sometimes Emily felt these reveries were indulgence, particularly now she could give way to them on the moors with Keeper as her only companion, or in the still house after Papa and Tabby had gone to bed. Guiltily she would remember Charlotte earning her living in Brussels and Anne and Branwell doing the same at Thorp Green, all exiled from home. She accused herself of idleness when she wrote to Charlotte, who replied bracingly, '*You* call yourself idle! Absurd, absurd!'

7

Sweet dreams of home my heart may fill.
That home where I am known and loved:
It lies beyond . . .
And morn and even, my yearnings flow
Thitherward tending, changelessly.
My happiest hours, Ay! all the time,
I love to keep in memory,
Lapsed among moors, ere life's first prime
Decayed to dark anxiety—

Charlotte Brontë

CHARLOTTE's second journey to Belgium had a different kind of excitement about it because she was alone. It was January, one of the worst months for travelling, and she was a poor sailor, but, although nothing went right about the journey, to do it utterly alone gave her a real if unnatural pleasure, a feeling of freedom, even of elation. And she completed it in excellent time despite setbacks, leaving the parsonage first thing on the Friday morning and reaching the *pension* by seven o'clock on Sunday night.

She travelled by train from Leeds to London, but instead of arriving in the early afternoon did not reach Euston until ten at night. Daunted by the thought of seeking admittance at the Chapter Coffee House at what by Haworth standards was such a late hour, she took a cab to the wharf where the driver left her and her trunk the moment she paid his fare. The black river reminded her of the Styx; lights from the high piles of buildings, which seemed to spring straight out of it, slid on its oily waters. She was rowed up to several vessels heaving on the tide before the Ostend packet was found, but the rough men on board refused to admit her, bawling down that no passengers were allowed to sleep on board. She stood up in the rocking boat, hearing the water slap against its sides in the strange blackness, and asked to speak to someone in authority. The steward permitted her to embark, and she spent the night on board, listening to the screech of the wood as it strained against the elements and, in the moments of eerie silence, to the hooting and whistling of the wind and the suck of water.

Back at the *pension*, into the frolicsome, noisy little world of school, she was greeted by Madame and Monsieur Heger. She had written Charlotte a kind letter when she had been at home and gave her now a warm welcome. It was always a refreshment to see Madame Heger with her unfaded hair, her eyes with their temperate blue light, her fresh colour like the wholesome bloom of a fruit. He was small, dark and square, with the Jove-like capacity to dispense shafts of sunlight or thunderbolts but, whatever his mood, always to thrill.

They told her she must consider their sitting-room hers, but in the daytime it was in constant use by the visiting teachers and in the evening Charlotte would have felt it intrusion to join a husband and wife with their children. She was teaching Monsieur Heger and his brother-in-law English. Both learnt rapidly, but Monsieur Heger was like lightning. Cheerful laughing lessons they were as the two men strove to imitate Mademoiselle Charlotte's pronunciation that was to make them speak like Englishmen.

Now that she was by herself, without the taciturn Emily, the Wheelwrights invited her to visit them. They had a flat in an *hôtel* in the foreign sense, a collection of dwelling-houses. The parents (he was a doctor) were a well-matched couple, nice looking and kindly. It was such a relief to be amongst compatriots that Charlotte was never so shy with them as she was in other households. Visiting the Jenkinses by herself was more pleasurable than it had been with Emily, and there were the rare calls on the Dixons, when she saw Mary.

Mary had come to a watershed in her life; the death of the father had shaken the stability on which the family fortunes had been reared, and now there was no Martha to confront life for, only herself. She corresponded with Charlotte and, although she did not complain, her letters did not strike Charlotte as those of a happy person; they had always been close. Mary of course had no one to be as good to her as Monsieur Heger was to Charlotte, to lend her books and talk to her.

Monsieur and Madame Heger were the only two people in the *pension* whom Charlotte could either regard or respect. She liked none of her fellow resident teachers. Her dissecting gaze appraised them from the ringside: Mademoiselle Blanche who hated Mademoiselle Haussé, Mademoiselle Haussé who frightened Mademoiselle Blanche with her white passions, Mademoiselle Sophie who disliked Mademoiselle Blanche because she was heartless, insincere and vindictive, with all of which adjectives Charlotte heartily concurred. Into the bargain she made the unwelcome discovery that Mademoiselle Blanche was Madame Heger's daily spy.

Charlotte gave her English lessons in a new schoolroom which had been built on to the house. The Belgians were an unruly herd, rebellious and stubborn, and it was suggested that she teach under the surveillance of either Madame or Monsieur Heger whose very presence would command order, but Charlotte preferred to enforce discipline by her own methods. Her chief disadvantage was that she taught her own language through the medium of her pupils', of which she had anything but complete mastery. Her class was large, anything up to sixty pupils at a time, many of whom were young women rather than girls, and these were the most unmanageable, but Charlotte was determined to succeed. She knew nothing spread quicker in the ranks than insubordination and that it was essential for her to win the first battles; therefore she concentrated her fire on the ringleaders, holding them up to ridicule. Once they were subdued their weaker followers fell into line and she had the mastery, a heightening of colour, a slight dilation of the nostrils the only outward signs of the inward effort it cost her.

She explored the ancient capital city, liking to walk through it after the dark rush of rain or a thick snowstorm had swept it empty and made a quiet path for her through the broad, grand streets, or when she saw its spires and towers sparkling in the brilliant sunshine of an unclouded day. The picture galleries were her especial delight, particularly when she could visit them alone. Accompanied, and having to talk about what she saw, exhausted her, whereas by herself she was stimulated, although the pictures and portraits she liked and came to love were the exceptions.

She rose early or went late to linger in the garden, for then she could have it to herself. Throughout the day it was restless with girls who in good weather almost lived out of doors amongst the rose bushes and fruit trees, working at their lessons or sewing while Madame Heger or one of the teachers read to them. She would pace the white gravelled walk beside the old wall, alone but for the birds flickering amongst the tufted shrubs and thick ivy, the branches of the trees above her making it into an arbour. Amongst the roots of the doddered orchard trees, their shapes weird with age, bright nasturtiums were like patches of sunlight. In the evening she would wait long enough to see the spires of the grey cathedral fade into a blue sea of mist and smell the strong sweet scent of flower and shrub as the bloom of the garden folded for the night.

Her salary was sixteen pounds a year. From this she had to pay the German mistress ten francs a month—exactly the same amount as she and Emily had paid between them when they shared the lesson. She wanted to become really proficient at German, for with that and her French, which was improving every day, she would be well equipped for the future. It really was a necessity for her to acquire a thorough knowledge of German, and this was the reason why she remained on in the *pension*. Ellen wrote that people were saying she had returned to Brussels because she was going to announce her engagement to someone over there! They could not believe that she crossed the sea merely to return as teacher to Madame Heger's. She received the tart reply that Charlotte never exchanged a word with any man other than Monsieur Heger, and seldom indeed with him.

She hungered for news of home, and it was to Branwell she turned to be fed as though, solitary in Brussels, she longed to re-establish between them the old comradeship of Us Two. She wanted to know if he was in better health and spirits, and Anne—did she continue to be pretty well? Would he give her a detailed account as to how he got on with his pupil and the rest of the family? He was to tell her everything he could think of. And for her, she was very well and wagged on as usual. Amongst the hundred and twenty persons who composed the daily population of this house, there were only one or two for whom she could have anything like regard. This was not owing to foolish fastidiousness on her part, but to the absence of decent qualities on theirs. They were very false in their relations with one another, but they rarely quarrelled, and friendship was a folly they were unacquainted with. The black swan, Monsieur Heger, was the sole veritable exception to this rule (for Madame, always cool and always reasoning, was not quite an exception). But Charlotte rarely spoke to Monsieur now, for, not being a pupil, she had little or nothing to do with him. From time to time he showed his kind-heartedness by loading her with books, so that she was still indebted to him for all the pleasure or amusement she had. Except for the total lack of companionship, she had nothing to complain of. It was a curious metaphysical fact that in the evenings when she was in the great dormitory alone, having no other company than a number of beds with white curtains, she always recurred as fanatically as ever to the old ideas, the old faces and the old scenes in the world below. 'Give my love to Anne, and believe me yours—Dear Anne, write to me, Your affectionate Schwester C.B.' She opened her letter to add the postscript, 'Mr Heger has just been in and given me a little German Testament as a present. I was surprised, for since a good many days he has hardly spoken to me.'

Branwell, overcoming his own homesickness at Thorp Green, did not answer her letter. They were now on opposite banks of the river with no bridge connecting them.

The carnival struck Charlotte as nothing but masking and mummery. Monsieur Heger took her and one of the pupils into the town to see the masks. It was animating to watch the immense crowds and the general gaiety, but she considered the masks were nothing. And after the carnival came the gloom and abstinence of Lent—coffee without milk for breakfast, vinegar and vegetables, with very little salt fish, for dinner and bread for supper. How she hated their Romanism which deemed a lapse in church-going worse than falsehood; *la lecture pieuse* which came at the end of each day and from which she escaped if she could; talk of mortification of the intellect, humiliation of reason and the flouting of down-to-earth common sense.

She had hoped when she came to Brussels that she would in time be introduced to connections far more improving, polished and cultivated than any she had yet known. George Dixon was a pretty looking and pretty behaved young man, so characterless he was apparently constructed without a backbone. As for Mr Jenkins— Charlotte described him to Ellen as that unclerical little Welsh pony. She had little opinion of the English clergy either at home or abroad and referred to her father's curates as 'the Holys'. The English living abroad, in their over-flounced tumbled dresses of costly silk and satin, did not show up well amongst the trim foreigners. Madame Heger's dark silk dresses fitted her as only a French semptress could make a dress fit, suave and smooth as their wearer gliding in and out on her noiseless slippers.

It was on holidays that Charlotte missed Emily most. Last year when they had been together fête-days had been times of veritable re-creation. But now it was very terrible to be left alone for hours at a time in the empty hive of a building with four great empty schoolrooms at her disposal. The silence and loneliness of the house weighed on her like lead.

Madame Heger never came near her on these occasions, yet she must have known Charlotte was quite by herself. She was not any colder to the English teacher than she was to the others, indeed Charlotte had heard that she praised her very much to everybody and said what excellent lessons she gave, but the others were less dependent on her than Charlotte was, for they all had relations and acquaintances in Brussels.

She wrote Emily that of late Monsieur and Madame Heger rarely spoke to her, and she really didn't pretend to care a fig for anybody else in the establishment. But Emily was not to suppose from this she had a *warm* affection for Madame Heger. Charlotte was convinced Madame did not like her—why, she could not tell, nor did she think Madame had any definite reason for her aversion. Monsieur Heger was wondrously influenced by Madame, and Charlotte would not wonder if he disapproved very much of Charlotte's unamiable want of sociability.

'I get on from day to day in a Robinson-Crusoe-like condition—very lonely', her letter continued. 'That does not signify. In other respects I have nothing substantial to complain of, nor is even this a cause of complaint. Except the loss of Monsieur's goodwill (if I have lost it) I care for none of 'em. I hope you are well and hearty. Walk out often on the moors.'

Madame Heger told her to cultivate happiness, but happiness was not a potato to be planted in mould and treated with manure. Happiness was a glory shining down from far heaven. Madame Heger of course did not 'know' Charlotte. For one thing she was under the quite mistaken impression that she was a bluestocking and warned her not to study too much lest the blood all went to her head. Her husband had a more accurate assessment of the English teacher's attainments. He had malign glee in pointing out with chuckles at every opportunity that Mees Charlotte's reputation for learning in the *pension* was little more than superstition.

He really was not at all a good little man, although he had good points. In the earlier days, when Charlotte's cleanly written composition, tied neatly with ribbon, was whisked away by the professor as he made his rapid tour of the desks, she had written an essay on the death of Napoleon. When she saw him knitting his brow or protruding his lip over one of her exercises, which had not as many faults as he could have wished, she used to think that in his eager grasp after supremacy, his ability to flash danger and discomfort around him, he had points of resemblance to Napoleon Bonaparte.

Yes, he liked her to commit faults, a knot of blunders was as sweet as a cluster of nuts to him. The jealousy he suffered from was not the tender kind of the heart, but the sterner, narrower sentiment of the head. He would accuse her of the most far-fetched imitations and impossible plagiarisms. She liked to see him jealous, it lit up his nature and threw all sorts of queer lights and shadows over his dun face. He could look like a wrathful cat when his black whiskers curled and his eyes had a cloud in their glitter.

Anne and Branwell were at home for the summer holidays. The Robinsons had given Anne a puppy when she pleaded with them not to drown it, a curly coated King Charles spaniel. She wrote and described it to Charlotte, so silky Anne called her Flossy, with a black and tan head and back, the loveliest dog anyone could imagine. As Keeper was Emily's, so Flossy belonged to Anne. All of them at home except Charlotte. She pictured them walking on the

moors in the clear upland air. In Brussels it could be
Asiatically hot. All her friends were leaving—Mary had
gone, the Dixons were going and the Wheelwrights
following. She longed to live once more among Protestants,
they were more honest than Catholics. A Romish school
was a building with porous walls, a hollow floor and a false
ceiling. Every room had its eyeholes, and what the house
was so were the inhabitants, very treacherous. They all
thought it lawful to tell lies, and called it politeness to
profess friendship when they felt hatred. How Madame
Heger's blue eye could graze one with their hard ray like a
steel stylet.

Soon it would be the holidays, five weeks of them, when
Charlotte would be practically by herself. Everyone was
joyous and animated at the thought of going home. For the
first time in her life she dreaded the vacation.

Her dread was such that the first half passed rather
better than she had expected. Her only companion was
Mademoiselle Blanche at meal times. The Englishwoman's
dislike of the Frenchwoman was so apparent that her table
companion now did not speak to her, to Charlotte's relief.

It was fine, but not so insufferably hot as the previous
year, so that she was able to tramp about the streets and
boulevards and the long alleys in the summer park. She
went on a pilgrimage to the cemetery where Martha was
buried, and walked far beyond it on to a hill where there
was nothing but fields. Death appalled Charlotte, no one
could tell how long or how terrible the moment of dissolution might really be. So when she thought of Martha it
was to remember her cold, coffined, solitary underneath
foreign sod, with the rain from the Sunday they had
visited her newly-made grave forever soaking into the
earth above her.

It was evening when she returned and she could not make
herself enter the silent *pension*. The thought of the solitude
and stillness of the long dormitory daunted her. Those
ghastly white beds were turning into spectres for her, each

pillow a death's head, huge and sun-bleached. The dread
dreams of an older world and a mightier race lay frozen
in their wide gaping eyeholes.

She found herself opposite St Gudule's Cathedral, whose
bell began to toll for the evening service. What prompted
her she never knew—she answered it by going inside. She
craved companionship, friendship, counsel, and could find
none in a deserted school or a forsaken garden grey with
the dust of a departed town summer.

A few old women were saying their prayers, and she
wandered about the aisles, hearing the mutter of their
invocations. The church was old, the pervading gloom of
its interior not gilded but purpled by light shed through its
stained glass. She waited until vespers began and remained
after they were over; sharing worship with the devout was
as welcome to her at that moment as bread to the starving.
Six or seven of the scattered congregation had remained
behind and were kneeling by the confessional, an upright
like a sentry-box with two grilles and a priest inside who
could turn from one to the other. Every door of the
church was shut.

Why should she not imagine herself a Catholic and make
a real confession—just to see what it was like, to know the
consolation each of these suppliants and penitents received?
She did not really care what she did as long as it was not
absolutely wrong, as long as it served to break the mono-
tony of her time and yielded a moment's interest. It was, she
supposed, an odd thing to do, but when people were as
much by themselves as she was they do have odd fancies,
and this atmosphere breathless with prayer created its own
pattern.

She watched the procedure, saw a penitent take the place
of the one who had been shriven and kneel on the steps.
The whispers between the hidden priest and the suppliant
were so low no one but the two communicating parties
could hear. Charlotte knelt down in the vacated niche, and
waited for ten minutes as the priest heard the confession on

△ Haworth Parsonage at the time of the incumbency of the Reverend Patrick Brontë.

▽ The Sunday School and churchyard at a slightly later date. The house on the right was built by Branwell Brontë's friend John Brown, the sexton, and Mr Nicholls lodged there.

THE BRONTË "GUN GROUP"

24052

△ Emily, Charlotte, Branwell and Anne, depicted by Branwell.

▷ Anne, Emily and Charlotte, painted by Branwell about 1835.

Title-Page of *The Young Men's Magazine*. Manuscript of twenty pages, $2\frac{1}{8}$ inches by $1\frac{1}{4}$ inches in size.

The Misses Brontë's Establishment

FOR

THE BOARD AND EDUCATION

OF A LIMITED NUMBER OF

YOUNG LADIES,

THE PARSONAGE, HAWORTH,

NEAR BRADFORD.

Terms.

	£.	s.	d.
BOARD AND EDUCATION, including Writing, Arithmetic, History, Grammar, Geography, and Needle Work, per Annum, ...	35	0	0
French, German, Latin .. .. .. each per Quarter, ...	1	1	0
Music, Drawing, ... each per Quarter, ...	1	1	0
Use of Piano Forte, per Quarter, ...	0	5	0
Washing, per Quarter, ...	0	15	0

Each Young Lady to be provided with One Pair of Sheets, Pillow Cases, Four Towels, a Dessert and Tea-spoon.

A Quarter's Notice, or a Quarter's Board, is required previous to the Removal of a Pupil.

Announcement of the Brontë sisters' school at Haworth Parsonage.

It is past Twelve o'clock Anne
and I have not tided ourselys, done our
work, done our lessons and we
want to go out to play we are going
to have for pinner Boiled Beef
Turnips, potatoes and applepudding the
kitchin is in a very untidy state
Anne and I have not done our music
exercise which consists of b major
Taby said on my putting a pen in her.
see ya pitter pottering there instead of
pilling a peaces I answered O Dear,
O Dear, O Dear I will directly with
that I get up, take a knife and
begin pilling (finished pilling the potatos
papa going to walk Mr sunderland
expected

Anne and I say I wonder
what we shall be like and
what we shall be
and where we shall be
if all goes on well in the
year 1874 —in which year
I shall be in my 54th year
Anne will be going in her 55th
year Branwell will be going in
his 58th year And Charlotte
in her 59th year hoping we
shall all be well at that time
we close our paper
Emily   and Anne

ond page of a diary paper composed by Emily and Anne, and written by
Emily; dated November 24th, 1834.

Pages from Charlotte's earliest known manuscript, about 1824. The original measures $2\frac{1}{2}$ inches by $1\frac{1}{2}$ inches.

205

18/1/49.

My dear Sir

In sitting down to write to you I feel as if I were doing a wrong and a selfish thing; I believe I ought to discontinue my correspondence with you till times change and the tide of calamity which of late days has set so strongly in against us, takes a turn. But the fact is, sometimes I feel it absolutely necessary to unburden my mind. To papa I must only speak cheeringly, to Anne only encouragingly, to you I may give me hint of the dreary truth.

Anne and I sit alone and in seclusion as you fancy us, but we do not study; Anne cannot study now, she can scarcely read; she occupies

Part of a letter from Charlotte to William Smith Williams which refers in dejection to the recent death of Emily and to Anne's illness; January 1849.

The Emigrant.

When sink from sight the landmarks of our Home
And - all the bitterness of farewells oer -
We yield our spirit unto Ocean's foam,
'And in the newborn life which lies before,
On far Columbian or Australian shore
Strive to exchange time past for time to come;
How melancholy then - if morn restore
[Less welcome than the nights forgetful gloom]
Old England's blue hills to our sight again
While we, our thoughts deemed weaning from her sil
The pang - that wakes an almost silenced pa
Thus, when the Sickman lies resigned to die,
A well loved voice, a well remembered strain
Lets Time break harshly on Eternity.

Northangerland.

May 26th
1845.

'The Emigrant'. A poem in Branwell Brontë's hand, signed 'North-angerland' and dated May 26th, 1845.

the other side. Then the little door behind her grating slid back.

She felt exactly as she had felt when alone on the Thames at midnight, strangeness all round her, with no precedent to direct or guide. There must be a formula by which one began a confession but she did not know it. The ear was turned formally in her direction. She heard herself say she was a foreigner and had been brought up a Protestant. There was a slight attentive pause; then she was asked if she was still a Protestant, and because she could not lie she replied yes.

He was not a Belgian, she could tell from his profile and intelligent brow he was French. Then, he said not unkindly, she could not enjoy the happiness of the confessional. But she had to confess. Not all the rites, prohibitions and formulas of his Church could deter her, or the inhibitions and restraints of her own. Startled, he agreed to listen because it might be her first step towards returning to the true Church.

When she had done he told her his address, and said that every morning she was to go to his house, where he would reason with her and try to convince her of the error and enormity of being a Protestant.

As soon would she have dreamed of walking into a Babylonish furnace, but she never thought of the priest without remembering his compassionate eye. She was sure he was a naturally kind man, with a sentimental French kindness, to whose softness she was not impervious in this mood of desolation.

Mary, who realized she was passing through a crisis very similar to what she had endured at Miss Wooler's, wrote her urgently, telling her to leave Brussels and join her. Charlotte replied she would certainly follow her advice, and was grateful to the great service Mary had done her by tendering it. Nevertheless she did not take it. Mary had noticed that before about Charlotte: she patiently tolerated advice but that did not mean she accepted it.

Instead, she put it quietly aside and did exactly as she thought fit.

Charlotte made herself believe she was not justified in taking such a step; leaving a certainty for an uncertainty would surely be imprudent to the last degree. But there was no denying that Brussels had soured on her. Although the holidays were over and the *pension* humming and busy once more with its full complement, she still felt completely alone, for all her friends and kind acquaintances had left and she could not count the Belgians anything.

It was October and no fires lit yet although it was cold. She dreaded the nipping severity of a Continental winter. When she felt she could bear her solitude in the midst of numbers no longer she went to Madame Heger and gave her notice. Madame Heger, who appeared a rosy sugar-plum but whom Charlotte knew to be coloured chalk, accepted it with alacrity: she was a politic, plausible and interested person. When Charlotte remembered the kind and affectionate letter she wrote her at Christmas last year it all struck her as very odd, but she fancied she was beginning to perceive the reason of this mighty distance and reserve. Sometimes it made her laugh, and at other times nearly cry.

The following day Monsieur Heger sent for the English teacher and vehemently pronounced that she should not leave. Charlotte had no wish to excite him to anger, and yielded. But it was a dreary life she was living, with only one person in the house worthy of being liked. In all other respects she was well satisfied with her position, and Ellen must say so to people who inquired after her (if anyone did).

The 1st December was a Sunday, and in the morning, when everyone else in the household was at their idolatrous Mass, she was in the refectory writing to Emily. At that moment she would have liked uncommonly well to be at home, in the dining-room, or in the kitchen, or the back kitchen. She would like even to be cutting up the hash, with the clerk and some register people at the other table and Emily standing over her, watching that she used enough flour and not too much pepper, and, above all, that she saved the best pieces of leg of mutton for Tiger the cat and Keeper the dog standing like a devouring flame on the kitchen floor. 'How divine are those recollections at this moment!' she wrote. 'Yet I have no thought of coming home just now. I lack a real pretext for doing so; it is true this place is dismal to me, but I cannot go home without a fixed prospect when I get there; and this prospect must not be a situation—that would be jumping out of the frying-pan into the fire.' Emily was to tell her if Papa really wanted her very much to come home, and whether Emily did too. She had an idea that she would be of no use there— a sort of aged person upon the parish.

On 19th December she was again writing to Emily: 'I have taken my determination. I hope to be at home the day after New Year's Day. I have told Madame Heger. . . . Low spirits have affected me much lately, but I hope all will be well when I get home—above all, if I find Papa and you and B. and A. well. I am not ill in body. It is only the mind which is a trifle shaken—for want of comfort. I shall try to cheer up now. Goodbye. C.B.'

8

I knew a flower, whose leaves were meant to bloom
Till Death should snatch it to adorn a tomb,
Now, blanching 'neath the blight of hopeless grief,
With never blooming, and yet living leaf;
A flower on which my mind would wish to shine,
If but one beam could break from mind like mine.
I had an ear which could on accents dwell
That might as well say 'perish' as 'Farewell!'
An eye which saw, far off, a tender form,
Beaten, unsheltered, by affection's storm;
An arm—a lip—that trembled to embrace
My angel's gentle breast and sorrowing face—

Branwell Brontë

THERE is no doubt that Madame Heger was glad to see the English teacher depart; indeed she was led by the cool Directress into submitting her final notice rather than tendering it. Miss Brontë's competence in the classroom had begun to be outweighed by her lack of cordiality outside it.

It was incomprehensible to the Belgian that there was something so far wrong with every member of her staff which made it impossible for Mademoiselle Brontë to strike up a friendship with one of them, and she placed the blame squarely at the Englishwoman's door. If that was how Miss Brontë felt, then Miss Brontë must be prepared to enjoy her own company since none of her fellow teachers was good enough to share it. It was her own temperament that was stoking the sense of grievance she appeared to be suffering under as time went on, and her melancholy. Also her opinion of the Roman Catholic religion might be unspoken, nevertheless it was conveyed to Madame, who was *devotée*.

But the chief reason for the chilling atmosphere was that
the married woman, naturally enough, was the first to
notice Charlotte's dependence on her husband.

A capable woman with a successful career of her own,
she was a second wife and five years older than her husband.
The fifth of her six children was born a month before
Charlotte left the *pension*. She was a Continental and the
more she saw of the Englishwoman the more of an unknown quantity she became, her frigid foreign reticence
was ice that glassed an ardour and abandon that were
startling. One could not explain away as a foolish romantic
an efficient teacher who kept a large class of unmanageable
girls in order without raising her voice, yet one could not
shut one's eyes to the fact that she was dominated by a
fixed idea which centred on the Directress's husband. Nor
could this be dismissed as adolescent fervour in the teacher.
Charlotte Brontë was not a schoolgirl, she was a mature
woman in her late twenties who reacted strongly against
counsel, inference or persuasion. Also Constantin Heger
was no longer her teacher, which made her attitude towards him of the suppliant pupil an irritation to his wife,
twelve years older than the Englishwoman.

Accustomed in their marriage to handle the reins, Louise
Heger was able to warn him of what was happening long
before he would have discovered it himself. This was the
period when Charlotte wrote to Emily that Monsieur was
wondrously influenced by Madame.

There is no evidence that he felt for Charlotte at any time
anything beyond the interest of a teacher in an unusual
pupil. He was only seven years older than she, but the letter
he wrote to Mr Brontë about both his daughters was
fatherly. He was to say, years after Charlotte was dead,
that he liked his little English pupil, but she had a warmer
feeling for him. Nevertheless his attitude to her was
different from that of his wife's. Like her he was Continental, he was also human, and the recipient of admiration
is in a more interesting position than is an observer. He

might chide Charlotte for being neurotic and having black thoughts, but he was kindly when his wife would have had him be brisk. This does not mean that he encouraged Charlotte in any way, but such occasions served to emphasize to her the difference between husband and wife.

The Hegers accepted that Mr Brontë's eyesight was now so poor it necessitated his eldest daughter's presence at home, and the sharpness of the break was tempered by the suggestion that if she was successful in setting up a school in England one of their small daughters might be sent as pupil. It was agreed that she could write to Monsieur at stated intervals to keep him advised of what was happening in the parsonage home and that he would reply. Before she left he gave her a diploma certifying her abilities as a teacher.

Charlotte wrote to Ellen that she suffered much before she left Brussels; never, as long as she lived, would she forget what the parting with Monsieur Heger cost her, he who was so true, kind and disinterested a friend. Constantin Heger was to remember from the vantage point of hindsight that she left Brussels disillusioned, after having tasted strange joys and drunk deep waters, the very bitterness of which seemed to endear them to her.

Home had always meant to her in the past both sanctuary and restoration, but that was not what she experienced now. This time her return was like that of an animal whose wounds made its lair unfit for a lying-place. Yet she completed the family circle, for Branwell and Anne were on holiday. And all was well with Branwell; he had been in regular employment at Thorp Green for a year, valued as highly as Anne by their employers.

They left to join the Robinsons at Scarborough a little later. Where was the glory and freedom of being at home? Accustomed to the stir of a busy school in a foreign city, to her the parsonage was now like living inside a clock that had stopped. It depressed her to notice the difference in Papa. His sight was very poor and was going to deteriorate still further, for a cataract had formed. It was very terrible to lose one's sight, to have to depend more and more upon others. Papa was never peevish or impatient, which said much for a man who had been red-haired. What distressed him was to know that a time was perhaps coming when he would no longer be anything in the parish.

Now she had returned home everyone asked her what she was going to do. Everyone seemed to expect her to start a school there and then, but although she now had the money and the qualifications she could not leave Papa. She should not really have been away from him for so long, she should not really have returned to Brussels after Aunt's death, her conscience had warned her that her duty was at home. And she had not listened, an irresistible impulse had seemed then to be drawing her back. She had done what she had wanted to do, and this was her punishment.

For everything, her ideas and feelings, had changed, her enthusiasm tamed and broken. What she needed was a stake in life; what she had was lethargy.

Sunday, baking-day and Saturday were the three days in the week different from the others because on Sunday they went to church, on Monday they baked and on Saturday prepared for Sunday, but their very inevitability flattened them into the same sameness as the other days. There was nothing to do but walk and walk and walk, Emily her companion, her mind a treadmill as she remembered what she had left in Brussels, the presence of her master, the chance of seeing him, hearing the sound of his voice. Her thoughts fed on her memories until they were necessary for her very existence, yet this was starvation diet as she hungered for the letter from him that did not come.

Her hour of torment was the post hour—she dreaded the rack of expectation, the sick collapse of disappointment. Yet so little would keep her alive, only a few lines from him. Afraid lest she forget her French, she learnt every day by heart a half page. She knew she would see him again; she did not know how or when, but her very longing would make of it a reality. And when that day came she must be able to speak with him, no barrier of language must be between them as there was a barrier of distance now. As she pronounced the French words in the silence of her room it seemed as if she were chatting to him as they used to chat.

With only two of them at home, she and Emily were thrown closer together than they had ever been. Not that this closeness made for more intimacy; Emily's self-sufficiency marooned her as the sea isolates an island from the mainland. She was happy in that the week, Sunday, baking-day and Saturday, sufficed her. Charlotte would go so far as to call her a recluse.

She did not think there was anyone she admired more than Emily, who was strong where she was weak, not dependent on anyone for her peace of mind, but it was admiration tinged with something like timidity. She and Tabby had waited, sick with dread, in the dark passage when they heard Emily drag Keeper, who had been found lying on the clean white counterpanes again, downstairs. Emily had sworn this was the last time Keeper would do that, but the watchers knew she had been warned that Keeper must on no account be struck or he would fly at her throat. The two women saw the girl plant the ugly strong dog in the corner and, before he could spring, pommel his fierce red eyes with her bare fist until he could not see. She bathed his swollen face afterwards and Keeper padded after her, more her dog than ever. Emily had mastered him.

Charlotte was offered a situation as first governess in a large school in Manchester at a salary of a hundred pounds per annum, but she refused it. Since leaving Papa was now out of the question, a new enterprise was entered into with varying degrees of enthusiasm by the three sisters—turning the parsonage into a small boarding-school. It was quite a large house, and with a few alterations could be made to accommodate five or six pupils.

This was certainly not Charlotte's dream; she longed to

travel, to live a life of action, to have movement around her. Haworth had once been a very pleasant place to her, but it was no longer so. But running their own school would be a worth-while occupation.

So she busied herself trying to set the wheels in motion. Her last mistress before she went to Brussels was written to and told of her plans, various other letters sent to any likely person. She even made so bold as to call on a lady she did not know very well. Ellen's and Mary's good offices were elicited, a prospectus drawn up when Anne and Branwell were at home for the holidays and cards of terms printed.

She was told that if the Whites had only known a month earlier they would have sent their daughter, also Colonel S.'s, but both now had been promised elsewhere. The lady upon whom she called regretted her children were already at school in Liverpool; she took a great interest in what she called a most praiseworthy undertaking, but feared Miss Brontë would have some difficulty making it succeed because of Haworth's retired situation. Charlotte bravely pointed out this was an advantage as, had Haworth been a large town, she would have had to charge high fees. Wisely no alterations were made to the parsonage until there was the promise of at least one pupil. As the months passed without fulfilment Charlotte bore the disappointment stoically enough, admitting that the aspect of Haworth would daunt both mamma and daughter.

Emily was not greatly taken with the idea; she welcomed nothing that would disturb the even tenor of her day, the maturing of one season into another. She heard the chuckle of spring in the autumn blackbird's throat and the loud, long song of the storm-cock on a still day when it foretold rain. Woven into her background, it provided the perfect stimulus for her thoughts and ideas which clothed themselves in her poetry, for the excitement of living in and through her Gondal characters. Nor did she like teaching, but she would look after the housekeeping, and of course the chief advantage of a school in the parsonage was that it would bring Anne home for good.

Anne was probably the one of the three to whom it meant most, to whom its abandonment was to be the sharpest disappointment. Although she filled her post at Thorp Green to her employers' satisfaction she had never been happy there. A school of their own would mean she was no longer an exile, that she could develop her personality in teaching, which she loved, in the congenial atmosphere of home. The Latin lessons would devolve on her, as well as helping Charlotte with German, and the pianoforte—Emily was the musician of the family, but she had not enjoyed teaching it in Brussels.

That Charlotte was in love with Constantin Heger is proved by the letters she wrote him during the two years after her return from Brussels, yet they were not love letters in the conventional sense. If he had not been a married man she would not have written them. She did not think of herself as a rival to his wife, who was the mother of his children to whom he was devoted. Such an idea would have struck her as the height of absurdity. In her superb novel *Villette* she described the passion her heroine felt as a closely clinging and deeply honouring attachment. This attachment longed to take upon itself all that was painful to the loved one.

So we find her in the first letter we have, which was not the first she wrote to him, writing in July in his beloved language that she was pleased on his account the holidays were approaching. She had heard he was working too hard and that his health had suffered in consequence. For that reason she refrained from writing a single complaint about his long silence—rather would she remain six months without hearing from him than add one grain to his already too heavy weight.

She referred to an earlier letter she had written which had been less than reasonable because sorrow was at her heart, but she would try to be selfish no longer. His letters were one of the greatest felicities known to her, but she would await the receipt of them in patience until it pleased and suited him to send her any. Meanwhile she might well write him a little letter from time to time—he had authorized her to do so. She was well aware it was not her turn to write, but, as Mrs Wheelwright was going to Brussels and was kind enough to take charge of a letter, it seemed to her that she ought not to neglect so favourable an opportunity.

It was not a little letter she wrote, it was a very long one. She told him of her, not their, plan for running a boarding-school in the parsonage. 'I do not say I should succeed, but I shall try to succeed—the effort will do me good. There is nothing I fear so much as idleness, the want of occupation, inactivity, the lethargy of the faculties; when the body is idle, the spirit suffers painfully.

'I should not know this lethargy if I could write. Formerly I passed whole days and months in writing, not wholly without result, for Southey and Coleridge—two of our best authors, to whom I sent certain manuscripts— were good enough to express their approval; but now my sight is too weak to write. Were I to write much I should become blind.'

Charlotte, like Branwell, had suffered from poor sight since her youth, but it is revealing that it is only in this letter that she mentions that it was worsening. Her father's increasing blindness was a terrifying warning of what might be in store for her, but her lethargy was not caused by weakening sight; her weakening sight, either imagined or real, was caused by her lethargy. In love with Constantin Heger, she had neither the concentration nor peace of mind to achieve creative work. Her output during this period consisted of some poems, one of fifty-eight verses and all on the same theme as that with its tell-tale title of 'Master and Pupil', poems which pass the borderline into bathos.

'This weakness of sight is a terrible hindrance to me', her letter continued. 'Otherwise, do you know what I should do, Monsieur? I should write a book, and I should dedicate it to my literature-master—to the only master I ever had—to you, Monsieur. I have often told you in French how much I respect you—how much I am indebted to your goodness, to your advice. I should like to say it once in English. But that cannot be—it is not to be thought of. The career of letters is closed to me—only that of teaching is open. It does not offer the same attractions; never mind, I shall enter it, and if I do not go far it will not be from want of industry. You, too, Monsieur—you wished to be a barrister—destiny or Providence made you a professor; you are happy in spite of it.'

Charlotte's letters were considered at the Pension Heger to be *exalté* and inappropriate. It was hoped that the lack of reply would tone down this excessive ardour until they ceased altogether. An intellectual correspondence would have been balm and stimulus to Charlotte, but neither Constantin Heger nor his wife was likely to contemplate such treatment. Their method was to attempt to regulate the sluice gates by doing nothing.

Anne and Branwell were at home for their summer holiday, which was made uneasy by Branwell's behaviour. His nervousness and irritability alarmed his family, who did not know what was wrong with him. His Halifax friends too, when he visited them, noticed his intensity and agitation. Instead of dreading, like Anne, the end of the holidays, he chafed to return to Thorp Green.

Mrs Robinson, his charge's mother, was suffering from the same malady that afflicted the majority of her sex of that day, the boredom of being a woman. In her forties, no longer fanned like her two older daughters by the prospects and expectations of the future, she had only the present, tied to the man to whom she had been married for twenty years. He was no longer active, but more or less of an invalid with the active man's dyspeptic invalidism of moodiness and bad temper.

Branwell had the same propensity for worship that Charlotte had. In Mrs Robinson's circumstances it was recompense to know that her son's tutor, some seventeen years her junior, admired her to the point of adoration. She became endowed with the very attributes with which he endowed her, sweetness, unselfishness, devotion to her invalid for which she was repaid by impatience and temper.

Branwell Brontë might be only her son's tutor, but he was no ordinary young man. The longer and more intimately she knew him the more remarkable he became, with the quickened sensibilities of the literary genius, an inspiring flow of language and a veneration for herself that made her feel holy.

The husband's opinion of his son's teacher diminished as his wife's increased. It was quite out of place for one's *employé* to pretend he could write, and peculiarly discomfiting to learn that he had received a complimentary letter from Macaulay on his literary ability. Mr Robinson's unpleasantness to Branwell made him not only uncomfortable but unhappy. It was on one such occasion that Mrs Robinson was particularly kind to him to make up for her husband's unkindness, an occasion that took her and Branwell unawares, for she revealed to him that what he felt for her she felt for him.

From then Branwell's position became fraught with danger, but the titillation, excitement and delicious moments hid its precariousness. That something was happening between her mistress and her brother became obvious to Anne, who was appalled and who never had a moment's peace for the remainder of her time at Thorp Green. 'Sick of mankind and their disgusting ways', she wrote at the back of her Prayer Book in tiny script for only her eyes to see.

When she received no reply from Constantin Heger, Charlotte assumed her letters were not reaching him; it is not difficult to know who she felt was intercepting them. In October, before she had been home a year, she wrote to him that she was in high glee that morning—and that had rarely happened to her these last two years. Mary and Joe

Taylor were going to Brussels, and Joe had offered to take charge of a letter for him, promising to deliver it to him himself so that Charlotte would be certain he had received it.

She had not time to write a long letter, also she was afraid to worry him. She only wanted to know if he had heard from her at the beginning of May (the unreasonable letter she referred to in the very long one she wrote in summer) and again at the beginning of August. She told him that for six months she had been awaiting a letter from Monsieur—six months' waiting was very long, you know. However, she did not complain, and would be richly rewarded for a little sorrow if he would now write and give his letter to this gentleman, or his sister, who would hand it to her without fail.

'My father and my sister send you their respects. My father's infirmity increases little by little. Nevertheless, he is not yet entirely blind. My sisters are well but my poor brother is always ill.' Charlotte's pen had the dramatization, the heightening for effect, of the born story-teller. Certainly Branwell's behaviour in summer had been unsatisfactory, but at the moment of writing he was as certainly not ill, nor had he reached the stage yet when he could be described as always ill. He was in settled employment, in a comfortable post that left him much time on his hands, where he had been for nearly two years. We know that Anne did not mention at home her suspicions or certainties regarding her mistress's flirtation with her brother, so that when the news did break upon the parsonage it came as much more of a shock.

And Branwell, when he returned with his sister at the end of the year for their holidays, was quite different from what he had been in summer, cool and collected, very much the master of the situation.

That was not what Charlotte felt when she asked Joe Taylor on his return if he had a letter for her and received the reply: 'No, nothing.' She made herself believe Mary would have it, but when she saw her friend she was told:

'I have nothing for you from Monsieur, neither letter nor message.'

She wrote to her French teacher at the beginning of January to tell him the effect his silence was having upon her. 'Day and night I find neither rest nor peace. If I sleep I am disturbed by tormenting dreams in which I see you, always severe, always grave, always incensed against me. Forgive me then, Monsieur, if I adopt the course of writing to you again. How can I endure life if I make no effort to ease its sufferings?'

During these winter months Charlotte's sun never passed its nadir. Mary Taylor was leaving England to join one of her brothers in New Zealand; there was some talk of her coming to Haworth to say goodbye, but instead Charlotte went to her for a few days.

Charlotte's headaches, sickliness and flatness of spirits made her a poor companion, and she felt miserably aware that her presence was a sore drag on the lively, talkative, gay company who always collected round the Taylors. Only Mary was grieved when she left, Mary whom she was never to see again, to whom she could speak as she could speak to few.

Mary's advice was on no account to stay at home. She predicted that if Charlotte spent the next five years at the parsonage it would ruin her; the solitude was undermining her health, and once that was gone she was lost. Charlotte admitted she did not like it, that she enjoyed the novelty of change at first, as she had enjoyed Brussels at first. But her nature and temperament made her afraid of happiness. As happiness was not meant for her, so she must not look for the kind of normal life others enjoyed, varied with contacts and companionship. 'Think of what you'll be five years hence!' Mary warned her, and was so dismayed to see the dark shadow cross over her friend's face as she thought of it that she said: 'Don't cry, Charlotte.' Charlotte did not cry, but went on walking up and down the room. In a little while she said: 'But I intend to stay, Mary.'

She was no longer young; in April she would be twenty-nine. And life was bearing away. She felt as if they were all buried at Haworth.

And now she was twenty-nine, in her thirtieth year. A new curate took the place of Mr Smith, a large unsmiling man called Nicholls who came from Ireland—Papa preferred Irish curates—but his Scots blood successfully subdued any Irish blarney or devilment. The critical Charlotte's initial mild estimate of him as a respectable young man who read out well was soon superseded by her opinion of all curates as a vain, empty, bigoted race. Anne and Branwell returned in June for their summer holidays, but Branwell was hardly at home before he went back to Thorp Green, the explanation being that he had to be with the Robinsons until they went to Scarborough. Anne delighted her family by telling them she had given Mrs Robinson her notice before she left and would not be returning with Branwell after the holidays. With Anne at home, Charlotte felt herself free to visit Ellen.

Brontë plans were discussed inside-out and outside-in by the whole family before a move was made, and no member ever left the parsonage without Papa's comfort being taken into consideration and his permission being granted. Ellen wrote to inquire if Charlotte could be allowed to stay for a further week than the allotted fortnight, and Emily replied that if Ellen had set her heart on it Charlotte had their united consent.

Branwell had now returned to spend the remainder of his holidays at the parsonage. Ellen's companionship, new sights and surroundings, did Charlotte a world of good. Her mind and thoughts were taken up with what was happening around instead of inside her, and the pain of waiting for something that did not come was eased. Only on the morning of her departure was she disturbed with a feeling strong enough to be called presentiment that she was returning to sorrow.

The journey home was pleasant, even exhilarating. The

moment she saw the gentleman who shared her railway carriage she knew he was not only a foreigner but a Frenchman. Charlotte had the boldness of the shy, also it was such a joy for her to speak again her master's language. She asked him: 'Monsieur est français, n'est pas?' Her companion acquiesced and was even more surprised when his fellow traveller correctly inquired if he had not spent most of his life in Germany. Constantin Heger might be a Belgian, but his ancestry was German, for originally the Hegers came from Vienna, which was why they wrote their name in the German way without an accent. To hear French spoken again as he would speak it was like music in Charlotte's ears.

It was ten o'clock at night before she reached home. Branwell was in bed after drinking himself into a stupor. There was nothing particularly unusual about that until Anne told her what had caused the bout.

On Thursday he had received a letter from Mr Robinson dismissing him, intimating that he had discovered his proceedings, which were bad beyond expression, and charging him to break off instantly and forever all communication with every member of his family.

9

He saw my heart's woe, discovered my soul's anguish,
How in fever, in thirst, in atrophy it pined;
Knew he could heal, yet looked and let it languish—
To its moans spirit-deaf, to its pangs spirit-blind.
He was mute as the grave, he stood stirless as a tower;
At last I looked up and saw I prayed to stone:
I asked help of that which to help had no power,
I sought love where love was utterly unknown—

Charlotte Brontë

IT IS difficult in an exaggerated character such as Branwell's, impregnated as it was with a lifetime of fantasy, to assess when Lord Percy is speaking through his lips and writing with his pen or when he is only imagining himself as Lord Percy. To him Mrs Robinson was a hybrid of dream and reality, and he had reached the stage of dissolution when he was unable to lose himself in dream or make contact with reality. The truth was further blurred by the fact that he was drinking and taking laudanum, with the result that his delusions, wild, insane or comforting, had the nightmare quality of reality.

One unbroken thread after his dismissal ran through all his rantings, fevers and fits, the collapse of his vaulting hopes, and that was his good opinion of Mrs Robinson. It never wavered. His friends all heard of this lady, her mental and physical attractions, her sweet temper and unselfishness. He loved to speak of her—even to a dog.

He had never dreamed that his love for her would be returned. 'She was all I could wish for in a woman, and vastly above me in rank, and she loved me even better than I did her.' Mr Robinson, who suffered from a chronic liver complaint, was dying. 'I had reason to hope that ere long I should be the husband of a lady whom I loved best in the world, and with whom, in more than competence, I might live at leisure to try to make myself a name in the world of posterity, without being fettered by the small but countless botherments, which like mosquitoes sting us in the world of work-day toil.'

Letters from her lady's maid and physician after his dismissal informed him of her firm courage and resolution that whatever harm should come to her none should come to him. It nearly drove him mad thinking of what she was enduring at the hands of a jealous husband for his sake. The probability of her becoming free to give herself and her estate to him did not abate her lover's fear of her going into a decline because of her tribulations. Through his orgies of self-pity he believed her fate was even worse than his own.

Branwell lived for three years after his dismissal, the ruin of a man, a danger to himself and those around him. During that time he made sporadic efforts at writing and painting and plagued his friends to find him a post, preferably where he could travel. What about abroad?—anything to get away from the shiver of the wind amongst the ash branches, the quietude of home, from his family who failed to understand what he was enduring. The descriptions of his sufferings fill his letters with doom. He was without life, an old man, his clock at twelve at night, too hard to die and too wretched to live, his constitution still so strong that it would keep him years in torture and despair when every hour he prayed that he might die, he was toasting daily and nightly over a slow fire.

Once or twice a startling shaft of revelation penetrated his befogged senses: 'When I fall back *on* myself I suffer so much wretchedness that I cannot withstand my temptations to get *out* of myself.' 'I have been in truth so much petted through my life, and in my last situation, I was so much master, and gave myself so much up to enjoyment.' His

Haworth boon companions considered in their rough ready way that what ailed him was the bottle and the cure lay in knowing when to stop, his artist friends such as Leyland tried to encourage him to finish his novel *The Weary Are At Rest* and his poem *Morley Hall*, an epic based on Leyland family tradition. The horror of his predicament was the loss of what he called the springy mind, to know that if he saw the Elgin Marbles again his eyes would roam over them like the eyes of a dead cod fish.

The Brontës always considered Branwell the victim and Mrs Robinson the cause of his ultimate downfall. Papa was to call her his son's diabolical seducer. Certainly her involvement in Branwell's story was not teased solely out of nothing or even little by his over-fevered imagination. Whether it ever reached actual liaison is an open question: I personally think this most unlikely in a household such as Thorp Green Hall. But her children, particularly Branwell's charge Edwin, were aware of the something that Anne was aware of and threatened Mama, if she did not give in to them, to tell Papa about Mr Brontë. Both Mrs Robinson and Branwell felt guilt where Mr Robinson was concerned. It must be remembered that they lived in an age when concupiscence was as evil as its satisfaction, vengeance belonged to God and hell fire was not a mere figure of speech. Also Branwell, the self-professed atheist, was a clergyman's son reared on the Ten Commandments, throughout whose life church, inn and graveyard were contiguous.

Probably what alarmed Mrs Robinson more than anything else was Branwell's sudden, unlooked-for return to Thorp Green after he and Anne had left for their holidays. That she, realizing matters were getting out of hand, complained to the husband of the tutor's unseemly behaviour and so was the instrument of his dismissal can explain her later placatory attitude to Branwell through her go-betweens. She had not only to keep him quiet at all costs but she had him, because of what had passed between

them and to use an expression current in her day, on her conscience. She was a woman of the world, a professional
compared to Branwell's amateur. She had cause to believe
in his love for her and harped upon that string for all she
was worth. That she was a clever performer who could
play two strings at the same time is proved by her husband's
personal cash account which he kept himself. No breath of
suspicion can have besmirched his wife as far as the bounder
of a tutor was concerned, for after he had dismissed him,
his cash book records repeated costly gifts she received
from her husband. The eldest Robinson girl was giving
trouble at this time with her rebellious headstrong ways,
and her mother may have implied to her husband that it
was with her namesake Lydia that Mr Brontë had forgotten
his station and to whom he had made his unbecoming
advances.

Anne used to believe that the year she reached twenty-five
would mark an era in her life. In 1845 she attained her
quarter of a century and wrote in her diary paper that she
could not well be flatter or older in mind than she was now.
It was Emily's birthday and four years since they had
written their last diary paper. Branwell had just been
dismissed and, at the time they wrote, was away from
home—he was in such a state after hearing from Mr
Robinson that Papa had sent him away for a week under
the care of John Brown. Anne recalled that when she had
written her last diary paper she had wished to leave Thorp
Green. How wretched she would have been had she known
that she had four more years to endure of it. During her
stay there she had had some very unpleasant and undreamt-
of experiences of human nature. Charlotte's restlessness
stirs through her sister's note as she records that she is
thinking about getting another situation and wishes to go
to Paris. It was a dismal, cloudy wet evening and they had
had so far a very cold wet summer.

Emily's diary paper was *allegro* compared with Anne's
andante. 'My birthday,' she began, 'showery, breezy, cool.

I am twenty-seven years old today.' Happily she described
the first long journey she and Anne had made by themselves together, leaving home on the Monday, sleeping at
York, returning on the Tuesday to Keighley, where they
stayed the night, and walking home on the following
evening. Anne's first sight of York Minster had made such
an impression upon her that she had noted it in a previous
diary paper, but Emily made no reference to this wonder in
hers. Instead she describes how they spent their excursion
'being' different Gondal characters. 'The Gondals still
flourish bright as ever', she wrote, and she and Anne
intended to stick firm by the rascals as long as they delighted
them, which she was glad to say they did at present. 'I must
hurry off now to my turning and ironing,' she finished. 'I
have plenty of work on hand, and writing, and am altogether full of business. With best wishes for the whole house
till 1848, July 30th, and as much longer as may be. I
conclude.'

The new plan was to write their next diary paper in three
years' time instead of four. As it turned out, the two they
had just penned were to be their last. The 'as much longer
as may be' ran short in 1848.

Both were writing poetry and prose. Anne was struggling
to finish her *Passages in the Life of an Individual* and writing
poem after poem in the pretty little book she had made
herself. 'Only dreams can bring again the darling of my
heart to me,' she wrote of her dead love, extracting what
comfort she could from what might have been. 'Cold in
the earth—and the deep snow piled above thee!' thrilled
Emily's more than life-size Rosina to Julius of Angora. She
had read out to Anne some of the Emperor Julius's life
she was writing, but not her poetry, not even to Anne,
who wondered what it was about. This was the peak of
Emily's most productive period, when her mind was like a
plough releasing power and fertility as it turned over the
earth of her thoughts.

And Charlotte was passing through the longest stretch of

her life unable to write, a tract sterile for her as a desert, with no oasis of hope. A boarding-school at the parsonage was now out of the question, with Branwell either frenzied or sodden with drink, a living moral of what not to become. The only time they were quit of him was when he was at the Black Bull.

His effect on Charlotte was more adverse than it was on anyone else; a time came when she could not bear even to be in the same room with him. This aimless, idle creature shambling about the parsonage or lurching from the Black Bull was now the symbol of all their shattered proud ambition, their star-gazing dreams, their cherished ideals and blessed hopes. She knew his short spurts of activity, his fumbling efforts at turning a new leaf, would never come to anything, the sudden flares of a guttering candle. He was a permanent incubus, a drain on every resource and an impediment to all happiness. All they had to be grateful for was when he was tolerably quiet, when he could not fleece anything more from Papa on the pretence of being pressed for a debt, when there was no guest at the Black Bull for him to go down the brae to entertain for his lawing. 'I never sent for him at all,' the innkeeper was to deny later, 'he came himself, hard enough.'

During that autumn Charlotte lighted upon the little book in which Emily wrote some of her poems. She was aware of course that Emily wrote poetry. They all did and had since their early days, so natural to them it was taken for granted. But she was careful to read them in secret because she knew that Emily would not like her to see them.

The bond between Brontë and Brontë was all the stronger because it was tacit; they shared everything but the inner life, which was sacred to its owner and which none of the others would dream of invading. This freedom they had enjoyed from their earliest days, when their father had supplied them with sixpenny notebooks but had not expected to see how they filled them, when he showed them with his big fingers how to make real books out of scraps of paper and

sugar bags and left them to the bliss of writing them. They
had shared the same characters and writing territories, produced plays in which they all took part, stories, romances
and magazines they all read, but always each had a hidden
reserve to which only she had the right of way. 'These are
our three great plays that are not kept secret', the thirteen-
year-old Charlotte wrote sitting at the kitchen table while
Tabby washed the breakfast dishes and Anne watched that
the cakes did not burn. 'Emily's and my best plays were
established the 1st December 1827, the others March 1828.
Best plays means secret plays; they are very nice ones. All
our plays are very strange ones.'

Now as she read Emily's poems they struck her as very
strange. She had not known that anyone, certainly no
woman, could write such poetry, the rare wild cry of a swan
who has winged over unknown country and into un-
charted spheres. They stirred her like the sound of a
trumpet, they were the signal notes proclaiming what she
had always felt. The Brontës were unknown, cut off from and
of no moment in the world, but they were different from the
common run, and Emily had the peculiar inborn quality of
genius. After reading her poems life could never be the
same for Charlotte.

And it was never again the same for Emily. That her elder
sister had read what had been meant for no living soul was
dispossession, violation, a rifling of her sanctuary. One
more great poem she wrote, 'No Coward Soul is Mine'.
A few weeks after Charlotte's discovery she penned the
first draft, her microscopic script·forming the thoughts
waiting for birth in the womb of her unconscious. As far
as her poetry was concerned, nothing of importance
followed. Her one novel, *Wuthering Heights*, was written
during that winter and spring, but like her poem 'No
Coward Soul' it had been conceived in her Golden Age.

Something had disturbed her spring, she was cut off from
her source, her Golden Age was behind her, she no longer
lived in its brightness.

Emily's poems stirred in Charlotte all the old ambition she thought dead and buried. With characteristic energy and tenacity she now applied herself to breaking down her sister's resistance. To try to mitigate Emily's implacable antagonism, Anne put into their eldest sister's hands her book of poems—since Emily's had given her pleasure, she might care to look at hers. With some of Anne's and her own, Charlotte realized they had enough to make a small volume, and publication need no longer deter them. Using part of Aunt's legacy, they could now afford to publish them themselves.

When the volume came to be compiled, twenty-three of Charlotte's poems were included, twenty-two of Emily's and twenty-one of Anne's. Charlotte's contributions filled seventy-one pages, Emily's thirty-three and Anne's thirty. Female authorship must be hidden from prospective publisher, public and reviewers, otherwise the volume was sentenced to nothing but patronage and prejudice. So the surname of Bell and the first names, each initial corresponding with their own, of Currer, Ellis and Acton were chosen. Charlotte, to whom it was left to find a publisher and to deal with him when she had, referred to herself and her sisters in her businesslike letters as the Messrs Bell.

When she chose her poems for inclusion she excluded all her Angrian ones, which meant she excluded the best of her output. All three were influenced by the ballads they had read in childhood, and a ballad tells a story. But Charlotte was a born novelist, not a poet, and poetry, which is formed from essence, was no medium for her genius to create character, scenes and plot.

Emily always referred to her poems as these rhymes, and saw to it that every Gondal clue and indication was rigorously expunged. She loved the night:

> *Oh stars, and dreams, and gentle night;*
> *Oh night and stars, return!*
> *And hide me from the hostile light*
> *That does not warm, but burn.*

It was at night time that the messenger of hope came to offer to the captive chained in prison eternal liberty for short life:

> *He comes with western winds, with evening's wandering airs,*
> *With that clear dusk of heaven that brings the thickest stars.*

She sings of her darling pain, of seraph's song and demon's moan, of the thaw-wind silently melting the snow-drift.

The wind sounds through all Emily's poetry, and all its keys are heard in Anne's, but most of her verse was cast in the form of hymns, metrical forms of worship rather than songs of praise, for in her the note of jubilee was seldom heard.

In November the six months of silence had run their course and Charlotte could once more write to Monsieur Heger without breaking her promise. It was nearly two years since she had left Brussels, and in that time she had received from her one-time master two letters on which she had had to subsist.

Now she wrote that it needed painful effort on her part not to break her promise, that she had done everything to try to forget him, busied herself with occupations, denied herself absolutely the pleasure of speaking of him—did the agony of the three words she added reach him?—'even to Emily'. 'Why cannot I have just as much friendship for you, as you for me—neither more nor less? Then should I be so tranquil, so free—I would keep silence then for ten years without an effort.'

'Your last letter was stay and prop to me,' she wrote, 'nourishment for half a year. Now I need another and you will give it to me; not because you bear me friendship— you cannot have much—but because you are compassionate of soul and you would condemn no one to prolonged suffering to save yourself a few moments' trouble. To forbid me to write to you, to refuse to answer me, would be to tear from me my only joy on earth, to deprive me of my last privilege—a privilege I shall never willingly surrender.'

'May I write to you again next May?' she asked when at last she made herself conclude: 'I would rather wait a year, but it is impossible—it is too long. C. Brontë.'

But she was still loath to put down her pen and added a postscript in English, wishing she could write him more cheerful letters, for when she read it over she found it somewhat gloomy. At last she drew even her postscript to an end with the words: 'I love French for your sake with all my heart and soul. Farewell, my dear Master—may God protect you with special care and crown you with peculiar blessings. C.B.'

She did not know as she penned these words that they were the last she was to write to him. Some Brontë biographers believe that when he received this letter, Monsieur Heger wrote her with the full connivance of his wife suggesting she should address any future letters to him at the Athenée Royale, the boys' school where he taught, both Hegers knowing that Charlotte, the soul of rectitude, would be insulted at such subterfuge and break off the correspondence therewith.

This explanation has sprouted with all its confusion from the thin soil of what did happen. The Hegers children were to attest that Miss Brontë's last letter was addressed to their father at the Athenée Royale because she obviously suspected Madame Heger was interfering with those she sent to the *pension*. It was the Hegers, not Charlotte, who broke off the correspondence once and for all.

BOOK THREE

YIELD-TIME

I

Because the road is rough and long,
Shall we despise the skylark's song?—

Anne Brontë

CHAMBERS of Edinburgh recommended C. Brontë, Esq., to try as publisher of the projected book of poems Aylott and Jones of Paternoster Row. The sum of £31 10s. was agreed upon and sent as cost of publication, but it had to be followed by an extra £5 for paper and printing, and £2 for advertising. Messrs Aylott and Jones obviously thought nothing of this £2—£10 at least would be necessary if the Messrs Bell wanted their book advertised in the best newspapers and journals. A further £10 was sent, then the sisters drew in their horns. Positively they must draw on no more of Aunt's legacy.

Letters to and from the publishers began to leave and arrive at the parsonage, enlivening the days with interest. No one knew anything about them except Emily, Anne and Charlotte, who acted as amanuensis. Always one of them was about when the postman called, which was simple enough, for Tabby had not been too well that winter and Martha had to go home because of an obstinate swelling on her knee. Branwell had lost all sense of time as he staggered from bout to bout. It would be too cruel if he who was incapable of doing anything but drink should discover that the dream of their lives was about to materialize: they were going to be published, hold in their hands the book they had made, see their own words printed on a page. But they had no difficulty keeping anything from him; for long enough he had been interested only in himself.

There was a bad moment when the curious postman asked Mr Brontë about Mr Currer Bell for whom so many letters were arriving, but Papa disposed of him with the authoritative pronouncement: 'My good man, there is no such person in the parish.' And a worse time when a batch of proof-sheets failed to arrive. Charlotte had to write to the publishers and ask them to address C. Bell c/o Miss Brontë.

All three sisters were writing novels in the evening when the day's work was done, after Papa tapped the weather-glass on his way upstairs to bed and called to them not to sit up too late. Anne was at last finishing *Passages in the Life of an Individual*—that was too long and ponderous a title for a short book, simply *Agnes Grey* was better. Emily, instead of the life of the Emperor Julius, was writing a novel too, a story set in Yorkshire—it could have taken place quite near to home, Upper Withins for instance. *Wuthering Heights* was the title she found for it; it really found itself, wuthering being a local word for wind. And Charlotte was engrossed in hers, about a schoolmaster —she called it *The Master* to begin with and later changed that to *The Professor*.

All three novels were written in the first person: Agnes Grey, the governess heroine, told Anne's; Emily related hers through Mr Lockwood and the servant Nelly; and Charlotte's mouthpiece was William Crimsworth, who sought his future as a schoolmaster in Brussels.

Agnes's reactions were all Anne's, her cheeks burned and her hand trembled when she was upset, she flushed easily, eased her irritation by poking the fire strenuously, was told by her mistress not to be touchy, informed her pupils when their uncle incited them to some devilment, 'Your Uncle Robson's opinions of course mean nothing to me', and detected that the thick-set, strongly built, lofty-minded, manly Mr Robson, the scorner of the female sex, was not above the foppery of wearing stays. Agnes married the clergyman Mr Weston at the end, but this culmination is handled by the author in almost a cursory way, as if the happy ending cut her story short.

Charlotte's descriptions of happiness in her novels are more than anything else wish fulfilments in which the author never quite believes. Her slightly repellent William Crimsworth notes that man is ever clogged with his own mortality and it was his mortal nature which now faltered and plained. He was tortured by the hypochondria which Charlotte had endured as a governess at Miss Wooler's and by her fear of death as physical dissolution. Francis, the Quaker-like heroine of *The Professor*, is also not unlike Charlotte with her perseverance and sense of duty, who liked to learn and hated to teach.

The Professor always meant a great deal to its author, perhaps because with it she was able to take up her pen again after years of infertility. She set out to write of an ordinary man who would work his way through life, and whose enjoyment was a mixed and moderate cup. Moderate is its key word. Her book was shorn of all the ornamentation and redundancies of her earlier style, of Angrian excitements and extravagances. The writer had her characters well in hand, she kept a level gaze on them, she made, did not create, them. It was impossible for them to run away with her.

Anne and Charlotte when they wrote their novels used the stuff of their everyday to fashion them. So did Emily, but her everyday was not circumscribed by schoolroom or parlour or bound by a horizon. As in her poems, she used words with their intrinsic meanings, so that the single word 'bright' sounds in her context as though new minted. That her characters Heathcliff and the first Catherine are elemental does not mean they are less real. They do not cast doubt on their own credibility or the credibility of those they move amongst. All the Brontës were brought up on the Bible. Emily had sewn with black thread into her sampler how wickedness had made an outcast of Agur, the son of Jakeh, a curiously applicable portrait of Heathcliff. Her characters lived in the nineteenth century, felt the

Yorkshire weather keen on their faces, moved across the Yorkshire landscape, but they are lit by the unimpeded light that fell on Cain, Abel and Esau in the dawn of the world.

Charlotte wished the winter were over, she longed for the mild south and west winds, she hated the east wind which Emily, too, thought both dry and uninteresting. Emily had invested their legacy for them in the York and Midland line when Charlotte was in Belgium—everyone knew railways were the coming thing. But Charlotte was uneasy. Certainly their capital had not diminished, yet she would have preferred their money to be in something less spectacular but more steady. As it turned out she was right, but Emily withstood any suggestion that they should sell their shares and re-invest them at a lower rate of interest, and Anne sided with her as she always did.

So the elder sister gave in. She would rather risk loss than upset Emily. They were not a demonstrative family, but she was well aware of the bond that bound her to her sisters and they to her. That was something she would never undervalue, there was nothing like it in the world. Their affection was twined with their very life and no shocks of feeling could uproot it; small disagreements only trampled on it an instant that it might spring more freshly when the pressure was removed, no passion could outrival it, even love itself could not do more than compete with it in force and truth.

Ellen, whose ear was always cocked in readiness to hear news of a romance for Charlotte, had to be written to with some asperity when she repeated a rumour that the eldest Miss Brontë and her father's curate were about to become engaged. Mr Nicholls forsooth! Charlotte would have Ellen know that a cold far-away sort of civility were the only terms on which she had ever been with him. The curates regarded her as an old maid, and she regarded them, one and all, as highly uninteresting, narrow and unattractive specimens of the coarser sex. Yet, either consciously or unconsciously, when the three sisters came to choose a *nom de plume* they chose Mr Nicholls's middle name of Bell. He, despite the fact that he had now been at Haworth for well over a year, was making little of it. The parishioners had not taken to him and he, behind his rigid, stiff front, aware of his unpopularity, was thinking of returning to Ireland.

The proof-sheets of their poems arrived and were dispatched duly corrected in March. In April Charlotte wrote to the publishers that C., E. and A. Bell were each preparing for the press a work of fiction which could either be published together in three volumes of the ordinary novel size, or each separately in a single volume, as was deemed most advisable. Aylott and Jones did not deal in fiction, but supplied a list of the principal publishing firms in England and Scotland.

In the first week of May their poems were published, and when their complimentary copies arrived they saw for the first time the small neat dark green volume. In July favourable notices appeared in *The Critic* and *The Athenaeum*, the latter critic noting that Ellis Bell possessed a fine quaint spirit and an evident power of wing that might reach heights not here attempted. But the October issue of the *Dublin University Magazine* carried the review that cheered the brothers Bell most, and Currer wrote to the editor to thank him for their indulgent notice. Yet only two copies were sold. One of the two purchasers was a song-writer who admired the poems so much he wrote to the publishers and asked for the authors' signatures.

Altogether the mere effort to succeed had given a wonderful zest to life which Charlotte determined must be pursued at all costs. Their three novels were sent out to the publishers on the Aylott and Jones list. When they were returned the address was scored out and the same paper used for the next attempt, so that each publisher knew exactly how many of his brothers in trade had rejected it already.

The seasons in their cycle do not so much revolve as evolve

one from the other, as the lives of those who weather them ripen from infancy to youth and mature into age. The plough was put into the ground round the solitary moorland farms in spring, turning the rugged earth upside-down as it prepared it for the seed. The most critical time for the seedling is when it has exhausted the food store germinating within it, when it has to depend on its own roots and leaves. Branwell had none of the hold of root and the thrust of blade that his sisters had, yet they shared the same environment with its seemingly so arid soil. The climate of character played an important part in their growth and garnering. A crop must be sown whenever the land is ploughed, otherwise it soon becomes green with every conceivable weed. Branwell's growth had that overrun luxuriance.

He was going from bad to worse. In May, the month in which their poems were published, he read in *The Leeds Mercury* the obituary notice: 'On Tuesday last at Thorp Green near Boroughbridge, aged 46, the Rev. Edmund Robinson. He died as he had lived, in firm and humble trust in his Saviour.'

Branwell saw paradise opening before him. According to him he had been loved intensely by a lady for four years, including one of absence, as he loved her, and each had sacrificed to that love all that they had to sacrifice. Now the hope they had held out to each other was about to bloom into reality.

When a messenger was sent up from the Black Bull to say a visitor had arrived to speak with him, Branwell knew he was from Thorp Green. It was remembered that he fair danced down the churchyard as if he were out of his mind. The Robinson's coachman awaited him, and Branwell saw him alone in the small back parlour.

The man rode away after paying his bill. Those outside the room heard a noise coming from within like the bleating of a calf. When they entered, it was to find the vicar's Pat in an epileptic fit.

The story Branwell was told by the coachman was corroborated by the Robinson's physician Dr Crosby and Mrs Robinson's lady's maid, who both wrote to him: Mr Robinson had added a codicil to his will to the effect that his wife would forfeit every penny of the inheritance and her children be removed from her care if she ever again saw Branwell or remarried. Mr Robinson had done nothing of the kind; what he had done was to cut his eldest daughter Lydia out of his will because she had eloped with an actor.

But it was essential that Branwell must never make his appearance at Thorp Green. A letter he wrote to the widow was returned unopened by Dr Crosby at the command of one of the executors, all of whom hated him and would see this diabolic will was carried out without mercy. The physician advised him to give up hope.

Branwell believed everything he was told by coachman, Dr Crosby and lady's maid: that it was a pity to see Mrs Robinson, for she was only able to kneel in her bedroom in bitter tears and prayers; that they feared for her sanity, so great was her horror at having been the cause of Branwell's wretchedness and her husband's death, who in his last hours bitterly repented of his treatment of her; that when the doctor, her confidante and Branwell's, mentioned Branwell's name she fainted, and when she recovered it was to dwell on her inextinguishable love for him; that she had been terrified by vows she had been forced to swear at her husband's death-bed. Her sensitive mind was totally wrecked; she was resigned to her doom and talking of entering a nunnery.

Branwell was to receive sums, £20 at a time, through the physician. His deterioration was such that within months he was writing to Leyland, when pressed for payment for an account he had run up at the Old Cock in Halifax, 'I will write to Dr Crosby, and request an advance through his hands which I am sure to obtain.'

Every day that passed he became more of a problem, with

all the cunning of the drug addict in finding ways and means of procuring opium. Even Emily said he was a hopeless being. He slept in his father's room, which was an added anxiety, for Papa could no longer see properly and his loaded pistol still lay beside his watch at his bedside to be discharged in the morning. Branwell in his cups had been heard to say that either he or his father would be dead before the morning. But Papa would not listen to Charlotte's fear for his safety. Branwell was his son, he must be beside him in the attacks he was beginning to have when he was like a soul in hell. Charlotte could not have despised anyone more than she despised her brother when she heard him say in the morning in his hateful slurring speech: 'The poor old man and I have had a terrible night of it. He does his best, the poor old man, but it's all over with me.' Her contempt for him reached Branwell in his saner moments.

Papa could no longer read or write. There was something solitary about him as he groped his way about the house, unable to tell one of his children from the other unless they stood against the light. He had allowed Charlotte to read to him and write his letters for some time; she, his eldest daughter, had his confidence as none of the others had and filled the place of his son. His congregation watched him being led up the pulpit stairs on a Sunday. He would not be able to see them as he stood there, so high above them, pitching his words into the darkness creeping ever closer. But he had never needed note or paper even when he had his sight, so that now he did not fail them. He was still their vicar, and they were his flock.

At the beginning of August Charlotte and Emily went to Manchester in search of a surgeon who could couch their father's eyes. They found a Mr Wilson. As he would have to see the patient before he could make a diagnosis it was arranged that Charlotte should take Papa to consult him, and if Mr Wilson judged the cataract ripe they would remain.

A fortnight later father and daughter arrived at the lodging in Boundary Street which Mr Wilson had kindly recommended and which was kept by an old servant of his. The surgeon, after examining his patient, pronounced that he thought most favourably of the case. He did not approve of couching but believed in the more serious operation of extracting the cataract. In 1846 there was of course no question of anaesthetics. Papa was seventy, and he doubted if he could survive the ordeal. When they were alone Charlotte heard his despairing cry: 'I shall never feel Keeper's paws on my knees again!'

So much depended on what was about to happen that every hour was weighted with its own portent. Nothing mattered but Papa, he filled the stage, yet the background was restless and uneasy with insistent anxieties. Everything here was unfamiliar and strange, Manchester a grey place composed of drab streets of small houses like the one where they lodged. Their rooms were comfortable enough, but Mr Wilson's one-time servant was recuperating from an illness in the country, which meant that Charlotte had to do the ordering. She had not the faintest idea what to suggest in the way of meat, and hurriedly wrote to Ellen asking for hints. Ellen was so practical. Their needs were simple enough, she could cater for them, but the nurse who was coming to attend to Papa would not be content with what satisfied them. Charlotte dreaded the thought of her and was intimidated, despite her obsequious manner, when she did make her appearance. She felt the nurse untrustworthy, yet she had to be trusted to carry out her duties. They would be here for at least a month before Papa was able to travel, whether the operation was successful or unsuccessful. This meant that for four long weeks Emily and Anne would be alone with Branwell. Toothache nagged her. The three novels they had sent out with such high hopes had returned to them again and again, like homing pigeons. Charlotte was sending out *The Professor* separately now and Emily her *Wuthering Heights* with Anne's *Agnes Grey*. Charlotte had just had hers returned once more with its sickeningly familiar rejection slip.

Two assistants attended Mr Wilson on the day of the operation. Charlotte remained in the room throughout, as was Papa's wish. He lay disciplined and resolute as a soldier while the surgeons worked with him and they marvelled at his fortitude.

It was over now. Mr Wilson said he considered it quite successful, all that remained to do was to wait. The patient was to speak and be spoken to as little as possible. His eyes bandaged, Charlotte at last left him in the darkened room.

She wrote to Emily and Anne. All that remained to do was to wait. No Brontë ever threw out even a scrap of paper, and she had always a squirrel's store of bits and pieces. They were her stock in trade. It was easier for her being so short-sighted to make her first rough draft on them, when she could bring them close to her eyes.

She would begin her new book, the one she had told Emily and Anne about, with its heroine as plain and small as herself, after they had said a heroine must be beautiful to be interesting. Her pencil began to write the first sentence: 'There was no possibility of taking a walk that day.'

2

He that does not grasp the thorn
Should never crave the rose—

Anne Brontë

ALL THE profligacy of genius is in *Jane Eyre*, no scraping of
the barrel but a cornucopia with its promise of more to
come. Maria and Elizabeth fused into the one character,
memories that still palpitated of the school at Cowan
Bridge, the moors with their consecration of loneliness;
Ellen's old home 'The Rydings' and its lightning-riven oak
tree, 'Stonegappe' where Charlotte had been unhappy as a
governess, although countryside, house and grounds had
been perfect, 'Norton Conyers' with its legend of a mad
woman caged up in one of its attics, all merged in the
crucible of her imagination into 'Thornfield', and when
she came to 'Thornfield' she could not stop. The temperate
Henry Nussey with his lack of stamina who had proposed
to her was transformed into St John Rivers, inexorable as
death. The whole book pulses with vitality, and it is this
force which carries the reader with it on an irresistible tide
as it carried its author, sweeping aside any absurdities,
rhetoric and the splash of purple passage, the force of
passion with its purging strength.

Despite or because of the isolation of their upbringing,
all three sisters were generations ahead of their contemporaries in their outlook. And for this their clergyman
father was unconsciously responsible, for he had left them
to think for themselves. Charlotte's four words, 'Con-
ventionality is not mortality,' removed the foundation-stone

on which the whole rigid Victorian structure of society was reared. Anne for the life of her could not conceive why a woman should be censured for writing anything that would be proper and becoming for a man. All three took for granted that a woman could love a man as a man loved a woman, and were startled to find that those pages in their books were considered coarse.

After a stay of five weeks in Manchester Charlotte brought Papa home. The operation had been successful, and although his recovery was slow it was marked. His congregation watched him climb into the pulpit unaided and spoke of a miracle. He made a crude little pocket-book for himself out of two pieces of leather and some leaves of paper in which he wrote items such as the date the well was cleaned out. In the joy of being able to see to write once more, he was unaware that his entries were as badly written as a child's.

Charlotte found Branwell more or less the same. There never would be any change there now except for the worse. When he was not insensate with drugs he was crafty and shifty with half hints of what he was going to do next. They never knew what would happen next. A sheriff's officer arrived at the parsonage with a warrant for his arrest because of non-payment of debt, and his sisters paid what he owed rather than see him removed to York jail.

The incident was kept from Papa; everything that could be was kept from Papa. Unable to sleep at night, Branwell was beginning to stay in bed during the day. Anne once found him in a heavy stupor with the bed alight—he had forgotten to blow out the candle he had intended to read by. When she could neither rouse nor move him she ran for Emily, who had the presence of mind to fetch a bucket of water before she flew upstairs. She was stronger than Anne and able to pull their brother from the bed when she tore down the burning bed-curtains and emptied the water over them. 'Don't tell Papa', she warned Anne.

Charlotte's excitement in writing her new book reached

uch a pitch that she wrote herself into a fever which
compelled her to pause. But it was only to draw breath.
The thought of those hours at night when the three of them
were alone was like the promise of food to a hungry man.
This was their kingdom. On the chime of nine they entered
their domain, although they might not have stirred from
the familiar room where they had meals during the day. It
was lively with firelight and Emily and Anne moved in and
out of it as they walked up and down or round the table
when Charlotte read out what she had written. She listened
attentively enough to any suggestion, but she seldom
altered anything—you did not alter what had taken
possession of you.

A cruel winter ended the year their poems were pub-
ished, and the cold in Haworth was dread. Charlotte could
not remember such a series of North Pole days—England
might have taken a slide up into the Arctic zone. The sky
looked like ice, the earth was frozen, the wind as cutting
as a two-edged blade. She could not keep herself warm and
they all had colds and coughs. Papa went down with
influenza and was much depressed, but Anne was definitely
ill with the worst attack of asthma she had had since
childhood. Her breathing was painful to hear, yet she never
complained, only sighed now and again when nearly worn
out.

Her younger sister's heroism of endurance struck Charlotte as extraordinary, something she could admire but
certainly not imitate. Three years earlier she had coupled
Anne with Ellen: 'You and Anne are a pair, for marvellous
philosophic powers of endurance—no spoiled dinners—
scorched linen, dirtied carpets—torn sofa-covers, squalling
brats, cross husbands would ever discompose either of you.'
Charlotte had written that to her friend in the year her sister
had composed her heart-break of a poem to her dead love:
'Yes, thou art gone! and never more/Thy sunny smile shall
gladden me.'

Anne's one-time pupils, the two younger Robinson girls,

resumed their correspondence with her in the new year. Their governess stood for something in their lives for which they felt grateful and, as the months passed and they found themselves thrown more and more on their own limited resources, necessary. The give and take of letter and answer had been interrupted by their father's death when they had been forbidden to write—their mother had not wanted uncensored information about herself to reach Branwell's ears. The Robinson daughters knew nothing of what Charlotte termed their mother's errors, by which she meant her affair with her son's late tutor, and the Brontë sisters took every care to ensure that the resumed correspondence was kept from their brother.

The girls wrote warmly of their mother after their father's death, but this affection sharpened into bitter criticism as the year progressed and letters, written from their grandmother's at York, reached the parsonage almost daily. They no longer had a home, for Thorp Green Hall was let, their brother sent to board with his new tutor in Somerset, their disgraced elder sister ostracized by the family, and their mother spending her days of mourning in the household of her relative Sir Edward Scott.

She was at this time forty-three, her host thirty years older and his wife an invalid whose early release from a long and trying illness was awaited with expectancy. Mrs Robinson was anxious to find husbands of any kind for her two marriageable daughters and thus have them off her hands to be free to marry Sir Edward when he became a widower. Painfully the Brontës realized that Branwell had been told a cock-and-bull story when it was asserted that Mr Robinson's will had provided for his widow to be cut off without a penny should she marry again. She was, according to her daughters, Sir Edward's infatuated slave. Her angel husband was forgotten and her affair with her son's late tutor like the ashes of a fire she had no wish to rake amongst for embers. The payments her physician made to Branwell from time to time were like the interest on a lapsed

account, small disbursements that took the form of
gratuities when the sum which might have been involved
was considered.

As sometimes happens after a hard winter and tardy
spring there was a radiant summer. Their three novels
were still making their unsuccessful rounds, together
again, when the incredible happened. A publisher accepted
Wuthering Heights and *Agnes Grey* and rejected Charlotte's
The Professor.

He was Thomas Newby of Cavendish Square, who agreed
to publish an edition of 350 copies if the two authors
shared the risk of publication costs to the tune of £50
which would be refunded as soon as initial expenses were
defrayed.

The £50 was sent. Although they had decided after the
expense of their poems not to pay out any more of Aunt's
legacy on publication, this was different. After all, Emily
and Anne were not being called upon to defray the whole
cost, Mr Newby was prepared to risk something, and it was
obvious, after a year and a half peddling their wares, that
this was the best offer they could expect. Mr Newby must
have great faith in the two books, for within a few weeks the
authors received proofs to correct.

What they did not know was that their two books were
set up in print but no attempt made to publish them. Newby
was greatly shocked by *Wuthering Heights*. He may have
thought when he read them in manuscript that the gentle-
ness of *Agnes Grey* would counteract the violence of
Wuthering Heights, which would have an appeal of its own
for a certain section of the public who patronized the
circulating libraries, but when he read *Wuthering Heights*
in cold print he, scandalized by what struck him as its
brutality, changed his mind.

Acceptance of her first novel encouraged Anne to begin
her second. Her theme, plot and characters evolve together.
It is a closely integrated book stamped with the three S's
essential for a best-seller, Sincerity, Surprise, Suspense. As

her poems have a limpid quality, so her prose has a clarity which makes it a joy to read. Its form is interesting, for it begins with Gilbert Markham telling in the first person of the new tenant who had come to deserted Wildfell Hall with her child. The mysterious Mrs Graham, the neighbour-hood discovers, is not after all a widow. A clergyman's daughter is writing the book, but Gilbert Markham feels, acts and thinks like a man. The story is continued through Mrs Graham's diary which she gives to Gilbert to read, and from which he learns of her injudicious marriage and that she has run away from her profligate husband because he was beginning to contaminate their son.

Anne's attack of asthma during the winter had made Charlotte fearful for her. If only she would stop stooping over her desk day after day writing her new book. Why, they had difficulty prevailing on her to take a walk, even to talk.

Charlotte strongly disapproved of its subject matter, it was a mistake from beginning to end, Anne of all people to write about dissipation and vice. She did her best to try to dissuade her from continuing, but Anne's silence was as little amenable as Emily's intractability. She was not writing her book to amuse the reader or gratify her own taste; she was depicting the scenes and happenings when wrongdoers did wrong, the misery they brought on those around them in the short run and on themselves in the long. She was not preaching, she was telling the truth, for truth conveyed its own moral to those who were able to receive it.

That the eldest sister's book had been rejected by the same publisher who had accepted those of the two younger was perhaps the first time Charlotte had to abrogate her position at the wheel of the family bark. There can be no doubt that she was glad of her sisters' success as there can be no doubt that it was a shock as far as her own work was concerned, but Charlotte was strong enough to live past her eleventh hour. *The Professor* was parcelled up once more and sent out—this time to Smith, Elder and Co., of Corn-hill, in London.

Within three weeks she received back the familiar packet, but with it, instead of the customary slip of two curt lines, a letter. Smith, Elder regretted to refuse the book and took the trouble to say why. Also it was too short to stand by itself, but if the author had another novel of three-decker size they would be pleased to consider it.

Charlotte replied, agreeing that it might lack variety and telling them she was completing a second book in three volumes. What about their publishing the unexciting book to whet the public appetite for the more exciting one to follow? Perhaps they would be kind enough to favour Currer Bell with their judgment on this plan.

Smith, Elder's judgment was negative, but they looked forward to seeing the new work when it was completed. It was dispatched within the month. This time the author had not to wait weeks for a reply. A letter arrived from Mr George Smith, the head of the firm, offering to buy *Jane Eyre* for £500.

Nothing in Charlotte's life can ever have come up to that moment.

A visit from Ellen that autumn added a note of festivity to the parsonage household. She had been sixteen when she paid her first of many visits to Haworth, and in these fourteen years many waters had tumbled over the rocky shelves of Emily's and Anne's secret waterfall. It was still the same, although its waters were forever changing, unlike the inhabitants in the parsonage. Mr Brontë was as upright as of yore, but after his operation even more venerable, and Branwell was no longer like a Hallowe'en lantern in a wind. He had begun to lose weight and his face to become hollow, so that his small eyes looked as if gummed to the back of his head; while Tabby was more like a loaf than ever, all crust now, her shrewd eyes making up for her loss of hearing as she hobbled from kitchen to parlour and from table to fire.

Pretty Ellen was thirty now, that anxious age for a woman of her era, but she was not as conscious of the years behind as Charlotte, who had accepted spinsterhood from the age ye: eleven. Despite Charlotte's irritable repudiation of gossip coupling her name with that of her father's curate, Ellen was more than ever convinced now she had met Mr Nicholls that he had personal feelings towards his vicar's eldest daughter. Ellen, who had a great respect for the cloth, tiresomely saw very little wrong with Mr Nicholls. Charlotte had no opinion of the clergy, apart from her father, and could not see those interesting germs of goodness in him which Ellen had discovered; his narrow-mindedness for one thing made him totally uncongenial to her.

The two women's friendship went back to their school-days, and had now consolidated into an affection which no transient irritation or sudden pique could disturb. Charlotte's correspondence with Ellen acted like a safety valve through the various crises that beset the parsonage, but there was a region where her friend, so well dowered with this world's goods, could never enter, and that was the region of imagination. Its precincts had been jealously guarded since she and Branwell had held sway in that dangerous, enthralling existence where the tree bearing forbidden fruit grew so exotically luxuriant, that existence which Us Two knew of as the infernal world.

Nor was Ellen allowed to know about any Brontë literary ventures. No one was, even Papa was unaware they had all written books that were going to be published. Mary Taylor on the other side of the world was the only exception Charlotte was to make. The sisters had an almost morbid anxiety to keep secret the fact that they wrote. With publishers Charlotte took elaborate precautions, if she had to mention the name Brontë, to ensure that it was merely a postal convenience and that the authors were the brothers Bell. Less than a year later, when *Jane Eyre* was on everyone's lips, Charlotte was denying most emphatically Ellen's report that she was an author—whoever said she was publishing was no friend of hers. Though twenty books were ascribed to her, she would own none; she scouted the idea utterly. The three sisters had pledged to one another that they would never reveal their secret; after all it was a combined one—if it was discovered about one, it would be discovered about all three. It was as though they felt that if it became known, virtue would go not only from them but from their work, and of the three Emily felt this most powerfully.

Ellen, however, might not be literary, but she had enough perspicacity to know that the Brontë sisters 'did' something and were clever enough to write books whether they had or not. So when she was walking on the moors with the sisters and they saw not one but three suns shining in the lightening sky she, in all the loyalty and pride of friendship, exclaimed as she gazed up: 'That is you! You are the three suns!' At once Charlotte silenced her, nervous lest she upset Emily. But Ellen did not feel she had upset Emily, who was half smiling to herself as she stood apart on a little knoll.

Autumn brought the harvest of that golden summer when the moors were royal with heather in bloom, when the farthest distance had the clarity of nearness and every hair on a thistle's stalk was illumined against the light. This was not sky, it was firmament which globed the world like a shell, vibrant with lark song or the cry of grouse and lapwing, across which armadas of storm clouds swelled and swept, or swan-white argosies sailed.

Charlotte paid a return visit to Ellen shortly after Ellen's to Haworth. It must have been trying in the extreme for the hostess to see her guest correcting what were obviously proofs without making the slightest reference to what she was doing. Otherwise the visit passed happily and Charlotte found all well at home on her return. Next day her trunk and boxes arrived, but with extras Charlotte had certainly not packed: a screen for Papa, a cap for Tabby, a collar Emily was pleased but rather surprised to receive, a jar

slipped into Charlotte's trunk which she was so infuriated
to find filled instead of empty that she could have hurled it
all the way back to Brookroyd until she found it was for
Anne and softened somewhat.

'We are getting on here much as usual,' she remarked in
her thank-you letter. Much as usual! The very next day,
on 16th October 1847, *Jane Eyre* was published, only eight
weeks after acceptance.

There were moments when Charlotte could scarcely
credit what was happening, that anything she had written
could give pleasure to the great, Sir John Herschel, Mr
Fonblanque, Leigh Hunt, George Lewes—and, crowning
all, Thackeray, the greatest genius of his day, the giant of
giants. Hardly a day passed without papers or magazines
with still more reviews arriving from her publishers. The
libraries could not satisfy the demand for it. The mail
which Jim Feather, the postman, delivered at the parsonage
reached voluminous proportions, sure to contain some new
excitement such as a letter from G. H. Lewes telling Currer
Bell with what delight he had read *Jane Eyre*, but caution-
ing him to beware of melodrama, letters that were a stimulus
to answer. At last she was in direct touch with men of
letters, the pulsating outside world, the literary life of
London brought over the very doorstep, and she never
ceased to be grateful to her first favourable critic—W. S.
Williams, chief reader to Smith, Elder who had been
unable to put her book down. Nor could praise ever touch
her as the few words her father said to Emily and Anne
when he came in for tea after they had at last prevailed on
her to give him a copy: 'Girls, do you know Charlotte
has been writing a book, and it is much better than
likely.'

But through all the triumph and excitement there nagged
in the background the anxiety about Mr Newby. There was
no sign of *Wuthering Heights* and *Agnes Grey* making their
appearance; although accepted last, *Jane Eyre* had been
published first. Mr Newby was a most unsatisfactory,

unbusinesslike publisher, quite unlike Smith, Elder. Charlotte's gratitude to her publisher knew no bounds—she
trusted they would always have reason to be as well content
with her as she was with them.

At last in mid-December, when everyone was talking of
Currer Bell, Newby saw fit to publish his two novels by
the brothers Bell, and Emily and Anne each received their
six complimentary copies. Their excitement turned to gall
when they discovered the published book was full of
printers' errors, whilst they might as well not have corrected
the proofs for all the attention that had been paid to their
alterations. Charlotte felt keenly for her sisters when she
thought of *Jane Eyre* with its good quality paper, clear type
and everything of the best. Certainly no one would care to
have Mr Newby for a publisher a second time.

She wondered very much how *Wuthering Heights* would
be received—she told Mr Williams she would say it merited
the adjectives vigorous and original much more than *Jane
Eyre*. As for *Agnes Grey*, it should please such critics as
Mr Lewes, for it was true and unexaggerated enough.

Three different novels published within six months of
each other by three different Bells not unnaturally caused
confusion amongst the reading public and critics alike, and
the question arose, were the Bells really three different
people—what about them all being the one and the same
person? After all, were there not similarities between all
three? Never before *Jane Eyre* had any novel portrayed so
revealingly the love of a woman for a man, a departure
which shocked the unconditioned public. 'Equal as we
are!' Jane says to Rochester. And then came *Wuthering
Heights* with its 'heroine' Cathy accepting her love for the
'hero' Heathcliff as naturally as she accepted the breath she
drew. If *Agnes Grey* did not break any new ground, as
Anne's second novel *The Tenant of Wildfell Hall* published
six months later was certainly to do, it had similarities with
Jane Eyre, for both were about a governess. Even *Agnes
Grey* did not escape the criticism of overcolouring which

was applied to both her sisters' books. Acton Bell must have bribed some governess, either with love or money, to reveal to him the secrets of her prison-house in her various employments, and surely such terrible children as Agnes's pupils could not possibly exist. It was not realized that the three novels might have come out of the same workshop, but by three different craftsmen whose individual personality stamped each work with an unmistakable hand.

At first *Wuthering Heights* and *Agnes Grey* were taken to be earlier productions of Currer Bell, who wrote to her publishers that she was far from being ashamed at having them attributed to her pen but must in all truthfulness deny the honour. Somehow it altered the picture for Charlotte when Smith, Elder warned her that Newby was sedulously spreading the rumour that *Jane Eyre* was the work of Ellis Bell, and critics began to follow suit.

That winter was as cruel with its cutting east wind as its predecessor had been, and all three sisters had influenza. Anne took the longest time to recover. She wrote her last love poem, 'And while I cannot quite forget/Thou, darling, canst not quite depart'. Branwell had a graveyard cough but could still manage sometimes to get to the Talbot and Old Cock at Halifax to meet his friends, excursions which usually had the effect on his return of making him fall down in a fit. After all he had put and was putting them through, Charlotte had no sympathy to spare; it all went on Papa, who was harassed night and day, and on themselves to whom he gave little peace. What would be the ultimate end, only God knew.

As the sales of *Wuthering Heights* and *Agnes Grey* increased, Mr Newby began to cosset his two authors. To Charlotte's dismay both Emily and Anne promised him their second novels. *Jane Eyre* went into its second edition in January and Charlotte could not understand how her sisters could continue with a shuffling scamp like Newby when they might deal with an upright firm such as Smith, Elder, who had served her so handsomely. But Emily—and Anne was swayed by her in such matters—probably felt that Smith, Elder was Charlotte's preserve while Mr Newby was theirs. He was in correspondence with both Ellis and Acton Bell, agreeing with Ellis that he should not hurry over his next book. And when Acton sent him the completed manuscript of *The Tenant of Wildfell Hall* he contracted to pay Anne £25 on the day of publication and a further £25 after the first 250 copies were sold. All that can be said for this is that it was more favourable payment than for her first book, which was a loss, but cannot be compared to the £500 Charlotte received from Smith, Elder.

Currer Bell inserted a short note to the third edition of *Jane Eyre* published in April to rectify mistakes which might already have been made and to prevent future errors. The title of novelist rested on this one work alone. 'If therefore, the authorship of other works of fiction has been attributed to me, an honour is awarded where it is not merited; and consequently, denied where it is justly due.' Surely that would settle that once and for all.

She had now begun her second novel whose heroine was Emily, not Emily a parson's daughter but Shirley of independent means. Shirley had Emily's characteristics of standing on the hearth-rug with her hands behind her and reading a book with her arm thrown round Keeper. She had Emily's eagle acuteness of sight, her small, slightly marked, distinguished features, her tapering fingers, her sprightly spirits, the aspect of a gallant cavalier; her moments when her thoughts, her simple existence, the fact of the world being around and heaven above her, yielded her such fullness of happiness that she did not need to lift a finger to increase the joy. But Charlotte was a subjective, not an objective, writer, she was at her best writing in the first person, not the third, and *Shirley* has none of the surge of *Jane Eyre*. Its author is not swept forward with it so that her pen can scarcely keep pace with her thoughts. *Shirley* is a self-conscious book; Charlotte is watching herself write it.

Mr Newby did not sit on *The Tenant of Wildfell Hall* as he

had sat on *Wuthering Heights* and *Agnes Grey*. He published it early in June. It created such a sensation that he was writing before the end of the month about a second edition. Its upper-class *milieu* of house-parties and entertaining Anne knew from her residence at Thorp Green Hall, when as a governess she had sat in the background of the drawing-room with her pupils as Charlotte had sat at Stonegappe and Jane Eyre with Adèle in Thornfield Hall. But the female guests in Anne's book did not wear turbans when they went in to dinner as they did in Charlotte's, no character said to the footman in *The Tenant of Wildfell Hall*, 'Cease that chatter, blockhead, and do my bidding', as Blanche Ingram said in *Jane Eyre*. In Charlotte's book there are no dissolute scenes as there are in Anne's: it is they which made her novel a *succès de scandale*.

To Anne's bewilderment she found her book described by some as coarse with its morbid revelling in scenes of debauchery and praised by others for these very scenes. She could not have told which type of review she disliked the more.

Mr Newby was now even more assiduous on the other side of the Atlantic than he was on this. There he let it be known that as far as he knew there was only one Bell, the author of *Jane Eyre* which was then having a great run in America. On the recommendation that his new novel *The Tenant of Wildfell Hall* was definitely Currer Bell's best work, he sold it to an American publisher.

A rival firm heard that Currer Bell's second book, which Smith, Elder had promised to them for a high price, had been sold above their heads, and they at once got in touch with their English associates, accusing them of breach of faith.

On Friday, 7th July, Charlotte received a letter from Mr George Smith. Although Smith, Elder were quite sure Mr Newby's assertion was untrue, stiffly Mr Smith made it plain to Currer Bell that they would be glad to be in a position to contradict it.

That afternoon Charlotte and Anne left for London to prove to Charlotte's publishers that they were two authors, not one.

3

A withered leaf on Autumn's blast;
A shattered wreck on ocean's tide—

Branwell Brontë

DURING the four-mile walk to Keighley across open fields they were caught in a freak storm which in July had even snow as one of its constituents. By the time they reached the station they were soaked through. They only just caught the connection to Leeds where they changed into the night train for London, indulging themselves by travelling first class.

This was the first time Anne had been so far afield, her first visit to London. Both were too excited to sleep as they sat in their wet clothes and were whirled through the darkness, hearing the deafening clangour of the train, the shunting, whistling, strident noises breaking up the empty silences of stations. They arrived at Euston at seven in the morning, and went to Papa's Chapter Coffee House in Paternoster Row—the only place Charlotte knew. As her elder sister paid the cab fare, Anne caught her first glimpse of St Paul's—first York Minster, and now this——

The Row was narrow, which made its buildings seem higher than they were, and it was quiet at that hour of the morning for a city street, for the atmosphere of the Chapter Coffee House was muted. Its low small rooms were dark after the airiness of the parsonage, the shallow wide staircase, which creaked under their footsteps, was shadowed. Heavy beams brought the ceilings even lower and the wainscotted walls made the rooms even smaller. It was an interior that gave the traveller the impression of being inside a disused instrument which could now twang or reverberate only to outside sounds.

It was a relief to find themselves in a stationary bedroom where they could wash and tidy themselves, instead of being shaken in carriage or cab. They kept close together as they made their way to a long, low room upstairs for breakfast where a grey-haired elderly man gave his unusual customers punctilious attention. Afterwards they sat for a short time on a window-seat at the far end, not wishing to arrive too early at Smith, Elder's, their excitement mounting silently as they dwelt on the interview before them. It did not enter their thoughts that, being a Saturday, perhaps neither Mr Smith nor Mr Williams might be at the office, nor did they think of hiring a cab. After all, Cornhill was only half a mile from Paternoster Row.

But making their way through crowds and across unfamiliar streets dangerous with traffic held them back so that it took them something like an hour for their journey. Cornhill was as bustling as the Strand, and Charlotte loved its vitality. The West End with its parks and squares was never to mean to her what the City did. It was so much more in earnest; its business, its rush, its roar, were such serious sights and sounds. The City was getting its living, the West End merely enjoying itself.

They found No. 65 was a large bookseller's shop. There were a great many young men and lads moving about who paid not the slightest attention to them. Anne left Charlotte to take the initiative, she always knew what to do. She stopped one man who was passing and asked for Mr Smith. Anne noticed he was surprised at this request, but he said he would see and found chairs for them at the counter. They seemed to sit there a long time, pretending to look at the books displayed, all published by Smith, Elder. Anne recognized several they had sent Charlotte as presents —they were a very generous firm, not like Newby. That was another interview they would have to face before they went home—Mr Newby. The clerk returned to ask for their names which Charlotte declined to give. Firmly she said they wished to see Mr Smith on a private matter.

At last he reappeared and led them upstairs to a small room with a very large skylight where a man awaited them. He was tall and young, two factors which, added to his reluctance to see them, somehow made him appear intimidating. Anne saw Charlotte peering up at him through her glasses and heard her inquire, to make quite sure, 'Is it Mr Smith?'

He agreed it was, whereupon she put his own letter she had received the day before into his hand. He glanced down at it and saw it was addressed to Currer Bell.'Where did you get this?' he asked with some sharpness.

Charlotte was laughing now at his perplexity and gave her real name, Miss Brontë; Anne was brought forward as the author of *Agnes Grey* and *The Tenant of Wildfell Hall*, and Newby was roundly anathematized by all three.

So these two quaintly dressed ladies, one very small, were Currer and Acton Bell, the literary sensation of London. Mr Smith hurried out and returned with a pale, mild, stooping man whom he introduced as Mr Williams and who, once he caught their hands to shake, forgot to let them go. He had a stutter which meant he spoke little, but Mr Smith made up for his lack of loquacity, and so did Charlotte. When she overcame her shyness Charlotte not only talked but talked well.

'We are three sisters', she explained to the two men. The moment she had said that she could have bitten off her tongue as she remembered Emily's insistence, implacable as taboo, that her identity should never be disclosed.

Mr Smith's amiability and ease of manner precluded any arrogance that his distinguished, handsome presence might have conveyed. He heard where his visitors were lodged and said at once that the Misses Brontë must come and stay at his home, well did he know how welcome his mother and sisters would make them, but Charlotte hastily declined this well-meant invitation with the excuse that they were not going to make a long stay in London. Only until they had seen Mr Newby, Anne thought, and that would have to wait until Monday now. Charlotte was impressing on both Mr Smith and his head reader that the name Brontë must not be used—if they had to be addressed or introduced would they kindly use the name Brown.

Mr Smith thought Acton a gentle, rather subdued person, by no means pretty yet of a pleasing appearance. Her manner, curiously expressive of a wish for protection and encouragement, was a kind of constant appeal which invited his masculine sympathy. His first impression of Currer Bell was that she looked interesting rather than attractive. She had little feminine charm, a fact of which as he came to know her better he realized she herself was uneasily and perpetually conscious. He was to penetrate her defences sufficiently to know that she would have given all her genius and fame to be beautiful.

By the time they arrived back at the Chapter Coffee House Charlotte paid for the excitement of the interview with a thundering headache and harassing sickness. They had been unable to sleep the night before and there loomed before them a prospect which forbade them to rest now. Had Mr Smith not said something about bringing his sisters to call on them tonight? They went out and each bought a pair of gloves and a parasol. As the impending visit drew near Charlotte in desperation took a strong dose of sal-volatile, but the little good it did her dissipated when their guests arrived in full evening dress to take them to the opera. Mr Smith thought he had made it clear that was to be the arrangement.

Anne wondered what Charlotte would do in such a predicament. The Misses Smith were very elegant in their low-cut evening gowns, and she and Charlotte had only their plain, high-necked Haworth garments. A certain recklessness took possession of Charlotte who determined to put her headache in her pocket—it was better to fall in with the arrangements for them than remain where they were and spoil the evening for everyone. They were not in London every day of their lives, with the chance of going to the opera.

When they arrived at the Opera House the feeling of recklessness gave place to thrill, even enjoyment, as she walked up the crimson-carpeted staircase beside the white-gloved Mr Smith and thought of the contrast they must make. The box-door was not yet open, and as they waited amongst that brilliant throng Charlotte was aware of the many supercilious glances cast at them from all sides, which she quite understood their clownish appearance warranted. She glanced at Anne, who did not appear to notice them but looked as tranquil and peaceful as if she were at home. 'You know I am not used to this kind of thing,' Charlotte confided to Mr Williams.

Happening followed happening so swiftly during the week-end that there was no time to savour anything, only to experience it. When they looked back they remembered it all in separate scenes like a kaleidoscope. Mr Smith's splendid drawing-room—fortunately no company to meet them, only his handsome mother and younger brother and sisters, all looking at them from their clear, pale faces. Dinner was a penance to both the guests; neither had any appetite for the procession of courses and both were glad when it was safely over. Charlotte always felt constrained and awkward at table and now was no exception despite the amiability of their host.

Nothing has gone wrong for you, she thought as she watched him; throughout your life you have been a man of luck, living in the glow of success. Some travellers encounter fitful and gusty weather from the start, breast adverse winds, are belated and overtaken by the early closing night. But you will always arrive on time, every term is your season. Some lives were thus blessed—it was the attesting trace and lingering evidence of Eden.

Mr Williams's home could not be compared to Mr Smith's for grandeur, but although humble it was a neat

residence, and his family of eight children made no demands
on the guests. Their father's lack of conversation did not
make Charlotte undervalue him, for she knew from his
correspondence how intelligent he was. Perhaps it was a
pity Mr Williams was not more practical, like Mr Smith.
The head reader was of the contemplative, theorizing order.
Charlotte came to the conclusion that Mr Williams had too
many abstractions.

He took them to St Stephens, Walbrook, but unfortunately the famous Dr Corly they wanted to hear was
not preaching that morning. There were a walk in Kensing-
ton Gardens where they were enchanted with the smooth
beauty they saw all around them, visits to the Royal
Academy and the National Gallery. Of the interview with
Mr Newby little is known! The second edition of *The Tenant
of Wildfell Hall* was due before the end of July and Anne
promised to send a preface for it on her return. It was left
to Mr Smith to try to extract from him what he owed Ellis
and Acton Bell, an attempt which, like everything else to
do with Newby, proved unsuccessful. Anne promised
Smith, Elder the refusal of her next book and they under-
took to bring out another edition of the poems by the
Messrs Bell.

There were presents to buy for all those left at home, for
Tabby and Martha, and a twelve-shilling volume of
Tennyson's poems probably destined for Emily. They left
on Tuesday, scared at the money they had spent, travelling
back second class in the daytime laden with presents of
books from Mr Smith.

When she reached home and Charlotte saw herself in the
looking-glass she thought how grey and very old was the
face staring back at her. She felt weak after the excitements
of the few days' visit to the capital, yet restless, and it was a
while before she settled.

There was a disturbing aftermath when Emily discovered
Charlotte had revealed to Mr Smith and Mr Williams there was
another sister at home. She could not endure to be known

to the outside world except as Ellis Bell and felt Charlotte had betrayed her identity. Bitterly Charlotte regretted the four words that had so inadvertently slipped out, that were against every feeling and intention of Emily. She warned Mr Williams not to mention her sisters in the plural when he wrote.

And Branwell was always there to return to. He was thirty-one years old now. He might still live under his father's roof, but there could no longer be any communication between him and his family when the whole of his personality was centred on scraping together a few pence for gin, or on inveigling John Brown to procure it for him on tick. It is unlikely that he had missed Charlotte and Anne at the week-end, for no longer were they a part of his life. His existence was himself. He slept most of the day and consequently lay awake at night, making it impossible for his father or family to have undisturbed rest. He never knew that his sisters had written books which had been published. His arch enemy was Dr Wheelhouse, whose sole prescription for an inebriate was to forbid him intoxicants of any kind. His thoughts were blasphemous when they dwelt on Dr Wheelhouse.

The landlord of the Old Cock and the landlady of the Talbot were both dunning him for arrears. Papa gave him ten shillings to pay off the Old Cock when Mr Nicholson wrote to him that unless his son's debts were paid he would proceed to law. Ten shillings—Papa did not realize it was not shillings but pounds his son owed. Desperately Branwell wrote to Leyland begging him to keep landlord and landlady quiet while he got in touch with Dr Crosby, who was morally certain to send the money. If they would not wait until he heard from him, Branwell was ruined. He had had five months of such utter sleeplessness, violent cough and frightful agony of mind that jail would destroy him forever.

He was now of scarecrow thinness: when he visited John Brown in his cottage in Parsonage Lane little Tabitha teasingly asked him if he was wearing his father's coat.

Sometimes his mind felt cold as a key in the draught of its lock, at other times his waking moments were infested with a nightmare quality, as when one evening he was told his old friend Grundy had sent up a message to say he was waiting for him in the Black Bull below.

He was in bed when the message came and he knew at once it was not Grundy waiting for him below; he would never see Grundy again. This was a call from Satan. Papa tried to discourage him from going, but he insisted upon dressing to rendezvous with what everyone believed was Mr Grundy, and when no one was looking he slipped a carving-knife up his sleeve. He was going to finish with Satan once and for all. The moment he entered the inn he would rush into the room and, taking him off his guard, stab its occupant to death.

It was the September of a wild and tempestuous autumn with violent changes of temperature. The world was cold, it was always cold now when he staggered out into it, and the wind shivered through him as though he were composed of nothing but short ends. It was only a short pace to the Black Bull, but the world and the wind were between him and it. And it was downhill—nothing went of its own momentum except something that was going downhill.

Satan was waiting for him in the private room. He turned the handle of the door as quietly as he could and looked round it cautiously to take Satan's and his own bearings. There he was in the guise of a stranger, greeting him cheerfully after a prolonged confrontation, welcoming him, elbowing him into the body of the room, beside the fire, pressing on him a glass, making him drink its hot contents, saying what good it would do him, just his own words to John when he pressed him to get some gin on the sly.

And it did not do him good. He wished he had not come. He felt frightened for himself sitting there in a room dancing with firelight. He told the stranger he should not have left his warm bed to come out into the cold night, and the stranger gave him another hot drink.

Of course he was not a stranger, Branwell was beginning to recognize his voice, he was Mr Grundy, young Mr Grundy the engineer, to whom he could play God when they walked the countryside round Luddenden, where trees grew like plants, philosophizing, moralizing, declaiming, holding forth on every subject under the sun just as he was doing now.

It was like old times again sitting down at a table with a friend—Branwell even took something to eat, which he had not done for too long. You were never hungry when you had an unslakable thirst gnawing at your vitals.

The evening began to fall apart when Mr Grundy at last made more than a bid to take his leave. It was in fragments as he said goodbye on the road outside the inn. He had a last picture of Branwell standing where he had left him, his figure bowed, tears dropping from his eyes, his unkempt, uncut red hair made still wilder by the wind.

They noticed a change in him at home when John Brown's brother brought him back up the lane. He was gentler, sweeter, his eyes no longer like a crazed cat's. All his life he had thought, talked and written of death, the tomb's eternal shade, the dark chambers of that unknown shore where night and silence sealed each guarded door, Charon's boat and Lethe's river, cold grave and church-yard stone, the battening worm and dismembering corpse. Yet now that it drew near him he was unaware of its enveloping presence.

He was in bed early on the Sunday when John Brown came in to keep him company as some of the family were preparing for church. As they talked together Branwell told him he had done nothing either great or good. The paroxysm of death came upon him suddenly as a clap. He seized the sexton's hand and cried: 'Oh, John, I'm dying!'

Brown saw from his face what was happening and called to the family to come at once. When they flocked into the room he slipped away, to leave the son and brother with his own. He stood in the belfry doorway, waiting to receive the

signal from the parsonage to sound the passing bell to tell
Haworth that t'vicar's Pat had gone.

As his father prayed at his bedside Charlotte heard her
brother say 'Amen', yet he had not been inside church
since Aunt Branwell's funeral six years ago. When he
started up in bed with the final spasm it was his father's
arms that caught him and it was in them he breathed his
last. The old man's broken-hearted cry of 'My son, my son',
tore at Charlotte's heart.

It was the first death scene she had ever witnessed, as it
was Emily's and Anne's, but it was Charlotte who suc-
cumbed to headache and sickness before the Sunday was
out.

The death throes she had witnessed, the final separation,
gave her more acute, bitter pain than she could have
imagined possible. Just when she felt she ought to be able
to collect her strength to support Papa she fell ill with an
attack of jaundice and was in bed for a week.

When the calm of death had settled after the struggle of
dying, he looked so noble with his fine features and brow,
like a marble his friend Leyland had chiselled. Her emotions as she viewed him were quite different from Papa's or
Emily's or Anne's. Their acceptance of his death startled
her. His altered mien, his return to religion towards the
end of his life, seemed to have expunged from their minds
all that had gone before, all that had brought him to so
untimely a death.

But for Charlotte there was such a bitterness of pity for
his life and death, such an aching for the emptiness of his
whole existence which she could not describe, which she
prayed time would lessen. She was to write a little later to
Mr Williams of the wrench to the natural affections, and it
was this wrench that affected Charlotte as it did not her
father or Emily or Anne. There had been but a year between
her and her brother, she had been closer to him than she
had ever been or ever would be to any other human being,
yet in these last years of his life she had been further from

him than any of them, despised and rejected him more heartily.

She of all the family was unable to be present the following Sunday when his funeral sermon was preached.

4

No coward soul is mine,
No trembler in the world's storm-troubled sphere:
I see Heaven's glories shine
And Faith shines equal, arming me from Fear.

There is not room for Death
Nor atom that his might could render void:
Thou—Thou art Being and Breath,
And what Thou art may never be destroyed—

Emily Brontë

MR NICHOLLS exercised Emily's Keeper and Anne's Flossy by calling at the parsonage each day and taking them for walks on the moors. It was his unobtrusive way of helping his vicar's family until their owners were well enough to undertake so pleasurable a task for themselves, for the Emily one had caught a chill on the Sunday her brother's funeral sermon was preached, and the cutting east wind made the weather too unfavourable for the delicate Anne to venture out.

Mr Morgan, the vicar's old friend, had buried the son of the parsonage on the Thursday, and on the Sunday Mr Nicholls had conducted the funeral service assisted by Mr Grant from Oxenhope. Even had he known Branwell in his happier days, there was no mutual attraction to draw the vicar's son and his curate together. As it was, Mr Nicholls witnessed him tipple himself to death, a weakling who scoffed at everything the curate stood for and believed in, who disrupted the lives of all his family and added to the burdens of the mistress of the house, his eldest sister.

Miss Brontë was now almost recovered from the severe

illness which had struck her down at her brother's death. The dour Irishman could have wished her normal health were stronger. It was of her he thought as he tramped the Yorkshire moors, not of her ailing sisters, wondering if he would see her on his return. She was always trim, her collars and cuffs fresh as though she had donned them only that day. She might be a child to look at with her tininess and delicacy, her fair straight hair and disconcertingly large eyes, but it was no child's tongue that flicked out a couple of sentences which cut the very breath from out of his mouth, and Bradley's, and Grant's, when they were drinking tea at the parsonage.

Nicholls had not been long at Haworth when it happened; he had little tea-talk but, reinforced by his two fellow curates, he could hold forth on the one subject which bound the three of them into kindred spirits as long as it lasted—the Dissenters. Carried away by the enjoyable pursuit of tearing ranting nonconformists to pieces, they, the established, standing four-square on a foundation stone that nothing could rock, heard themselves silenced by their hostess in a couple of sharp sentences delivered with the rapidity of pistol shot. So withering was his daughter's fire that even Mr Brontë had been shocked.

Yet it was she who kept Mr Nicholls uneasily at Haworth where he had never felt welcome, curate to a vicar with whom he was on as formal terms after three years as when they first shook hands. He suffered of course as far as the parish was concerned from the same drawback as had his predecessor: he was not Mr Weightman. He was not unhandsome, but he had none of the cheerful good looks or buoyant spirits which had made Willy Weightman popular in every house he entered. He was serious to the point of solemnity, reserved to the point of stiffness. Because of his vicar's illness, much of the work of the parish devolved on him; he did his best with the humbling and unrewarding realization that he was a poor substitute from both his vicar's and the parishioners' point of view.

He lodged at the sexton's in Parsonage Lane, scarcely a stone's throw from the parsonage itself, which had never had the open door for him that it had had for Willy Weightman because he was Arthur Bell Nicholls with an inability to feel at ease. Even after three years he still felt a newcomer in the parish, a lodger at the Browns, and the parsonage was not the likeliest place in Haworth or elsewhere where he could feel at home. Yet the Brontës were his contemporaries, he was the same age as Emily. At thirty he did not consider himself youthful, but he always thought of the two younger parsonage daughters as girls. Emily avoided him as she did all strangers, and if he happened to come across her she looked the other way, and the youngest was as silent as he was himself.

As the October days shortened into those of November, and he was still exercising Keeper and Flossy, he knew that the continued ill health of the Brontë girls was an increasing anxiety to their eldest sister. Because he was in love with her he wished he could do something to alleviate the strain. She had so much to bear; the heaviest weight of the overburdened household fell on her who was its mistress, the prop and stay of her father in his old age, the eldest daughter who filled the position of the son of the house even when her brother had been alive.

And the Emily one was making things no easier for her, refusing all medical attention, saying no poisoning doctor would come near her, that they were all quacks, refusing to take medicine or treatment of any kind, saying nature should be left to take its own course, rising in the morning at seven as she had always risen, staying up until ten at night, the earliest she had ever gone to bed, spending the day doing exactly what she had always done as though there were nothing wrong with her.

The curate knew all about what was happening in the parsonage. After all, he lodged at the sexton's which was but a hop, skip and a jump away for the young Brown daughters who went to help in the square, unadorned house, and their twenty-year-old Martha now shared the kitchen as a permanency with the aged Tabby. The Emily one was the favourite with the Brown girls, because they worked more to her hand, the curate concluded, and so did not see so much of Miss Brontë. As far as he was concerned there was no comparison. The opinion of the sexton's household was that Emily was grieving for the loss of her brother—did everyone not notice that she had not set foot outside the door since she had been to church on the Sunday to hear his funeral sermon?

It was December now and bitterly cold. No longer could the curate take the dogs so far on desolate moors blasted by winds edged with ice. Haworth of course was an exposed place and the parsonage at the top of the hill most vulnerable of all. Every time the front or kitchen door was opened the winds, pressed against it waiting for entry, tore into the house to chill it before whipping upstairs. Martha had seen Emily thrown against the wall by the force of it. She had always been thin but now she was like a shadow, yet when they sent for the doctor and he was in the very house she refused to see him. Mr Nicholls considered the best place for her was in her bed, being looked after instead of making it harder for everyone round her. He could see that Mr Brontë was very despondent about the outcome—the Browns told him there had been two older daughters who had died of galloping consumption long ago when they were all young.

At first it was Anne Charlotte was fearful for, Anne who had always been delicate. They all had harassing colds and coughs. Papa did not quite escape, but he stood up to it better than any of them, to Charlotte's surprise. She made herself believe it was the intolerable east wind, blowing wild and keen as it had for days over their cold hills, that was responsible for everything.

But it was not Anne, it was Emily. She did not throw off the cold and cough they had all had. Charlotte felt sure she had a pain in her chest, she caught a shortness in Emily's breathing when she moved quickly, but Emily would not brook being questioned. Once when her pulse was taken it was found to be 115 a minute—she did not allow it to be taken a second time. She would permit no one to help her, withdrew further and further from them as they made their ineffectual essays towards her. She was now so thin that she seemed to be wasting away before their very eyes, and Papa was beginning to lose heart, but Anne and Charlotte still hoped.

Emily could not be dying, not Emily; they could not imagine life without Emily, as they could not imagine Emily without life. Their love would tether her to them, but even as they thought that they knew that their love could not reach her in her isolation. The very harshness of Emily's character made Charlotte want to cling to her more, made Emily more necessary to her. When she was ill there was no sunshine in the world, she was the nearest thing to her heart, dear to her as life.

Everything the elder sister could think of she did. What about Ellen to cheer them all for a short visit? But Emily's agitation at the suggestion made her drop it at once, she was not well enough to stand the upset that even Ellen's presence would create. Both Charlotte and Anne had longed to have her, perhaps Emily would listen to an outsider, be persuaded to see a doctor, but they might have known. Charlotte noticed she took no interest in the last packet of books sent by Smith, Elder, but she reminded her to thank Ellen for the crab-cheese she had sent which she was not well enough to eat. The weaker she became bodily, the stronger she appeared mentally. Charlotte put Mr Williams's letter, in which he advocated homoeopathy, into her hands without saying a word. The very last thing you must do with Emily was to give your opinion, for that was sufficient for her to say exactly the opposite. She returned the letter with the remark: 'Mr Williams's intention is kind and good, but he is under a delusion. Homoeopathy is only another name for quackery.' All they could hope for was that she might have second thoughts; Emily's second thoughts were often wiser than her first.

Charlotte wrote to the famous Dr Epps, a leading homoeopath recommended by Mr Williams, asking for his advice in a letter which told of her sister's most obvious symptoms, such as no appetite but a continual thirst with a craving for acids. She could not be as explicit as she would have wished because of the patient's reserved nature. What she was able to give drew forth the reply that the case was grave and medical advice should be sought at once. Emily imagined as favourable one of the distressingly weakening symptoms Charlotte was able to list, for she believed this was nature's way of ridding her of the disease.

Charlotte wrote to Ellen that her own health kept tolerable at present, which was as well, for Anne, however willing, was too delicate to do or bear much. But Anne had to bear what Charlotte was bearing, the sight of her beloved sister dying before their eyes and they unable to help her in any way, not even allowed to allude to her illness, unable to share their sorrow with her suffering. What was so alarming was the rapidity with which she lost ground—it was not three months since Branwell had died between the hay and the harvest. Now they knew why it was called galloping consumption. There was something intimidating about Emily during these last days, going out into the yard to feed the dogs as she had always done, exacting from her weakening frame what it had given her when she was strong, conscious her breathing was becoming noisy, daring them by her very silence to hear it too. It was now so loud it told them her whereabouts in the house.

Her cough kept her awake at night and in the morning she was at her worst, drowsy and exhausted with lack of sleep. But they noticed that in the evening she seemed to revive somewhat. They did not realize that this was because then her temperature soared.

The clock of the year was moving towards the shortest day. As they sat together one evening in the parlour

Charlotte read out from one of the books that had come in the latest parcel from Smith, Elder. Not only was Emily long past the delight of opening their parcels to see what they had sent, but also of reading what had come. It was an essay of Emerson's the elder sister now chose, but even as she read she realized Emily was not listening. She repudiated the thought that perhaps Emily could not hear and laid it aside decisively by marking the place and thinking she would finish reading it out to her on the morrow. The room, warm and cosy with firelight, had the sudden languor of a room in use all day when the very flickering of flames and the subsidence of firewood sounded protracted.

Emily was sleeping in the big room which Aunt had made her own where a fire could be lit. Her sisters heard her moaning in her sleep that night. Charlotte rose very early when it was still dark and went on to the moors to search for one little spray of heather, even a single piece, to take back to Emily, to remind her of the moors from which she had never before been parted for so long while she had been at home, the moors which were Emily's home, waiting for her to return to them.

She had to go farther than she expected until she found a tiny piece, sheltering in a crevice, with its faded bells still on it. She hurried home in the unfamiliar half light of a winter dawn when objects did not loom as in twilight before they faded but diminished as daylight strengthened. Perhaps that was because such immensity of space dwarfed landmark and boundary.

It was not seven by the time she reached the parsonage. She went into Emily's room and placed the sprig on her pillow. A pang she was never to forget shot through her as she saw Emily's listless eyes look at it and realized she could not see.

But the habits of a lifetime still prevailed and Emily rose as though this were an ordinary day. She sat to comb her long hair at the fire and the comb dropped from her nerveless fingers. 'See, Martha,' she gasped, 'my comb has fallen into the fire, and I cannot get it.' It was already scorched by the time the little servant retrieved it. Step by step she came down the stairs she was never to climb again. After breakfast Anne and Charlotte sat with her in the room lit with the level cold light of December. Anne was sewing and Charlotte writing to Ellen. Emily, seated on the black horsehair sofa, took up some sewing but her hands fell heavy on her lap.

'I should have written to you before if I had one word of hope to say,' Charlotte was writing, 'but I have not. She grows daily weaker. The physician's opinion was expressed too obscurely to be of use. He sent some medicine which she would not take. Moments so dark as these I have never known. I pray for God's support to us all. Hitherto He has granted it.'

She knew Emily was dying, they all knew that, but she did not realize as she wrote that every breath her sister drew was struggling towards her last. Emily knew. She said: 'If you send for a doctor, I will see him now.' But when her sisters tried to take her upstairs to bed she cried out, 'No, no!'

These were the last words she spoke. She died shortly afterwards, sitting on the old horsehair sofa they could all remember as far back as they could remember anything.

5

There is a rest beyond the grave,
A lasting rest from pain and sin. . . .
Show me that rest—I ask no more.
Oh, drive these misty doubts away;
And let me see that sunny shore,
However far away!
However wild this rolling sea,
However wild my passage be,
Howe'er my bark be tempest-tossed,
May it but reach that haven fair,
May I but land and wander there
With those that I have loved and lost—

Anne Brontë

ALMOST hourly Papa said to his eldest daughter: 'Charlotte, you must bear up, I shall sink if you fail me.' Not only was Emily the most like him in looks of all his children, but there was much in her temperament that was in accord with his, and her death so soon after that of his only son told on him grievously. But he had a hardihood that Charlotte, in her lifelong preoccupation about his health, never realized.

He led the four mourners across the graveyard into the church on the funeral day, following the coffin with Keeper padding beside him, and he allowed Emily's dog to share the family pew with Charlotte and Anne, Tabby and Martha. Mr Nicholls conducted the service and when the little group, bereft of Emily, prepared to return to the parsonage, her dog had to be coerced into leaving with them instead of remaining behind with her.

Emily had never lingered over any task to which she had set her hand, and two short months had been all the time she had taken over dying. To Charlotte she appeared to have made haste to leave them. But so terrible had been these two months to witness that finality brought temporary easement. Emily died on 19th December 1848; on Christmas Eve Charlotte wrote some verses which in their resignation were like the foam thrown off by the tide of emotion:

> *My darling, thou wilt never know*
> *The grinding agony of woe*
> *That we have borne for thee.*
> *Thus may we consolation tear*
> *E'en from the depths of our despair*
> *And wasting misery.*

There are various theories to explain the manner in which Emily met death, varying from those who believe she deliberately courted it as liberation to those who believe, and Charlotte appears to have been of this number, she loved life to such an extent that she refused to succumb to death.

Charlotte could not forget the 19th of December. Like the hands on a clock her thoughts came round to it again and yet again until it became a more fixed, a more frequently recurring idea in her mind than ever. Always she used violent terms to describe it. 'It was very terrible, she was torn conscious, panting, reluctant though resolute out of a happy life.' 'Hope has proved a strange traitor,' she wrote to Mr Williams; 'she kept whispering that Emily would not, *could* not die, and where is she now? Out of my reach—out of my world—torn from me.'

She did not couple Anne or her father with herself when she mentioned its effect. Yet Emily and Anne had been like twins since their girlhood, two sprays on the one bough, drawing sustenance from each other as well as from the same source, and now the stronger, the more sheltering of the two had been cut off, leaving the other alone. 'O Thou hast taken my delight/And hope of life away,' Anne wrote in these early grey days of the New Year.

The second time Charlotte had travelled to Brussels she had felt a pleasurable excitement, even elation, because she was making the journey utterly alone. Unselfish, devoted and self-effacing—she was all of these things, but when the curtain was rung down she, with the intensity of her emotions and strong sense of drama, trod the boards of her secret stage and played out her part alone.

There was no fear of her not bearing up, she was needed too much. Her heart gave within her whenever her gaze fell on her younger sister. 'I now look to Anne,' she wrote to Ellen the day after the funeral. 'If only' must be the two saddest words in the language, with the drag of heartbreak upon them. If only Anne were well and strong, but she was neither. Her sorrow for the loss of Emily was too deep for words, and her silence made a moat of stillness round her.

Never had Charlotte needed the consolation of a friend's presence more than now, and Ellen did not fail her. She came at once in answer to her plea, her very advent breaking up the shut-in atmosphere of the parsonage compact with grief, bringing with her the normality of the outside world, Charlotte's confidante and a companion for Anne. Emily and she had said all those years ago on her first visit they had never seen anyone they liked so well.

Once Ellen asked Anne why she was smiling to herself as she read a magazine. 'Only because I see they have inserted one of my poems,' came the shy reply. Now there was no Emily to disturb in case their secret should be discovered, Ellen was allowed to know about the Bell brothers, and Charlotte gave her a copy of *Wuthering Heights* to take home with her.

Anne was known as Miss Annie in the village, and no one in Haworth needed to be told that the visitor who called at the parsonage a bare fortnight after the Emily one's death was Dr Teale, a specialist from Leeds. The vicar was taking no risks with his youngest, but Haworth had always held she was the most delicate of them all, the one likeliest to have gone first instead of his lad and middle lass.

After the doctor's examination of his patient, he was closeted with Papa and Charlotte and the local doctor in the study. Ellen kept Anne company. She was flushed and Ellen thought how pretty she looked. They walked round the room together, the invalid leaning on Ellen's arm and talking animatedly, not like the usual silent Anne at all.

They heard the bustle of Dr Teale's departure, the unfamiliar voice bidding goodbye, Papa's familiar one wishing him safe journey. Then Papa came into the room. He sat on the couch and drew his youngest child towards him. 'My *dear* little Anne', he said. She did not need to be told what that meant.

Dr Teale could offer no hope. The disease—both lungs were badly affected—had taken too strong a hold to be stayed. All he could do was prescribe to alleviate suffering and warn the unsuspecting inhabitants of the parsonage of the danger of the patient's condition to others. Miss Brontë could continue to share her bedroom but must on no account any longer share her bed, and he took it upon himself to contact Ellen's people telling them to terminate her visit at once.

So Charlotte and Anne were together again without Ellen between them. Those lovely moments in the past when Charlotte and Ellen, their skirts turned back over their knees, in the warmth of firelight, had put their hair in curlers for the morrow. Anne sat in Emily's chair now. Like Emily she did not stay in bed but came downstairs, even after the painful blisters were applied to her side. Unlike Emily she took everything prescribed for her, the nauseous cod-liver oil and carbonate of soda which smelled and tasted like train oil. Unlike Emily she was better in the morning, worse in the afternoon and evening. Like Emily her cough troubled her at night and disturbed her sleep.

Anne wrote her last poem during these January days. The first quatrain of the sixteen was written two days after Dr Teale's visit and begins 'A dreadful darkness closes in/ On my bewildered mind'. She had begged to serve God

heart and soul, to sacrifice to Him no niggardly portion but
the whole of her identity.

I hoped amid the brave and strong
My portioned task might lie,
To toil amid the labouring throng
With purpose keen and high.

But God had fixed another part for her. She prayed to learn
patience from every blow, to gather fortitude from pain,
and woe to teach her hope and holiness.

If Thou shouldst bring me back to life,
More humbled I should be,
More wise, more strengthened for the strife,
More apt to lean on Thee.

Should death be standing at the gate,
Thus should I keep my vow;
But hard whate'er my future fate,
So let me serve Thee now.

The whole poem of sixteen verses in her small script did not
take up anything like the half sheet of notepaper on which
it was written. Carefully she folded it into three, leaving
two parts blank to be filled in with any future compositions.

Anne did not want to die, she wanted to live, yet
Charlotte could write later that from her childhood she
seemed preparing for an early death. Dearly as she loved
her youngest sister, there was never the bond between them
that there was between Emily and Anne, and instead of the
appreciation Charlotte showed of Emily, she had towards
Anne an unconscious attitude if not of depreciation at least
of incomprehension. Even when they were both adult, the
difference between the eldest and the youngest still separated
them. Anne had been a queer little thing in these days—
just like the toy soldier of Branwell's she was allowed to
call hers and which was not a patch on Charlotte's or

Branwell's or Emily's choices and which they christened Waiting-boy.

It was always in subdued terms that Charlotte described her: still, thoughtful, long-suffering, self-denying, reflective. Her constitutional reserve and taciturnity kept her in the shade and covered her mind and especially her feelings with a sort of nunlike veil which was rarely lifted. But this is not the description of the spirited Agnes Grey or of the girl who created her, or of the woman who wrote *The Tenant of Wildfell Hall*. The sort of nunlike veil certainly covered her sister for Charlotte, and as far as she was concerned Anne never quite moved out of the shade, static as Waiting-boy with his legs painted in the one piece.

Of the three sisters and one brother, Anne was the only one to make a success of her calling. Shortly before Emily died the Robinson girls—Mary, now newly married, and Elizabeth, Anne's special charge—had made the tedious awkward journey to Haworth to visit their one-time governess. Attractive, stylish-looking girls, Charlotte reported to Ellen, overjoyed to see their Miss Brontë, clinging to her like children, bubbling over with all the news they had to tell her. Lady Scott had died and Mama was now married to Sir Edward and in the highest spirits.

Hope in the parsonage fluctuated with the patient's condition. In January it was at its lowest, in February there was a slight improvement and Charlotte remembered that spring lay before them, then summer—surely they might hope a little—dreaded March was a wrestle with its days and nights of frost, in April Anne wrote to Ellen asking her if she would accompany her to the sea, not as a nurse but as a companion.

She longed for Scarborough where she had first seen the sea, Scarborough which was so near that other miracle in her life—York Minster. After all, it was months since Dr Teale had seen her in the middle of winter and forbidden her to travel. It was spring now and she was impatient of delay. May might be a trying month as everyone said, she

agreed the earlier part was often cold, but she knew from
experience that fine warm days in the latter half were almost
certain, when the laburnum and lilac were in bloom,
whereas June was often cold and July generally wet.

It was a known fact that change of air or removal to a
better climate hardly ever failed of success in consumptive
cases if the remedy were taken in time. She, the most
unemphatic of people, underlined the word *time*. She would
not like to commit that error. Certainly she suffered much
less from pain and fever than when Ellen was with them,
but she was decidedly weaker and very much thinner.
Under all the circumstances she noted she thought there
was not time to be lost.

She hoped very much that Charlotte, who greatly needed
a change of air and scene, would after all be able to accompany her, but there was of course the responsibility of
leaving Papa. She thanked Miss Nussey and her mother
and sisters for their kind and often repeated invitation to
Brookroyd, but she would not think of inflicting her
presence upon them as she now was.

Charlotte wrote privately to Ellen and told her to
temporize in her reply. The elder sister felt Anne would
never stand the journey, she was now thinner than even
Emily was at the very last. There must be some improvement before she could feel justified in taking her away, for
now it was settled that if Anne went, Charlotte would
accompany her and Ellen go with them.

She was prevailed upon by Anne to consult Dr Teale
about the advisability of a change; to the invalid's joy he not
only said yes but recommended Scarborough. Reluctantly
Charlotte had to make arrangements for their visit.
Although Anne was up all day, she had hardly enough
breath to climb the stairs at night; although with the
betterment of the weather she had been able to go out for a
little, she crept rather than walked.

Should it be a boarding-house or lodgings at Scarborough? Anne was in favour of a boarding-house—she

thought it would be much more lively. What about Wood's Lodgings on St Nicholas Cliff? She had been there more than once with the Robinsons and could tell Charlotte all about them. The large house with its commanding view of the sea comprised groups of lodgings for every size of family, each with its own housekeeper and staff. Wood's, in the most expensive quarter of the town, was a household word in Scarborough, and Anne could well afford the best for the three of them as her godmother had recently died and left her a legacy of £200.

The date for travel was settled, 23rd May 1849, a Wednesday. Papa would not hear of any special arrangement being made while he was alone such, as Mr Nicholls's moving into the parsonage. Charlotte could only wish her judgment sanctioned the step and all it entailed more fully than it did. Would Ellen meet them at Leeds station when they arrived off the Keighley train and all three could then catch the afternoon connection to York. It was essential to break the journey for Anne, so it was decided they should spend the night there. Neither of the Brontës was furnished with clothes suitable for a fashionable watering-place, and Ellen had advised York rather than Scarborough for shopping. They had made a list of their requirements to be in readiness—bonnet, corset, black silk stockings, dress, gloves, ribbon for neck.

Ellen was in plenty of time on the Leeds platform where the Keighley train was due shortly after two. Charlotte had warned her that she would be shocked at the change in Anne's appearance, but Ellen of all people could be trusted not to betray what she felt.

The two sisters were not on the first Keighley train. Something must have happened and they would be on the next. But although she waited throughout the afternoon they did not come. Deferred hope made a mockery of even the beautiful weather. Twice Ellen watched a coffin being removed from the Keighley train and carried to a hearse waiting outside the station.

In 1849 there was no method which she could use to
contact the parsonage or the parsonage to contact her. There
was nothing for it but to return home for the night. Early
next morning she set out for Haworth, dear Ellen who so
many years ago had driven out of the blue to sweep Charlotte
away with her on holiday. As always she arrived in time—the
gig was outside the parsonage door and Charlotte and Martha
Brown were helping Anne into it. Mr Brontë was not there.
He knew when he kissed his youngest daughter goodbye before she left the house that he would never see her again, as
old Tabby, alone in her kitchen, knew. She was very deaf
now, but sounds, like remembrances, were trapped forever
within her. The youngest of her bairns away—her footfall
had ever been the lightest on the stair.

Only when the invalid was safely packed into the gig
and hidden from view did Martha break down. As the
vehicle moved downhill they left her there at the opened
door, crying as the young cry, without concealment.

Anne had been too ill the previous day to travel. Today
she had rallied sufficiently to make the effort. She was so
happy to be on her way that as the journey progressed she
revived instead of tiring. It was as though everything were
happening in concert to wish her God speed. The weather
was perfect, mild and balmy with the radiance of spring
lying over the countryside. No physical effort of any kind
was demanded from her—at every stage of the way railway
officials or members of the public came forward to assist
her.

At York they took a coach to the George Hotel where
they were to spend the night. It was an old building, its
exterior ornate with frieze and lively with stone cherubim
holding convoluted cornucopias. Its courtyard had all
the stir of a coaching inn, restless with departures and
arrivals. They arrived shortly after midday and had dinner,
which Anne greatly enjoyed.

She knew what she wanted to do in the afternoon and a
bath-chair was hired for her. She was their guide and

mentor as they passed through old streets and narrow alleys. This was a place she loved and she had much she wanted to share with them. York Minster had always been a landmark in her life; even to think of it made her thoughts soar. Now the sight of its stone, mellow with the honey tone of past summers, overwhelmed her. 'If finite power can do this, what is the——?' they heard her ask. She did not need to say more; York Minster answered her question before she had time to finish it.

Anne was the happiest of the three of them when they went shopping; she and Charlotte spent £2 16s. between them on their bonnets, an appreciable sum in those days. Next morning they travelled by train the hour's journey to Scarborough, Anne eagerly leaning forward in her seat to point out to them all the places she remembered.

On Saturday morning she wanted to go to the Baths and insisted on their leaving her with the attendant, walking back the short distance to their lodgings by herself. It was only afterwards they learnt that she fell with exhaustion when she reached the garden gate because she enjoined those who helped her not to tell her friends.

In the afternoon Ellen accompanied her to the shore where a donkey-carriage was hired for her. She dismissed the donkey-boy, as she felt he was over-zealous urging on his charge, and drove herself contentedly up and down the sands now the tide was out. She did not want to be a tax on Charlotte and Ellen and she was not lonely by herself. She was twenty-nine now, and in her youth, when she was twenty-two, a lifetime ago, she had dreamed in this place of Willy Weightman, lived again the moment when he had bidden her goodbye at Haworth and dared to think of their next meeting. She had heard of his death when she returned to Thorp Green. The shadow from it had not fallen athwart Scarborough and it was here she made Mr Weston in her book propose to Agnes Grey.

The following day was Sunday and she longed to go to church. Her overbright eyes glittered at the thought of it, but her companions dissuaded her. To them there was something fey about Anne's happiness.

In the afternoon she walked a little, then sat down to rest in a sheltered place. She not only wanted to be alone but she wanted them to see the marvels of the Saloon built round the original Spa which had made Scarborough famous.

Never had Ellen seen a sunset like the sunset that evening. Its glory filled the sky and they watched it together from the window of their sitting-room. Anne's uplifted face was illumined as though the sunset were shining full upon it. She remembered that the time for evening service was drawing near and urged Ellen and Charlotte to go to church in her stead, but not for the world would they leave her.

When she returned to her seat at the fireside she suddenly asked Charlotte if she did not think they should return home. Not for her own sake, but if she died here it might cause more suffering to those who were left than if she died at home. They knew she was thinking of Charlotte having to make the unbearable journey back with her coffin, but Charlotte, aware that Anne would never survive the return, gently brushed the suggestion aside.

Anne was the first of the three to rise next morning, at seven, when Emily used to rise. Charlotte let her do most of her dressing by herself because she knew that was what she preferred. She was the first to leave the bedroom, but later when Ellen went outside she found her still at the top of the stairs, unable to negotiate them.

There was no talk of going out that morning. Anne sat at the window until she said quietly she felt a change. Again it was of them and Papa she thought. She said it would be better if she saw a doctor, and waited for him still sitting at the window; she asked him if he thought she would reach home alive should she start out at once. Noticing his hesitation she, reliant and serene, told him not to fear speaking the truth, for she was not afraid to die—

how long did he think she would live? He held her hand as he said the angel of death was very near her. Later he was to tell Charlotte that in all his experience he had seen no such death-bed and it gave evidence of no common mind.

He came back once or twice to see her during the next hour, but she was alone with Charlotte and Ellen at her passing. The sound of Charlotte's grief reached her as she was borne from them and they heard her say, with startling clarity and strength, 'Take courage, Charlotte, take courage.' Life ebbed from her, breath by gentle breath, and she died without a sigh.

6

The shadow and sun-sparkle vanish,
The cloud and the light flee away;
But man from his heart may not banish
The thoughts that are torment to stay.

The reflection departs from the river
When the tree that hung o'er is cut down,
But on Memory's calm current for ever
The shade without substance is thrown—

Charlotte Brontë

CHARLOTTE wrote to Papa the day after Anne's death and told him she was to be buried on the morrow at Scarborough. She timed it thus to save him the anguish of a third funeral, but she looked upon the burial at Scarborough as a temporary measure. Anne must lie with her own in Haworth church, not permanently in the newly dug grave in this bright airy churchyard in full view of the sea. Charlotte had to do what was best for the present, and Papa could stand no more.

Neither could Charlotte; after all she had been through she could not face the return home. It was probably the doctor who attended Anne who ordered her to remain at the seaside. Papa in his reply sanctioned her to make a longer stay to gather her strength. He had known he would never see his little Anne again, and the knowledge of his resignation eased Charlotte. It never failed to surprise her how well he sustained shock, but his nervousness about his health was like the shaking of leaves to a stout tree whose roots spread deep and wide.

She could not bear to remain longer in Scarborough than was necessary, and she and Ellen moved to Filey and from there to the farmhouse near Bridlington where they had spent a happy stay ten years before, when Charlotte had seen the sea for the first time. Scarborough had been where that miracle had happened to Anne.

'Her quiet, Christian death did not rend my heart as Emily's stern, simple, undemonstrative end did,' Charlotte wrote to Mr Williams. 'I let Anne go to God and felt He had a right to her. I could hardly let Emily go. I wanted to hold her back then, and I want her back now. Anne, from her childhood, seemed preparing for an early death. Emily's spirit seemed strong enough to bear her to the fulness of years.' But despite the comfort in knowing that Anne had died in Scarborough which she loved, despite the peaceful sun that had gilded her evening and the calmness of her passing, there was to Charlotte something unbearably sad about her youngest sister's death. She could not have told whether it was sadder to think of her tranquillity or of Emily turning her dying eyes reluctantly from the sun. Yet the death of neither of her sisters had the effect on her that Branwell's had had, when she had feared the nights because of their tormenting dreams and could not put into words the emotions she felt during the day. Remorse did not chivvy her after Emily's or Anne's death as it had after Branwell's.

She was the eldest sister, the one who had always taken the lead, who had struck out not only for herself but for the others. Yet she was more vulnerable than either of her sisters. She was to want so much more than either of them and she was even lonelier without them than either would have been had she been the one to be left solitary.

She dreaded the return but was too brave to postpone it, and she refused Ellen's offer to accompany her to Haworth. She arrived home that midsummer evening before eight. The house seemed very bright to her, everything fresh—just as it used to be. Papa was so glad to see her, and old

Tabby and young Martha; she should be able to draw
consolation from their affection.

Papa was well and he thought she looked stronger, her
eyes not so sunken. Emily's Keeper and Anne's Flossy
went wild when they saw her; she knew why. They thought
if she had returned, Emily and Anne would be sure to
follow. Papa told her Keeper still went to Emily's room
every morning, snuffling below the door, the slit of a room
above the front door where they had gathered when there
had been six of them and their drawings on the walls
corresponded with their varying heights.

She left Papa and went into the dining-room, *their* room
after nine o'clock when they had it to themselves. She shut
the door and tried to be glad she was home. She had always
been glad before, except that once when she returned from
Brussels. But there was no joy in this silent house with its
empty rooms. Emily, Anne, poor Branwell—each occupied
his own narrow dark dwelling. With the feeling of
desolation came bitterness that it was so, and agony that
what was to be undergone could not be evaded.

As she had written a poem on Emily's death so, on the
night of her return to Haworth, did she write a poem on
Anne's:

> *There's little joy in life for me,*
> *   And little terror in the grave;*
> *I've lived the parting hour to see*
> *   Of one I would have died to save.*

> *Calmly to watch the failing breath,*
> *   Wishing each sigh might be the last;*
> *Longing to see the shade of death*
> *   O'er these beloved features cast.*

> *The cloud, the stillness that must part*
> *   The darling of my life from me;*
> *And then to thank God from my heart,*
> *   To thank Him well and fervently;*

Although I knew that I had lost
The hope and glory of our life;
And now, benighted, tempest-tossed,
Must bear alone the weary strife.

The sound of the clock on the stairs was no longer a companionable part of the house because unnoticed; now its every tick was emphatic in the silence, drawing attention to itself so that she was unable to forget it or get away from it as long as she remained indoors. But the moors were no solace; she saw Anne in the blue distances and Emily in the sullen hollow on a livid hillside. There was to come a time when she could no longer take the field-path behind the house into these solitudes bright with heath but haunted with the happiness of other years.

Work was her salvation in these months to come. She wrote the last volume of *Shirley*, and she thanked God she had it to do. She had already written twenty-three chapters in the sunshine of the days after the success of *Jane Eyre*. Now she headed chapter twenty-four 'The Valley of the Shadow of Death'.

Smith, Elder had seen the first volume and approved of the way it was working out, but had offered some suggestions. They were of the opinion that the first chapter, depicting the now famous scene of the three curates, should be scrapped entirely as an irrelevant piece of caricature.

Charlotte might ask for and even believe she welcomed criticism, but she reacted strongly against it whenever it was given. Her three curates caricatures! She could assure Mr Williams that they were real as the Bible, positive photographs, and she refused to give them up.

It was not likely she would forego the satisfaction of depicting the three Holys exactly as she saw them. Her flaying pen had picked each off with precision under guard of a fictitious name. Mr Nicholls was introduced towards the end of the book under the name of Mr Macarthey and, compared to his three fellow curates, got off lightly, but her description of him was certainly no panegyric.

'Being human, of course, he had his faults', she wound up the paragraph allotted to him; 'these, however, were proper, steady-going, clerical faults; what many would call virtues: the circumstance of finding himself invited to tea with a dissenter would unhinge him for a week; the spectacle of a Quaker wearing his hat in the church, the thought of an unbaptized fellow-creature being interred with Christian rites—these things could make strange havoc in Mr Macarthey's physical and mental economy: otherwise he was sane and rational, diligent and charitable.'

Only too well did Charlotte know that happiness and achievement in this imperfect world were always diluted. Fame and authorship had brought their own dissatisfactions, responsibilities and penalties.

There had been the confusion caused by all three being taken for the one individual passing off earlier work on the wake of success. There was the curiosity about their identity—were they three Manchester weavers, as some believed on the best of authority; was Currer Bell male or female? This curiosity, natural and legitimate enough, always struck Charlotte as intrusive.

Then there were the reviews. All their books had raised strong antagonism in certain quarters: Emily had been called a man of uncommon talents but dogged, brutal and morose, Anne had been told there was nothing kindly or genial in her powerful mind, and the *Quarterly Review* stated that *Jane Eyre* was anti Christian.

The *Quarterly Review* notice was monstrous, and Charlotte would not have been human had she not been affected by it, but in a subjective character such as hers she could not separate even a fair critic from his criticism. Therefore all adverse reviewers were to her incompetent, ignorant or flippant and the writers of favourable notices keen-eyed, quick feeling and talented.

Charlotte had not dreamed when she wrote in the unfamiliar rooms at Manchester about little Jane at Lowood School that readers would instantly recognize it as the school at Cowan Bridge. Not unnaturally Jane's inquisitor, the terrible black marble Mr Brocklehurst, was accepted as a facsimile portrait of the founder, the Reverend Carus Wilson, whose retirement was shadowed by this unwelcome notoriety.

She had always worshipped genius and had dedicated the second edition of *Jane Eyre* to Thackeray as a tribute from an unknown admirer to a master, unaware that Thackeray's wife was deranged like Rochester's bestial wife in her book. At once gossip circulated through London's coffee-houses, drawing-rooms and parlours that Currer Bell was governess to Thackeray's children.

She was anxious about the success of her second book, nervous in case it let down her publishers. In her gratitude for what they had done for her she was inclined to forget what her best-seller had done for them. She received for *Shirley* what she had received for her first book, a down payment of £500. It could not have come at a better time, for their railway shares, in which Emily had invested their money, had depreciated to the point of vanishing. Charlotte's small competency was gone, news so grave it had to be broken to Papa by degrees.

She trusted, vainly as it turned out, that her second book would stamp Currer Bell as male once and for all. Reviewers patronized the work of an authoress; if they believed Currer Bell was a man they would be more just in their criticism. The style and treatment of *Shirley*, brisk with true stories of Luddite risings which Miss Wooler had told them in those far-off Roe Head days, were surely strongly masculine.

Mr James Taylor, of Smith, Elder, called at the parsonage in person for the completed manuscript on his way back to London from his summer holiday. He was a Scot, and like so many of his hard-headed countrymen had worked himself up to an important position in the English firm. Charlotte had given her permission for the closely guarded secret that Currer Bell was Miss Brontë to be divulged to him and he had written to her after reading the earlier parts

of *Shirley*, to criticize with Mr Williams its beginning and
the unreality of her heroes.

Charlotte discovered he was a small man with red hair,
not prepossessing by any manner of means; indeed, to his
hostess there was something repellent about his native
harshness. He had a determined, dreadful nose in the
middle of his face, the usual place for a nose she had to
admit, but when he poked it close to her (he, like her, was
probably short-sighted), she felt herself recoil from him.
Decidedly he was not a gentleman with the finer qualities
of good breeding; as decidedly he was horribly intelligent,
quick, searching, sagacious, with a tenacious memory—
all the attributes necessary to reach the top of his particular
tree. Compared to his granite, Mr Williams was like soft
down, Mr Smith warm fur. Altogether he was an unusual
visitor to be taking tea with her in the parsonage parlour,
and his advent was a diversion with which to employ her
thoughts.

His opinion was not hedged with the modifications of
hers for him. When Mr Smith had given him a manuscript
called *Jane Eyre* to read, he had sat up half the night with
it. Subsequent results had more than justified his judgment
and the enthusiasm of his colleague Mr Williams. Lately
he had entered into correspondence with Currer Bell, in no
wise a one-sided affair but a spirited duel with a contestant
worthy of his steel who stood her ground and yielded
nothing. And now he had met Miss Brontë, small, decorous
and feminine. He found the combination of Currer Bell and
Charlotte Brontë quite irresistible.

He was to meet her again when she came to London
towards the end of the year. *Shirley* was published before she
made the trip and, although it did not create the furor of its
predecessor, was an undoubted success. It has not the
greatness of *Jane Eyre* and its impact had not the shock of
greatness, but it did create stir and excitement, and her
publisher prevailed on her to visit London before they
subsided. Charlotte employed the Haworth dressmaker to

make her a frock or two for the visit, quite plain, but she wished Ellen could have looked them over and given her advice.

This was the first of four visits she paid to London in four years, and each time she stayed with the unmarried Mr George Smith and his family. Other houses were open to her, but it was always to the Smiths she went, who would have been offended and deeply hurt had she done otherwise. The best-selling Currer Bell was a prized feather in any publisher's cap, and it was natural enough even from a business point of view that Mr Smith should claim her as his guest.

Ellen Nussey averred that George Smith proposed to her friend, but it is unlikely that a provocative friendship such as theirs ever culminated in anything so definite as declaration. He was some seven years younger than Charlotte, which to her separated them like a generation, while his good looks, different fortune and *milieu* placed him on another plane. However tantalizingly near they were drawn together at times, Charlotte never believed they could share the one orbit.

'You are to say no more about "Jupiter" and "Venus"—what do you mean about such heathen trash?' she wrote sternly to Ellen on her return from her first visit, up to her old tricks suggesting Mr George Smith as a prospective wooer. 'The fact is, no fallacy can be wilder, and I won't have it hinted at even in jest, because my common sense laughs it to scorn.' She wrote in the same letter that the idea of the little man, meaning James Taylor to whom the incorrigible Ellen had obviously also referred, shocked her less. That would be a more likely match if matches were at all in question, which they were not, and strenuously she underlined *they were not*.

On her next visit to London the following year she was happier than she had been since Emily and Anne died, describing in detail to Papa all she was doing and staying for a month instead of the planned fortnight. He hoped that she would be able to obtain a sight of Prince Albert's armoury before she came home so that she could tell him about it. At Mr Smith's request she sat to Richmond, the artist, and her publisher sent the portrait and a framed one of the Duke of Wellington as presents to Mr Brontë. They looked solitary and slightly out of place on the bare walls of the parsonage. Some contemporaries thought Richmond's charming picture of Charlotte flattering, but not Tabby, who pronounced it not good enough. The old servant could not understand that the other likeness portrayed the Duke of Wellington, but insisted it was her master.

Later that summer Charlotte travelled to Edinburgh to meet Smith, who had gone there to fetch home his young brother. These two days in the northern capital, which included a visit to Abbotsford and Melrose, whose very names possessed music and magic, were a halcyon memory to Charlotte. The four Brontës had been beglamoured by Scotland from their earliest days, this land of ballad and minstrelsy, with its presiding geniuses the Wizard of the North and the Ettrick Shepherd. Edinburgh compared to London was like a vivid page of history compared to a huge dull treatise on political economy. To Charlotte after her journey north London seemed a great, rumbling, rambling, heavy epic while Edinburgh was like a lyric, brief, bright, clear and vital as a flash of lightning.

In January of the following year Smith suggested she should later accompany him on a trip up the Rhine, an astonishing suggestion which she was later to refuse. 'That hint about the Rhine disturbs me,' she wrote to Ellen, still using her friend as a catalyst; 'I am not made of stone, and what is mere excitement to him is fever to me. However, it is a matter for the future, and long to look forward to. As I see it now, the journey is out of the question, for many reasons. I rather wonder he should think of it—I cannot conceive either his mother or his sisters relishing it, and all London would gabble like a host of geese.'

She was a difficult guest, though not to the household where she stayed, for her quietness and considerateness made her a general favourite, whether it was the Smiths in London, or Mrs Gaskell in Manchester, the formidable Miss Martineau at Ambleside or the Shuttleworths at Gawthorpe Hall. But when her hosts had guests to meet her or took her out visiting she suffered acutely, excitement and exhaustion making rough work of her nerves.

The literary world of London was agog when it learnt that Currer Bell was in their midst. Everyone who was anyone pulled every conceivable string to meet an author whose passionate, daring books had set them all talking, reading, speculating. Those wonderful books. There was wild excitement as they waited for the entrance of the guest of the evening. And tiny Currer Bell entered in mittens, in silence, in seriousness.

No lion ever vented so weak a roar to justify its existence. She had no small talk, and was incapable of seizing the friendliest lead. The simple question 'Do you like London?' was flattened by the reply of three words after thought, 'Yes and No'. Nor could she acquire the parry, thrust and counter-stroke of the literary coterie.

Dinner parties which should have been a brilliant success because of the company drew to an end, dismal failures. As the evening flagged to a close and the lamp began to smoke a little, she would make a point of seeking out the governess where she sat unobtrusively in the background of the drawing-room and entering into conversation with her. However well meant this gesture, it must have been embarrassing to her host and hostess, and most of all to the governess.

'Extremely unimpressive to *look* at', was Jane Welsh Carlyle's comment after she had met the famous authoress. Harriet Martineau described her as the smallest creature she had ever seen except at a fair, young looking in her deep mourning neat as a Quaker's, fine eyes and a sensible face indicating a habit of self-control. Matthew Arnold saw her as past thirty and plain, with expressive grey eyes. Mrs Gaskell's initial verdict was that she was altogether plain, her brown eyes very good and expressive, looking straight at you, large mouth, square broad forehead rather over-hanging. She saw her as having a reddish face. Thackeray's small daughter remembered her as pale with fair straight hair and steady eyes. The impression she made on George Lewes was of a little, plain, provincial, sickly looking old maid. A greater man than he measured her more surely: an impetuous honesty seemed to Thackeray to characterize this woman; she gave him the impression of being a very pure, and lofty, and high-minded person.

Contrary to the author's expectation, reviewers of her second book no longer suspected she might be a woman; *Shirley*'s treatment of male characters told them she was. Harriet Martineau of course had known from *Jane Eyre* the sex of its author when she came upon the passage about sewing brass rings on to the curtains after the fire at Thornfield. Only a woman could have written that, or an upholsterer—and he was not likely to write *Jane Eyre*. George Lewes insisted on addressing Currer Bell in his private letters before he met her as a woman despite his correspondent's protests, and in his review of *Shirley* referred to its author as female, an unpardonable breach in her eyes. As for Thackeray, before they met he was her genius, hero and prophet, standing head and shoulders above his fellow writers. After they met he was still a Titan, but a Grand Turk and great pagan as well. She had difficulty knowing when the Lion of Judah was in jest or in earnest, and he was incorrigible in the way he would address her in public as Currer Bell or introduce her as Jane Eyre no matter how soundly she rated him for this betrayal in private. This revealing of her sex was like exposure to Charlotte, to whom her masculine *nom de plume* acted as armour.

Each visit she made was easier than the last, less beset (although never entirely so) by the feverishness and exhaustion that meeting people always exacted from her, and she struck up a strong attachment with the two women writers Mrs Gaskell and Miss Martineau, who was said to be the ugliest woman in the world. Both had brains, but Harriet Martineau's were not veiled with ultra-feminine charm like Mrs Gaskell's; they were dominatingly, aggressively male. Her fusillade of a personality shoots itself across every memoir or biography of her time. Charlotte found her both hard and warm-hearted, abrupt and affectionate, liberal and despotic. Mrs Gaskell was a good, a great woman, and both were noble souls, although Miss Martineau, brought up a strict Unitarian, proclaimed herself an infidel.

Miss Wooler did not approve of her one-time pupil's friendship with a professed atheist, but Charlotte's loyalty withstood even the shock of Miss Martineau's heretical *Letters On The Nature and Development Of Man.* The break between them came later when Charlotte's third book *Villette* was published and she implored her friend to tell her what she thought of it. Miss Martineau had no option and wrote what Charlotte described as a fair, right and worthy letter except for one sentence—that she did not like the so-prevalent love in *Villette*, either the kind or the degree of it. That finished Charlotte. The break on her side was decisive and nothing the other could do could effect a bridge.

But there was never any rupture in her friendship with Mrs Gaskell. She was grateful for the companionship of this talented woman with her cheerful, pleasing, cordial manners, and her kind and good heart; Charlotte not only visited her but Mrs Gaskell came to the parsonage. She could have an intimacy with the womanly clergyman's wife that neither she nor anyone could have with the formidable Miss Martineau, isolated at the other end of her ear trumpet.

As the two women sat talking together in rooms that to Charlotte always seemed filled with the rustling of leaves

and the perfume of flowers, or in Haworth parsonage where
Mrs Gaskell was conscious of the deep repose that nothing
disturbed, the Brontë legend took birth. The melancholy
that has been allowed to enwrap the parsonage family
emanated naturally enough from the sole survivor of the
boat-load of six who, in the shadow of the tomb, looked
back at them so that their past had become darkened by
what lay in front of them. In fact their childhood had
much that was idyllic about it. Mrs Gaskell never tired of
hearing about Emily. What she heard made her think
Emily must have been a remnant of the Titans, great-grand-
daughter of the giants who used to inhabit the earth.

Emily, Emily, Emily. So attuned were Charlotte's
thoughts to her sister that she heard notes of her in different
voices. She corresponded with Mrs Gaskell and Miss
Martineau before she met them, and felt mournfully
pleased because she fancied in both a remote affinity to
Emily. She wept when she saw Richmond's finished
portrait of herself because it reminded her of Emily's
kindling look. George Lewes appalled her when he leaned
across the Smiths' dining-table to announce: 'There ought
to be a bond of sympathy between us, Miss Brontë, for we
have both written naughty books.' Yet, whatever Lewes
did or said, she could not hate him because he reminded
her so wonderfully of Emily. His face almost moved her
to tears, for there she saw Emily's eyes, her features, the
very nose, the somewhat prominent mouth, the forehead,
even, at moments, the expression.

If each visit to London became less nerve-racking, then
each return home became more onerous, the return to
deadly silence, solitude, desolation, the craving for companionship, the hopelessness of relief. It was Emily and
Anne she yearned for and missed with every fibre of her
being, not Branwell. Her sisters' lives had been twined with
hers from their beginning to their end, whereas her affinity
with her brother had long since evaporated as though he
had died years before he had. But the solitude of the room

she and Emily and Anne had used pressed on her with a
weight she found well-nigh intolerable. To walk round and
round the table by herself at night and remember because
of her very solitariness when there were three of them.
'Burd-alane,' the Scots called the only surviving child of a
family. She was burd-alane, the last leaf on the tree feeling
every whistle of the wind, the left-over arrow in the quiver,
useless because the bow was now unstrung.

Papa had never been a companion to his children: he
occupied his own territory in the household, his study-
sitting-room where he had his meals, and they the other
public room. More than ever Charlotte was plagued by the
fear that she might lose him, the last, the only near and dear
relation left to her in the world. Any indisposition he
suffered from depressed her as much as it did him, and she
had to hide her own persistent ill health because of the
uneasiness the very mention of it caused him.

With what had happened to Maria and Elizabeth still a
living memory, he had foreseen the end as Emily and
Anne sickened. When Martha now fell ill he at once declared she was in imminent danger. Charlotte, her spirits
lowered with constant headache and a nagging pain
between her shoulders, had Martha on her hands and old
Tabby whose lame leg was causing her pain again. Fretted
and waylaid on every side, it seemed they would never be
out of the wood. But Martha recovered, Tabby improved,
Papa walked to Keighley and back—nearly eight miles with
the return uphill all the way—and Charlotte was able to
visit Ellen for a week; also to travel to London on her first
visit to the Smiths, where her kind hostess saw that she had
a fire in her bedroom and wax candles on her dressing-
table. But happiness quite unshared could not be called
happiness—it had no taste.

Tabby was seventy-eight compared to Papa's seventy-
three, very lame, very deaf, her sight dimming. The kitchen
was still her domain and Martha, bright and blooming with
youth, was not allowed to help her with certain duties

which Tabby considered her prerogative, such as peeling the potatoes—now there was no Emily to wave a pen in her face and promise she would do them directly. Charlotte, when Tabby was not looking, had to take away the bowl and pick out the 'eyes' the old servant had left in. Her master's family belonged to Tabby as it could never belong to an incomer like Martha. She did not approve of the young servant inspecting the mail, and made it a point to seize the letters from the postman herself and carry them safely to the mistress of the house. In the parsonage where she would have to shout, Charlotte could scarcely impart anything private to Tabby, greedy for family news. So together mistress and servant would go for a walk on the moors and there, each sitting on a tussock of heather, Charlotte would tell her everything she wanted to hear.

'I've heard such news, ma'am!' Martha came in one day, puffing and blowing with excitement. 'You've been and written two books, the grandest books that ever was seen.'

Charlotte had certainly been living in a fool's paradise when she thought the name Currer Bell would hide her identity in Yorkshire. The topography of *Shirley* alone, described with such veracity, led readers unerringly to the Roe Head district where many of the happenings in the book had actually taken place. She had assured her publishers before publication that the originals of certain characters would never recognize themselves. The vicar of Birstall would no more suspect her of putting him into a novel under the name of Cyril Hall, or indeed of writing a book at all, than he would suspect his dog. But the vicar of Birstall not only recognized himself but half a dozen other characters as well. He wrote to Ellen, his parishioner, signing himself Cyril Hall, to ask her, as an intimate friend of the unknown Currer Bell, to supply him with a key to the rest—and would she at the same time deliver his respects to Mr Brontë.

'God help, keep and deliver me!' Charlotte wrote to

Ellen. What would the three curates, 'real as the Bible', who appeared in the first chapter of her book, say? She did not quite know how to take the news about the fourth, Mr Nicholls. The sexton's wife as she moved about the house wondered if their peaceable lodger, Mr Brontë's curate, had gone right off his head—such roars of laughter issuing from his room where he sat alone, such a clapping of his hands and a stamping of his feet on the floor. The next thing she knew he was out of the house with a book in his hand making a bolt for the parsonage—to read aloud to Papa the scenes about the curates and enjoy them with him. To Charlotte's surprise Mr Nicholls triumphed in his character as Mr Macarthey. Granted she had let him off lightly compared to the others, but she had when all was said and done drawn him as the bigot he was, and the bigot gloried in her delineation. What Mr Grant, whom she had described as a frontless arrogant slip of the commonplace, would say was another matter.

But not one of the three that she termed the fighting gentry betrayed the slightest resentment. It was all rather disconcerting. Mr Grant indeed after reading *Shirley* came to the house oftener than ever, and was remarkably meek and assiduous to please. It might be politic of course—to refuse to wear the cap. Or each characteristically might find solace for his wounds in crowing over his brethren, but she felt chagrin when her victims, instead of being cut to pieces by her pen, sallied up to the parsonage full of good humour.

But if the curates were equable about the manner in which she had treated them as wearers of the cloth, other readers were not. Her kind godmother who had sent her to Roe Head ceased to correspond or have anything further to do with her. She did not approve of a clergyman's daughter writing novels in the first place, and certainly not novels ridiculing the clergy of the district. Miss Wooler wrote what Charlotte described as a foolish letter, saying that in spite of *Jane Eyre* and *Shirley*, their author still retained a place in her esteem. Charlotte's reply was delivered with the authority of a headmistress putting a forward pupil smartly in her place.

Mr Brontë, sharing with Mr Nicholls the enjoyment of scenes from his daughter's book, is the one picture we have of any intimacy between the vicar and his curate, but now the older man had become used to the younger, who spent time with him each week in his study discussing the work of the parish. Charlotte usually remembered to include him in the letters she wrote home to her father: 'Hoping you are well, dear Papa, and with kind regards to Mr Nicholls, Tabby and Martha, also poor old Keeper and Flossy.' For his part Mr Nicholls felt assured enough to invite himself to a farewell cup of tea on the eve of leaving for his holiday in Ireland, and proved himself to his hostess on that occasion good, mild and uncontentious.

Sightseers and curiosity hunters began to make pilgrimages to Haworth, to go into raptures with the wild scenery they had read about in *Jane Eyre* and *Shirley*. They came to church on Sunday, and paid John Brown a silver collection for pointing out the famous authoress.

Haworth, basking in reflected shine, took a proprietary interest in their Miss Brontë, quick on the defensive at any implied criticism of Yorkshire or Yorkshiremen from outsiders. The Black Bull could put a name on most of the celebrities who rolled up at the parsonage. Yon was Sir James Kay-Shuttleworth and his lady from Gawthorpe Hall, neighbours you might call them, although only now did they make the eight-mile journey across the moors, and although they did come from Lancashire and therefore the wrong side of the border. Him with the two brace of grouse in his hands as a present for the parson, who came in that big party of ladies and gentlemen, was Lord John Manners, and his companion Lord Strangford's son.

What Mr Brontë had never dreamed would or could happen was happening; the world was coming to his door, discovering him. The high and the mighty were seeking him out in his Haworth fastness because he was the father of

Currer Bell. If his daughter did not appreciate and shrank from this concourse of visitors, Papa went more than half way to welcome them. An unknown suppliant, whose only claim to see Miss Brontë was that he was a patron of authors and literature, captivated Miss Brontë's father and called Charlotte and her visitor Mrs Gaskell a couple of proud minxes because they considered his appearance on the parsonage doorstep a presumption. When the Kay-Shuttleworths pressed Charlotte to visit them Papa would not hear of her refusing: before they left Charlotte found herself tied down to a three-day stay.

It was not as bad as she had dreaded but was bad enough. Because of Papa's insistence and their persistence, she paid more than one visit, but she was never entirely at ease with them, probably because they had nothing in common. Not all the amiability in the world could disguise the fact that he was a lion hunter and she his quarry. The stalked was forced to make friends with the stalker, but that did not make her like him, a host who showed his white teeth in too frequent a smile.

She dreaded the harsh Haworth winters, locked in upon herself with nothing but her memories for company. Grief was a two-edged sword, it cut both ways: the memory of one loss was the anticipation of another. She was never well, her low spirits acting on her physical health and her poor health dragging down her spirits, dreading the sleepless night before her as she dreaded the dawn of another day she must endure. She was urged to take holidays from home, but this remedy she looked upon as weakness. There was Papa to consider, and each visit she paid to the Smiths made it more difficult to say goodbye as she thought of the loneliness awaiting her. She wished the leave-taking were over as the criminal on the scaffold longed for the axe to descend. She told them she did not visit them oftener because of the pain of the last goodbye, the unforgettable handshake.

The autumn months of 1850 were unspeakable because she

had the task of going through her sisters' twin desks, of turning over their papers, of coming across what only they had used, Emily's goose quill and Anne's wafers. It was work she could undertake only by day, for she found when she did it in the evening that she could not sleep that night. The mementoes and poems of Anne struck her as unutterably sad, they coloured her sister's mind for her with a melancholy rather than poignancy.

Mr Williams suggested that Smith, Elder should reissue *Wuthering Heights*, *Agnes Grey* and *The Tenant of Wildfell Hall* with a biographical preface by Charlotte making it indisputably clear about their three pseudonyms. The old error that all the novels were written by the one person had been revived by a brilliant laudatory notice in the *Palladium* by Sidney Dobell entitled 'Currer Bell'. He placed *Wuthering Heights* above *Jane Eyre*, and Charlotte, the first to recognize her sister's genius, was touched and deeply grateful for his percipience. But his article made her all the more anxious to fall in with Mr Williams's proposal that her sisters should receive their just meed. 'This notice has been written', she finished her moving memoir to the new edition, 'because I felt it a sacred duty to wipe the dust off their gravestones, and leave their dear names free from soil.'

She rejected the suggestion about a reprint of Anne's second book—she wrote Mr Williams that it hardly appeared desirable to her to preserve *Wildfell Hall*. She called Anne inexperienced, but neither of Anne's books was written by an inexperienced hand. Indeed the beauty of her work is that it is woven all of a piece, and to achieve such texture does not betray the lack of skill. But the elder sister still thought of the younger as the youngest who never quite attained maturity.

Reading *Wuthering Heights* again frankly staggered Charlotte. For the first time she realized the shock it must have been to the average reader. Re-reading it confirmed her certainty of Emily's genius, but she felt a product such as *Wuthering Heights* called for explanation and the explanation

she gave in her Preface to the new edition was that the
writer who possesses the creative gift possesses something
of which he is not always master. 'Be the work grim or
glorious, dread or divine, you have little choice left but
quiescent adoption. As for you—the nominal artist—your
share in it has been to work passively under dictates you
neither delivered nor could question—that would not be
uttered at your prayer nor changed at your caprice.'

Charlotte had forgotten that some eight years before
Monsieur Heger had warned her of the dangers of her
theory that genius was a gift from God with which its
possessor had nothing to do. Not that Charlotte thought it
was God who had inspired *Wuthering Heights*, but some Geni.
It was probably this unquailing spirit of Emily's that made
Charlotte timid of her sister although she was younger.
Emily had always been a law unto herself. Charlotte had
stressed the Christian quality of Anne's death. Emily's
death had not had anything about it of Christian
acquiescence or acceptance.

In her Preface she excuses Ellis Bell to the reader.
Currer Bell did not know whether it was right or advisable
to create beings like Heathcliff, she scarcely thought it was.
Had Ellis Bell but lived, she wrote, her mind would have
grown like a strong tree, loftier, straighter, wider-spreading,
and its mature fruit would have attained a mellower
ripeness and sunnier bloom; on that mind time and
experience alone could work. But this contradicts her own
theory in the same Preface that the creative artist is not
always master of his material. Charlotte did not realize that
what she was dealing with was not growing but had grown.
Elements do not mature, they are. Emily was not possessed,
she possessed.

Agnes Grey did not call for amendment or explanation,
but Charlotte felt *Wuthering Heights* did. She modified the
Yorkshire dialect and she subdued the more passionate
scenes. The same incomprehension was met with when she
chose from Anne and Emily's unpublished poems a

collection to be printed at the tail end of the new edition. She altered some of Emily's and wrote explanatory notes for others to make them, she must have hoped, more intelligible. But the poet speaks for himself, and needs no interpreter.

Charlotte was not a mystic and she felt the need to personify the inanimate. She abounds in capital letters and makes Shirley describe Nature as a woman kneeling at her evening prayers in a rhapsody incongruous when it is remembered that Shirley is supposed by her creator to be Emily. To Emily nature was the sun and air, the twisted heather root, the blast of the wind and the light on the hill, the tripping walk of a bird and the honk of a grouse.

Charlotte received the *Athenaeum* regularly from James Taylor but, as she told the highly diverted Ellen whom she kept posted, she did not consider herself placed under any personal obligation by accepting this newspaper from him for it belonged to the establishment of Smith and Elder. She had not expected to receive any more letters from him, having thought nine months ago that there would be no further correspondence from that quarter. Obviously James Taylor had made some overture towards her which she turned aside on her first visit to stay with her London publishers. However, she was not averse to hearing from him again.

The following year he was appointed to open a branch of the firm in Bombay. Charlotte could have no doubts why he asked if he could come to Haworth to bid her goodbye. He was going to ask her if, on his return after five years, she would reconsider her decision and marry him.

He looked much thinner and older than she remembered. He was very near to her, and once she saw him through her glasses when she was forcibly struck by his likeness to Branwell. She was close enough to see the lines of his face which showed inflexibility and unattractive hardness of character. Her veins ran ice when he looked at her in his keen way and it was all she could do to stand her ground tranquilly and steadily, and not to recoil as she had done before.

Papa was not aware of any of these drawbacks. Charlotte listened to him wishing their parting guest well, exhorting him to be true to himself, his country and his God. Whenever he alluded to him it was always with significant eulogy, brushing aside with some impatience Charlotte's objection that he was no gentleman. She believed Papa thought a prospective union deferred for five years with such a reliable personage would be a very proper and advisable affair. However, they did not discuss the matter: father and daughter were not on an intimate enough footing to ask questions of each other.

Physically James Taylor was repugnant to her, and it is unlikely she could ever have overcome this repugnance to marry him, but in the unsettled months that followed she was to wonder if she had been wise to refuse the little man. 'Would Mr Taylor and I ever suit?' she asked herself, though she wrote to Ellen and catalogued the reasons why they decidedly would not, a formidable list. But his absence and the exclusion of his idea from her mind left a blank she had not expected, and she felt lonely and despondent in consequence.

He wrote to her from Bombay, describing in one letter the processes of a Turkish bath which he had gone to see though not to indulge in. She thought he could have omitted some of the more realistic details, but she found his letter amusing enough in spite of herself. In her reply she sympathized about the deficiency of all intellectual attractions in Bombay. She began to look for Indian mail and was disappointed when she did not find it. All was silent as the grave, she replied to Ellen's query, and she asked her friend not to refer to the subject again.

In the couple of weeks between James Taylor's call and her second last visit to London Charlotte indulged in a shopping spree. So many things she found it absolutely necessary to have, several bodices and a lace mantle to go with her black satin dress. She bought a black one in Leeds, but when she took it home saw it was a mistake for it looked brown and rusty over the black satin, so she exchanged it for a white one which not only looked better but was cheaper. She went to Hunt and Hall in Leeds for a new bonnet and chose a quiet and grave one from all the feathered and flowered splendours she saw, to be horrified to discover when she took it home that it had a gay pink lining. The same nervousness overtook her when she handled some beautiful silks of pale sweet colours for a new dress—they were too dear, she felt, at five shillings a yard, and she bought instead black silk at three shillings. It is said one never regrets an extravagance and Charlotte regretted her thriftiness over the black silk, particularly when Papa said he would have lent her a sovereign if he had but known.

Smith, Elder had a staunch ally in Papa in their anxiety for a new book from Currer Bell, but Charlotte had not the vitality or urge for creative work, which distressed her for she felt she was failing her publishers. She laboured under an exaggerated sense of obligation to Smith, Elder. But health returned when at last she was able to make a start, although external happenings continually blocked and stemmed the flow of inspiration, and without the inflatus she was becalmed.

Old Keeper died, three years after his mistress in the same month of the year, December. Charlotte dreaded the anniversary of her death. There was something infinitely sad about losing the old dog, and Flossy was dull and at a loss without him. His death could not be hidden from Papa as could the death of one of Flossy's puppies. Charlotte had been shocked earlier that year when she was in London and heard from the parsonage, which was being re-roofed while she was away, that Papa had had the piano removed from the parlour, his study, and dragged upstairs into a bedroom. A piano in a bedroom struck her as absurd; besides, it had been so convenient for his books in the parlour. She did not understand that her father could not bear Emily's piano standing silent in his room, and Keeper's death was the severance of a living link between Papa and his second daughter.

Charlotte would not permit herself to holiday with the Smiths in London in 1852—she felt she could only earn such indulgence after she had finished her book. There were periods when, sick with solitude, she wondered if she would ever finish it, for it was a gruelling year ushered in by a virulent attack of influenza.

She had not seen the tombstone she had ordered to be put on Anne's grave, and towards the end of May went to Filey by herself and remained for a month in the rooms she had shared with Ellen after her sister's death. It was a pilgrimage she felt she had to make alone, which was a pity when she could so easily have had her friend's company, and she wrote to Ellen that her heart longed for her. There was in Charlotte's nature a strong tendency to depend on her own strength and to kiss the cross. This was apparent later in the year when she denied herself the comfort of a visit from Ellen until she finished her book, but the strain was such that she had to yield, to be cheered almost at once by her friend's presence.

At Filey she swam once or twice, which did her good, and walked for miles on the sands, trying not to feel desolate and melancholy. It was Anne she thought of here, Anne who had loved the sea. She wrote to Ellen about her headaches and the pain in her side, but not to Papa whose own health had really been wonderful that winter, good sleep, good spirits, an excellent steady appetite, all making for vigour. She told him that she had watched a dog swimming in the sea like a seal and wondered what Flossy would say to that. Mr Nicholls would certainly have laughed outright if he had attended the church Charlotte had in Filey, where the singers turned their backs on the congregation and the congregation on the pulpit!

Tabitha and the Browns never forgave Charlotte for leaving Miss Anne at Scarborough and not bringing her home. It grieved Charlotte too and she still thought of it as a temporary measure, but the time was not opportune and the wound still too open for Papa.

He had a seizure soon after her return, and for a time the worst was feared for him. Since his operation he seldom let a day pass without expressing his gratitude for the restoration of his sight. Now, his pulse bounding at the rate of 150 a minute, there was partial paralysis, although his mind remained clear, and complete blindness. He had to be kept very quiet—Charlotte knew that to mention apoplexy would be to kill him. His pulse was reduced to 90, the paralysis and blindness proved temporary and the doctor pronounced him out of danger.

As the year drew to a close Charlotte finished her book. Smith, Elder had seen and approved on the whole of the first two volumes, and Charlotte worked herself into something amounting to agony as she waited to hear what their verdict would be on the third.

She was anxious for this new book to be published under another *nom de plume*. She had not the stomach for poor reviews, and in her queasiness felt certain reviewers had a vendetta against Currer Bell. Also she had worked into *Villette* all her Brussels experiences and had used not only Monsieur but Madame Heger as characters. Her Madame Beck, gliding about her school on noiseless slippers, was Madame Heger as she appeared to Charlotte, a living catherine-wheel of compliments, delight and affability in company who could rifle drawers to read private letters in secret; yet a most consistent character, forbearing with all the world and tender to no part of it.

Villette is the greatest of Charlotte Brontë's novels. George Eliot wrote after reading it, 'There is something preternatural in its power', and it is this transcendence that makes it rank, unequal as it is, as one of the great love stories in any language.

It is written in the first person, and its narrator, Lucy Snowe, is naturally closely identified with her creator—not that Charlotte was leniently disposed towards her creation, but then she was not leniently disposed towards herself. She admits Lucy has about her an external coldness, and from the beginning never meant to give her an easy time or pleasant fate. It was Papa who could not bear the tale to end unhappily, so Charlotte temporized by leaving it to the reader to picture reunion and a happy ending.

Lucy was in love with Dr John, and Dr John was George Smith as Mrs Bretton was Mrs Smith. Lucy often saw him hard-worked yet seldom over-driven, and never irritated, confused or oppressed. What he did he accomplished with the ease and grace of all-sufficing strength, with the bountiful cheerfulness of high and unbroken energies. Strength dispenses with subtlety. He took pleasure in homage, some recklessness in exciting it and some vanity in receiving it. And Dr John wrote to the lonely English teacher in the foreign school good-natured letters, nothing more, but to Lucy in her loneliness they were godlike. Long pain made patience a habit and she buried the letters under Methuselah, the pear tree at the farther end of the walk in the *pension* garden, when she discovered Madame Beck had read them.

But Lucy's abortive love for Dr John had always the grey of renouncement upon it. It had none of the excitement of exchange, the riposte of the duel between her and the professor Monsieur Paul Emanuel, when contestants were closer than affinities and affinities as challenging as contestants. The love between Lucy and the irascible Paul Emanuel on his estrade is what makes *Villette* great.

Harriet Martineau's criticism of the book was that all the female characters in it were obsessed with the one thought—love. In her rational view there were other interests for women of all ages apart from this one passion. Charlotte's reply was hot with indignation: 'I know that *love* is as I understand it; and if man or woman should be ashamed of feeling such love, then there is nothing right, noble, faithful, truthful, unselfish in this earth, as I comprehend rectitude, nobleness, fidelity, truth and disinterestedness.'

Charlotte's exaggerated sense of obligation to her publishers was weighted by the fear that her new book would not come up to their expectations, that it would not sell well, that the critics would doom it. On delivery of the third volume she received from them payment but no letter. At once she jumped to the conclusion that this betokened disapproval, and determined to travel to London on the Monday to discover what had struck her publisher mute. Fortunately she received a letter from Mr Smith on the Sunday which saved her the journey and earned him a rebuke.

He and Mr Williams criticized parts of volume three, but their general judgment was favourable. Charlotte replied most reasonably to their criticism but did nothing to alter the manuscript. Lucy must not marry Dr John, she wrote to George Smith, he was far too youthful, handsome, light spirited and sweet tempered, and must draw a prize in life's lottery. As she had once taken upon herself to describe to Henry Nussey the wife he should marry, she now told George Smith that his prototype's wife should be young, rich, pretty—he must be made very happy indeed. As for George Smith, when Currer Bell demanded his opinion of Pauline whom Dr John marries in her book, he replied she was an odd, fascinating little puss but he was not in love with her, and refused to answer any further questions about *Villette*.

Naturally enough her publishers would not hear of its being produced under any other pseudonym than Currer Bell, and Charlotte realized why when they pointed out the obvious reasons. She contented herself, therefore, with having printed on the title page 'The author of this work reserves the right of translating it' and believed this would safeguard her. A one-time schoolfellow, who had been at the Heger *pensionnat* when Charlotte was there, read the book soon after publication and, although unaware of the identity of Currer Bell, at once recognized, from the vivid descriptions of the old garden and the *allée defendue* where so much happened, her one-time school in Brussels.

For *Villette* Charlotte received a total payment of £500, which was a disappointment to both Papa and the author. They felt her third book justified a larger sum, and they were right. £1,500 was not adequate for three best-selling novels, particularly when this sum included the American rights. She certainly was due for a rise for *Villette*, yet Smith, Elder were a generous firm. The explanation probably lay in Currer Bell's attitude towards them which unconsciously coloured theirs towards her. They had come to look upon themselves as her benefactors and thus never considered raising her payment.

Charlotte finished *Villette* in November and it was arranged that she should pay her long deferred visit to London in January for its publication. The few weeks' interval was a curious time of aftermath for her. She had put so much of herself into her last book that she felt as spent as a mother who has given birth to a child she is not allowed to keep. She had now written out the emotion she had once felt for Constantin Heger, there was no longer even friendship between her and James Taylor, and the *rapport* between her and George Smith had reached a stage when, by reason of its very tentativeness, it was neither going to consolidate nor likely to snap.

It was as though the mirror of life had tilted slightly and she had to adjust herself to the different slant, a change in positions. Mrs Smith did not mean to her what once she had done when Charlotte, braced to meet a crowd of strangers, felt without a word being spoken between them the support of her presence. She had written her usual kind letter of invitation, but Charlotte could not look upon that kindness as once she had done. It had been very pleasant to her in the past, but this was no longer the past, it was the irksome present.

At home everything was the same, the same canker of solitude, the same daily round bringing the anniversary of

Emily's death near once more, the same winter weather with a wind sobbing when it was not howling round the house, the same aches and pains. And it was December, an evening like any other. Mr Nicholls came to tea, which they had as usual in Papa's study, and as usual she left the two men together and retired to the dining-room for the usual evening alone. As usual Mr Nicholls sat with Papa until between eight and nine, when she heard him leave her father's room, and as usual she waited for the slam of the front door as he drew it behind him. But tonight it did not come.

Instead there was a pause outside the room where she sat, then a tap. And in the flash of that moment she knew what was coming even before he entered and stood before her.

He was deathly pale and trembling from head to foot. His voice was low but vehement. He loved her, but he knew she did not love him, which was why despite the vehemence he spoke with difficulty. He was asking her to marry him.

7

I have bloomed in my last summer's sun—

Emily Brontë

IT GAVE Charlotte a sense of shock to see someone ordinarily so like a statue standing trembling, stirred and overcome before her, telling her of what he felt, how he could endure his suffering no longer, throwing himself on her mercy, pleading for some hope.

All she could find to say was to promise him an answer on the morrow and to entreat him to leave her now. She did ask if he had spoken to Papa, to which he replied he dared not. And Charlotte remembered Papa's unsympathetic sarcasm about his curate's recent low spirits, his threats of returning to Ireland, his symptoms of impaired health, rightly divining he was in love but never for a moment dreaming it was with her.

She was a woman of thirty-six; nevertheless the minute her suitor was out of the house she went to her father's room and told him what had happened. No decision could be taken by her either way without Papa's sanction.

Her parent's reaction was instantaneous, his temper inflamed his agitation and his agitation increased his temper. That Nicholls, his curate, a man earning £100 a year, should have the effrontery to propose to his vicar's daughter was almost past belief. The more he thought of it, and it reached such a pitch he could think of little else, the more enraged he became, the more heinous the other man's presumption.

Such a marriage would be degradation; if Charlotte

married at all it must be very differently, not throwing herself away. Again and again he returned to Mr Nicholls's lack of wealth until Charlotte began to feel her father considered ample endowment the most important quality a suitor could have, whereas her objection to such a union was incompatibility. But Papa worked himself into such a state, betraying all the old familiar signs, that she feared another seizure and promised her answer on the morrow would be a decided refusal.

But for the first time she and her parent were in opposition. She felt her blood boil as she heard him belabour his curate with epithets. If she had loved Mr Nicholls she could not have borne to have listened to such injustice or heard him so miscalled.

But she did not love him. To her he had always been unlit and uninteresting as only a narrow-minded man could be. Yet the realization that this stiff, monosyllabic man was capable of the emotion he felt for her made her for the first time pity him.

Every action her father took alienated his daughter further from him. He treated his curate with a hardness not to be bent, and a contempt not to be propitiated. Not content with her promise to say no, he wrote to Mr Nicholls himself, a cruel letter which Charlotte could only describe as a pitiless dispatch. She sent a note dissociating herself from the vehemence of her father's expressions. Mr Nicholls's tacit reply to the pitiless dispatch was to resign his curacy, and to Charlotte's note to take no further steps to implement his resignation. Mrs Brown reported that her lodger was not eating a bite of the food she set before him. Charlotte began to find it all galling and irksome. She wrote to Ellen that she wished Papa would resume his tranquillity and Mr Nicholls his beef and pudding.

All Haworth knew what was happening; gone were the days when the uncommunicative Tabby was the only liaison officer between them and the parsonage. Now they had the whole Brown family keeping them supplied with news. No one was neutral, you were in either one or the other camp, and the vicar's supporters, generalled by the Browns, far outnumbered the curate's.

Martha Brown hated him, and she should know the ins and outs of it all, living as she did under the same roof where everything was taking place. Her father, the sexton, said he would like to shoot him. Haworth of course had never really taken to Mr Nicholls, but no one had thought he would so far forget himself as to propose to the vicar's daughter, who was a famous authoress. It was her putting him into one of her books that had turned his head and given him ideas. It was said he had property in Ireland, but no one believed it. Vicar and curate had not met since 'it' had happened; they said what they had to say through letters carried by someone else. Mr Nicholls, who at his best had never been cheerful like Mr Weightman, now went amongst them wrapped in gloom, and on a Sunday when it was his turn, supplied a substitute rather than fall in with the vicar. What the upshot would be no one could tell, but everyone's money was on the old one. Miss Brontë was off to London at the beginning of the year, so Martha told them, to see her new book being printed, and anything could happen except reconciliation between the pair of them whilst she was away.

Papa was most anxious for her to pay the visit; she knew he wanted her out of the way, and Charlotte was glad to escape from the over-charged atmosphere. She elicited a promise from him before she left that he would not refer to Mr Nicholls in his letters, a respite from the subject was essential for her. She was the only person who pitied the curate, all the more so because everyone else was leagued against him. He had written asking permission to withdraw his resignation, and Papa had agreed if the curate gave his written undertaking never again to broach the obnoxious subject to him or to his daughter. Mr Nicholls, with a certain dour skill, had evaded doing any such thing, so when she left everything was in a thoroughly unsatisfactory, unsettled state with dark hints coming from the Browns' lodger that he was thinking of emigrating to Australia.

It was her quietest visit to London; she was no longer the literary wonder of the day. George Smith was engaged to be married and very busy, but assiduous as ever making arrangements for his guest to visit all the places of interest she chose. Papa only partially kept his promise, writing two letters purporting to be from Flossy in which she was given a canine view of the curate which exactly tallied with her master's. Charlotte felt she could not face the home-coming without support, so Ellen met her at Keighley to accompany her to the parsonage.

Villette was published on 28th January, a few days before Charlotte left for home, and on 28th January Mr Nicholls wrote to London to offer himself as a missionary to the thousands of his fellow countrymen who had emigrated to Australia and who were in a great measure deprived of the means of grace.

Mr Brontë supplied the Missionary Society with a testimonial before Charlotte's return, vouching that the Rev. Arthur Bell Nicholls had behaved himself wisely, soberly and piously during his curacy, was a man of good abilities and (Australia called for physical strength) a good constitution, very discreet, wary and prudent, sound and orthodox in principles. In the writer's opinion he would, under Providence, make an excellent missionary.

Mr Brontë was mercifully spared the sight of the testimonials his curate's fellow clerics provided for him. Mr Grant, whom Charlotte had pilloried in her first chapter of *Shirley*, informed the Missionary Society that eight years ago when Mr Nicholls came to Haworth the church was in a very sad state, and called upon them to consider its improved condition now. The Society were told by a friend of Mr Brontë's that the Haworth vicar had often detailed to him his curate's invaluable services. The vicar of Bradford provided the information that Haworth was a very wild and rough part of the parish and Mr Nicholls's exertions among a rude and dissenting population had allowed the church to gain ground.

Charlotte on her return with Ellen found the tension between the two men as bad as ever, but the notices for *Villette* which began to arrive received it with acclaim. She could write that the reviews made her heart swell with thankfulness to Him Who takes note both of suffering, and work and motives. Papa was pleased too, and an important event took place in the same month which drove his curate into the background where he belonged. The Bishop of the diocese honoured the vicar by spending a night at the parsonage.

His hostess found him charming, the most benign little gentleman who ever put on lawn sleeves. Martha waited at table very nicely, and Charlotte engaged extra help in the kitchen for the occasion. Papa kept up fully as well as she expected, although she doubted if he could have borne another day of it. Altogether the visit could be rated a complete success but for the unseemly behaviour of Mr Nicholls.

The local clergy were invited to tea and supper to meet their Bishop, and Mr Brontë could scarcely exclude his curate. But his demeanour was anything but pleasant. For one thing he made not the slightest effort to mask his depression, indeed the blackness of his mood drew attention to it; for another, when he spoke to Papa he showed temper. Charlotte could see that the Bishop was very puzzled by it all.

When the rest of the party trooped from one room to another, Mr Nicholls stopped dead in the passage to waylay Charlotte, but she drew away from him and went upstairs, whereupon he gave what Martha, watching him from the kitchen, could only describe as a flaysome look.

Charlotte felt that if Mr Nicholls was a good man at bottom, it was a pity he had not the faculty to put goodness into a more attractive form. He was never agreeable or amiable and was less so now than ever. She did not know

him well enough to be sure there was truth and true
affection in his feeling for her, or only rancour and corrod-
ing disappointment at the bottom of the chagrin. She
found it most unpleasant being dogged up the lane by him
after the evening service. She might pity him, but she did
not like his dark gloom and would be thankful when he was
well away. When the Inspector called, he managed to get
up a most pertinacious and needless dispute with him. All
her old unfavourable impressions revived as she listened,
and she was afraid her face revealed exactly what she was
thinking.

Mr Nicholls thought better of going to Australia and
withdrew his application. They heard he had a new curacy
but did not know where. Charlotte hoped the news was
true. He and Papa never spoke if they met; Papa had a
perfect antipathy to him and he, Charlotte feared, to Papa.
He sat drearily in his rooms in the sexton's house, so
gloomy and resigned he was shunned by all—except Flossy,
who called for him every day, and every day the cheerless
curate took his only friend for a walk.

In April Charlotte made her escape to visit her two
closest confidantes, Mrs Gaskell and Ellen. Mrs Gaskell was
her solitary remaining link with the literary world it had
cost her so much to storm. She had written a frosty note
to Mr Williams asking him to send no more books as the
courtesies must cease one day. A new curate, a young man
called George de Renzy, had been engaged to take Mr
Nicholls's place when he left soon after.

Charlotte was home on Whit Sunday in time to attend his
last service. As she moved forward to take the sacrament
Mr Nicholls was seen to struggle, falter and lose command
of himself. He stood before the woman he loved and in full
sight of the congregation white, shaking and voiceless. The
parish clerk whispered something to him and he was seen
to make a tremendous effort, but could only with the
greatest difficulty whisper and falter through the service.
Charlotte thanked God Papa was not present, but either the

parish clerk or the sexton must have repeated to him what had happened. As his daughter heard his angry exclamations of 'unmanly driveller', she felt that compassion or relenting was no more to be looked for from Papa than sap from firewood.

But public opinion had now swung against the vicar and towards his curate. No one could deny that Mr Brontë was an obdurate man, once he made up his mind, as well they all knew. Before you could shoo a goose he had filled Mr Nicholls's place and Haworth was beginning to wonder if they wanted a stranger, a young one at that, about their doors instead of the man they knew. What was wrong with Mr Nicholls anyway? Haworth was not going to let him take his leave without showing their esteem for one who had always done his duty by them. The gold watch bore the inscription: 'Presented to the Revd. A. B. Nicholls, B.A., by the trustees, scholars and congregation of St. Michael's, Haworth, Yorkshire, May 25th, 1853', and the presentation was made to him at a public meeting. Papa was not very well that day, and Charlotte advised him not to attend.

Mr Nicholls left one morning at six o'clock and had called at the parsonage the evening before to hand over the deeds of the National School, and to say goodbye. He did not find Miss Brontë in her sitting-room, which was upside-down being spring-cleaned, and only his vicar was in his study, for Charlotte refused to speak to him in her father's presence. But when he left the house she ran out after him to say goodbye. She found him leaning against the garden gate crying as women never cry. Never again could she question his love or constancy and she felt punished for her former doubts, but she could not give him what he implored her to give, hope and encouragement.

Charlotte was not in love with Arthur Nicholls, but love, as she had once theorized to Ellen, was not necessary for successful marriage; better for that to come after, when it would be rooted in respect, than run all to flower beforehand. Her father's repugnance to her marriage with his curate ruled it out of the question, but unconsciously she had taken advantage of his disapproval to be entirely passive. Now she was no longer passive.

Mr Brontë's reasons for refusing his permission were threefold. The predominant one was that he could never allow his daughter, who had written masterpieces, whom titled and great people sought out and revered, who had been fêted by London, to demean herself by marrying a nobody. The second was the very real fear that he would be left alone, a fear that had communicated itself to other members of the household. During one of Charlotte's London trips there had been consternation in the parsonage when her return was delayed, as it was feared a secret marriage might be the cause of it. While she was absent on her last visit early that year Mr Brontë had unloaded on the unfortunate Mr Nicholls his unease about Mr George Smith by making his curate fiercely jealous of the unknown London man. Although an arrangement might have been effected if she married Nicholls whereby her father would not be left alone, Mr Brontë, like many another Victorian parent, considered marriage of his progeny quite unnecessary and unsuitable when it interfered with his comfort and upset his routine. The third reason was that he did not believe Charlotte was strong enough for marriage; she had been thirty-seven on her last birthday, no one could call her robust, and he had already lost five of his delicate brood of six.

Neither father nor daughter was well during the summer months. Charlotte had influenza and recurring splitting headaches, Papa's sight gave cause for alarm as it always did when he was upset. And there was much to upset the old man. The young curate was not working out well and the village did not like him. For the first time the vicar realized how much Mr Nicholls had taken upon himself and done for him.

He did not know that his former curate returned to the neighbourhood from his new curacy at Kirk Smeaton. He stayed with his friend Mr Grant, the headmaster of Haworth Grammar School, one of the shower of curates to open the first chapter of *Shirley* in a spray of satire. Mr Grant must have known of his guest's few meetings with Miss Brontë and their correspondence, and he was definitely on their side. It was his one-time vicar he did not like, and he took pleasure in going to the parsonage when the first unfavourable criticism of *Villette* appeared to show it to Mr Brontë.

In September Mrs Gaskell paid her long-postponed visit to the parsonage. Charlotte, who had visited her friend in her large, cheerful, airy house with its garden pervading the pleasant rooms, felt self-conscious about her own home which she had described when they first met rather as she would have described a tombstone—as a grey, square, cold, dead-coloured parsonage. Now Mrs Gaskell was warned that coming to Haworth would be to her like coming to the backwoods of America, that she would be leaving civilization behind in exchange for barbarism, loneliness and liberty.

The guest did not think she had ever seen a spot more exquisitely clean than Haworth parsonage. Even the way the table was set for a meal had this simplicity of grace about it. It was a cold country and the fires cast a pretty dancing light all over the house. The room where she and her hostess had their meals (Mr Brontë's were sent in to him) was the perfection of warmth, snugness and comfort. Crimson was the prevailing colour, to make a contrast for the cold grey landscape outside with its leaning and horizontal gravestones. The daughter of the house had been able to refurnish it with some of the money from her books, she had even dared to hang curtains at the windows —that had not pleased Papa with his dread of fire, but he had not forbidden it.

No one came to the door, hardly a voice was heard, only the ticking of an unseen clock and the wind piping and wailing round the square unsheltered house in a strange unearthly way. Mrs Gaskell's bedroom was upstairs and glimpsed the moors, a view that looked beautiful in certain lights, especially moonlight.

That year the heather had been blighted by a thunderstorm, and instead of a blaze of purple glory was all of a livid brown colour. They had long delicious walks against the wind on Penistone Moor. Oh, those high, wild, desolate moors up above the whole world, and the very realms of silence!

Walking and talking together hour after hour might sound monotonous, but it was not so in reality. There were some people whose stock of facts and anecdotes were soon exhausted, but not Miss Brontë. She had the wild strange facts of her own and her sisters' lives, and, beyond and above these, most original and suggestive thoughts of her own, so that the attentive novelist felt on the last day that, like the moors, their talk might be extended in any direction without getting to the end of any subject.

Mr Brontë was a tall, fine-looking old man who had a sort of grand and stately way of describing past times which tallied well with his striking appearance. Despite his poor sight he refused to allow his daughter to accompany him on his walks, accusing her of treating him as if he were in his second childhood. He came back tired, having lost his way, and moaning, 'Where is my strength gone? I used to walk forty miles a day.'

He was very polite and agreeable to his daughter's guest, but once or twice she caught a glare in his stern eyes as he looked over his spectacles at his daughter that made her know her man. Obviously he still considered Miss Brontë a child to be guided and ruled; she submitted to this with a quiet docility that half amused, half astonished the more sophisticated woman. Charlotte confided to her that she had met Mr Nicholls since he had left Haworth and was corresponding with him; she was excited about what was happening but troubled that the meetings and correspondence had to be clandestine.

A young inexperienced curate could never take the place of an active and assiduous co-worker such as Mr Nicholls. With his enfeebled eyesight the vicar needed someone who did not have to be told what to do or, as he had discovered with de Renzy, be warned into the bargain what he must not do. After a more lamentable lapse than usual on the part of the young man, Charlotte told her father she was in touch with Mr Nicholls. All she asked was the opportunity to become better acquainted with him, and as he was coming shortly to stay with the Grants she could have that opportunity if her father would but give his permission.

'Papa,' she said, 'I am not a young girl, not a young woman even—I never was pretty. I now am ugly. At your death I shall have £300 besides the little I have earned myself. Do you think there are many men who would serve seven years for me?'

He turned on her then, harshly demanding if she would marry a curate.

'Yes, I must marry a curate if I marry at all; not only a curate but *your* curate; not merely your curate but he must live in the house with you, for I cannot leave you.'

He silenced her then by saying, 'Never. I will never have another man in this house,' and walked out of the room.

For a week he did not speak to her. It was Tabby who asked him if he wanted to kill his daughter, and then hobbled to Charlotte and blamed Mr Nicholls for not having more brass.

The old man gave way to the extent of agreeing to see his former curate when he came to Haworth. It was not a pleasant interview. Papa remained very, very hostile and was bitterly unjust.

By April the battle was won. 'Mr Nicholls has proved himself disinterested and forebearing', Charlotte wrote to Ellen. 'He has shown, too, that while his feelings are exquisitely keen, he can freely forgive. Certainly I respect him, nor can I withhold from him more than cool respect

In fact, dear Ellen, I am engaged.' She called him Arthur now.

There was little expectation of happiness. Her husband to be was an affectionate, conscientious, high-principled man and she told herself, as Lucy Snowe might well have taken herself to task, that she must not yield to regrets that he had not fine talents or congenial tastes or thoughts. She admitted it cost her a good deal to come to this, he was not intellectual but a Puseyite and very stiff, but she would never let him make her a bigot.

Ellen, although years ago she had favoured such a marriage, was not happy about the engagement. It struck her as a dreary end for one who had borne so much. Tartly Mary Taylor retorted from New Zealand that Charlotte was quite entitled to decide for herself, whatever Ellen thought. She was never to think without gloomy anger of her friend's sacrifices to the selfish old man who was her father. Miss Wooler, the unmarried woman, considered the advantages of marriage. Mrs Gaskell, the happily married woman who, unknown to Charlotte, had tried to bring her engagement to Mr Nicholls about, considered some of the disadvantages. Charlotte stayed with her when she was engaged and she could not but be affected by the lack-lustre of the bride to be. A creative writer herself, she could not envisage Currer Bell writing another masterpiece with the shadow of Mr Nicholls athwart the page. But it is unlikely, even without Mr Nicholls, that Charlotte could have written another great book. The fragment *Emma* which she left is like a burnt-out cinder compared to the glowing, kindling, flaming genius of her three published novels which even sparks her earliest, *The Professor*, published posthumously. Into all four she had put herself; when she wrote the last word 'Farewell!' of *Villette* she had no more to tell.

Now that the Rubicon was crossed, Papa's health improved daily. He was preaching twice on Sunday, as well and strongly as ever. In all the preparations and arrangements for the marriage, his comfort and convenience were the first to be considered. He began to realize that there were going to be positive advantages in having not only another man but his curate living under the same roof, a curate so touchingly grateful for his permission to marry the woman he had always loved that he was anxious to prove his gratitude by every means in his power, who was into the bargain going to subscribe so generously to the household expenses that the marriage would be Papa's gain, not loss.

No one could ever again question Arthur Nicholls's love, for to return to the curacy of Haworth he rejected several offers of promotion. The Bishop, who had of course to be consulted, gave his blessing. He was not only a good and dear Bishop but a penetrating one as well, for he had divined the reason for the Haworth curate's extraordinary behaviour to his vicar on his visit last year.

The small room behind the sitting-room where peat was stored was emptied and made into a study for the future son-in-law. Charlotte chose sprigged wallpaper for it, and green and white curtains to match the paper. Papa now admitted he had been far too stern, even unjust. Charlotte realized that what had disappointed him was ambition, paternal pride, and paternal pride was ever a restless feeling. She felt she could almost cry sometimes that in this most important happening in her life she could not better satisfy his natural pride. Her destiny would certainly not be brilliant, but Arthur was conscientious and affectionate and she felt very grateful to him. She meant to try to make him happy, and Papa too.

The wedding was hastened to the end of June to foil the designs of Mr de Renzy, so smooth and fairspoken to Papa, so acrimonious behind his back, which were to leave the vicar without a curate for some weeks when he left earlier than his legal due. But Arthur with his usual trustworthiness took upon himself all the bother of providing substitutes while he was on his honeymoon. Wedding cards were ordered to be sent out after the ceremony, for they

were information not invitation. Arthur thought sixty would
be required—there seemed no end to his string of parson
friends. Eighteen sufficed for Charlotte. They wanted the
wedding to be as quiet as possible, no sightseers, and
Arthur, the soul of discretion, arranged for it to take place
at the unlikely hour of eight in the morning when nobody
would be about.

But Haworth knew how to put two and two together.
Mr Nicholls was staying the night with the Grants, and he
had the Reverend Sutcliffe Sowden along with him. Now
why would that be unless Mr Sowden was going to marry
him? The parsonage had sent to the Devonshire Arms for a
cab to meet the afternoon train at Keighley. Haworth did
not need a Brown to tell them the identity of the two
passengers when it lumbered up the brae. The younger one
was Miss Nussey—they had seen her oft enough sitting in
the parsonage pew of a Sunday. She would be Miss Brontë's
bridesmaid. The old one they might have seen only once
but they knew who she was all right—Miss Wooler, their
headmistress when they were both girls and that wasn't
yesterday. They were to be the only two at the ceremony,
and they were to be but eight sitting down to the wedding
breakfast in the parsonage, and that eight included the bride
and groom and the bride's father. Mr and Mrs Grant were
invited to the breakfast but not the ceremony. They were a
real close set, the Brontës.

Charlotte showed her two guests her wedding dress, a
white embroidered muslin with a little lace mantle and a
white bonnet trimmed with green. Everything was prepared and in order for the morrow when she went in to say
goodnight to Papa, only to hear that he would not after
all be in church to give her away; all he could manage was
to attend the wedding breakfast.

It was the last hurdle Charlotte had to take before she was
married, and at that hour of night, when the wedding was
to be first thing in the morning, it seemed insurmountable.
Miss Wooler and Ellen shared her consternation. To be

given away was written into the marriage service—the officiating priest asking, 'Who giveth this woman to be married to this man?' Who—did it say the 'who' had to be male? They looked up the Solemnization of Matrimony in the Common Prayer Book to discover to their immeasurable relief that it simply said 'who'. Charlotte was saved: there was nothing then to prevent Miss Wooler giving her one-time pupil away.

On that dim quiet June morning Haworth was waiting to see Parson's Miss Charlotte come out of the church after the ceremony. She looked like a snowdrop, they said to each other after she had passed.

Bride and groom left that day for their honeymoon, which was to be in Ireland. From Dublin they travelled across the country to the shores of the Atlantic, that wild coast bound with rocks and its limitless expanse of sea. Charlotte asked her husband, as she had asked Ellen when she saw it for the first time, to leave her alone that she might contemplate it by herself. Glengariff, Tralee, Cork—the scenery exceeded all she had ever imagined. They did not visit the home where Papa was born, the thatched hut with its mud floor, one chimney, one window and one door. But before they left Ireland they spent some days at Arthur's old home at Banagher where his uncle, who had brought him up since the age of seven, was headmaster of the Royal High School.

The property in Ireland was not a myth. Arthur, who already was her dear husband, appeared in a new light in his own country, for on every side she heard his praises sung, and it was she who was thought the fortunate partner of their marriage. Family servants and retainers told her she had one of the best gentlemen in the country, and she liked her new relations who obviously came as something of a surprise. The one shadow to fall across the honeymoon was when she heard from home that Papa had not been well, which made her, always duty bound, glad it was time to return.

Arthur left Ireland twelve pounds heavier than when he

entered, Papa recovered from his indisposition when his daughter and son-in-law came home, and never had Charlotte enjoyed such good health. She could not remember a time when she had been so free from headaches and all the old symptoms. She wrote to Ellen that the colour of her thoughts had changed since her marriage, she knew more of the realities of life than she once did. It was a solemn and strange and perilous thing for a woman to become a wife.

It was like a leaf out of someone else's book. Arthur and Papa agreed so well there was never a misunderstanding or wrong word. Papa had always lived apart from the rest of the household and now this prized seclusion was not interfered with in any way. Charlotte's dear husband became her dear boy who grew daily dearer and her days were mellow with happiness occupied with being a wife as well as a daughter. The very normality of her life left not a minute for introspection. She marvelled how some wives grew selfish—matrimony, in her experience, tended to draw you out of and away from yourself. A married woman could call but a very small portion of her time her own, and it was this sharing of every day, the companionship of husband and wife, that blessed her married life. Callers, mostly clerical, came to the parsonage and there were return visits to be made together. Arthur liked to do so as much as they could together, and was jealous of any encroachment upon his prerogatives. He was so shocked when he read one of Charlotte's letters to Ellen in which she referred with indiscreet levity to flighty Amelia Taylor that he sent a stern message to Ellen that she must burn all her friend's letters. Indignantly Ellen retaliated by saying she would promise to burn Charlotte's letters when he promised not to read them.

Mr Brontë had always been interested in the causes and cures of diseases and his copy of Graham's *Modern Domestic Medicine* was liberally strewn with his question marks, underlinings and marginal comments. Mr Nicholls on the other hand was interested in health and its preservation. His panaceas were not tinctures, antidotes and specifics but fresh air and exercise. He deplored the shut windows of the parsonage, particularly those in the bedrooms. A strong, vigorous man, he started each day with a sharp walk to tune up his constitution, terminating his constitutional at the school on the beat of nine to take the Scripture lesson and insist on all the windows being opened summer and winter. During the day he liked his wife to accompany him on his walks on the moor. 'I have not a minute', she wrote blithely to Ellen.

One afternoon in November he interrupted her letter-writing to take a walk. Although it had been fair in the morning it was wild and cloudy now and they did not intend to go far, but Arthur suddenly suggested the waterfall—after the melted snow it should be a fine sight. Often Charlotte had wished to see their waterfall in its winter power and, spectacular in spate, it did not disappoint her. It began to rain while they were watching it racing, white and beautiful, over the rocks, but although they returned under a streaming sky, she counted the walk of seven to eight miles well worth while.

But she was shivery that evening, and caught a cough and sore throat it was difficult to throw off. Poor little Flossy, Anne's beloved spaniel, drooped for a single day and died quietly in the night without pain. Charlotte admitted the loss even of a dog was very saddening, but was comforted by the thought that no dog ever had a happier life or easier death than Flossy. Much had happened to Charlotte in the three years since Keeper's death had plunged her into a morass of misery.

She confided to Arthur that she would like Anne to be brought home but he advised strongly against it, and she deferred to him. Perhaps it was better after all for Anne to remain where she was, undisturbed beside the boundary wall, where the salt sea winds sighed and shrilled.

The two Nichollses visited the Kay-Shuttleworths in

January for three days and Charlotte's obstinate cold was aggravated by a walk in thin house slippers on damp grass. Sir James offered the Haworth curate the advantageous living of Padiham near Gawthorpe Hall, but Arthur of course was tied to Haworth parsonage as long as Papa lived.

It was in January that Charlotte reported to Ellen that she had never before felt as she had done lately. Dear Nell was told not to conjecture as it was too early yet, and to keep the matter wholly to herself.

The Haworth doctor was called in to attend to her cold and confirmed she was going to have a child. She was confined to bed but able to write to the doctor and ask him to send medicine for dear old Tabby, who was ill. It had always been meant that Tabby should die at the parsonage which was her home, but it was impossible for young Martha, even with the help of a younger sister, to nurse two invalids and attend to two men. Tabby's nephew took his aunt to his small cottage at the foot of Kirkgate, where she died at the age of eighty-four. The birch rocking-chair where she used to sit at the kitchen fire was empty now, yet the curious thing was that none of her bairns ever saw it without her.

On 17th February 1855, the day that Tabby died, Charlotte made her will, testified by Papa and Martha Brown, in which she left everything she had to her husband and their issue.

Arthur wrote to tell Ellen that Charlotte's intended visit to her at the end of January was out of the question. They had sent for Dr MacTurk of Bradford, who pronounced the invalid very ill and likely to remain so for some time, but he foresaw no immediate danger. At about the same time Papa was answering a letter from Sir James Kay-Shuttleworth on behalf of his daughter, telling him that their village surgeon visited the invalid daily and that they had had a visit from Dr MacTurk of Bradford, both of whom thought her illness was symptomatic and that, after a few days, they hoped her health would again return.

Charlotte made herculean efforts for Papa, forcing herself to sit up when he came into her room and saying, 'See, Papa! I am a little better; don't you think I look better?' But she was so worn and thin that the light showed through her hand when it was lifted up, and when the Brown sisters tried to cheer her with the thought of her baby, she would reply, 'I dare say I shall be glad some day, but oh, I am so ill and tired.'

She was still able to scratch a note to Laetitia Wheelwright, her friend from the Heger *pension* days, and to her dear Nell. She knew there was scant sympathy between her husband and her dearest friend and she wanted her dearest friend's heart put at rest that she could not have a more tender, good, helpful, patient nurse than he. 'My heart is knit to him', she wrote. He was the tenderest nurse, the kindest support, the best earthly comfort ever woman had, whose patience never failed.

Her symptoms were distressing, sickness with scarcely a reprieve, which meant she could not take sufficient nourishment to hold her strength. Yet she did so want to live and, towards the end, when she was delirious, she unconsciously craved for food and would open her mouth like a little throstle.

At the end of March, after nine months of married life, Mr Brontë wrote to Ellen, because Mr Nicholls was not strong and composed enough to do so, to tell her that his dear Daughter was very ill, and apparently on the verge of the grave. He asked her to be kind enough to write to Miss Wooler.

That night when Charlotte awoke from her stupor she heard her husband at her bedside praying to God to spare her. 'Oh,' she breathed, 'I am not going to die, am I? He will not separate us, we have been so happy.'

She died in the short, dark hours of that night, but she did not speak again. The last word she said was the word happy. It grows like a rose on her grave so that we remember it and forget the thorn.

BIBLIOGRAPHY

BIBLIOGRAPHY

Charlotte Brontë by E. F. Benson. Longmans, London, 1932.

The Brontës by Phyllis Bentley. Home & Van Thal, London, 1947.

Life of Charlotte Brontë by Augustine Birrell. Walter Scott, London, 1887.

In the Footsteps of the Brontës by Mrs Ellis H. Chadwick. Pitman, London, 1914.

Haworth Parsonage by Isabel C. Clarke. Hutchinson, London, 1927.

Les Sœurs Brontë by Ernest Dimnet. Paris, 1910; English translation Jonathan Cape, London, 1927.

Emily Brontë by Mary Duclaux. Allen & Co., London, 1883.

Life of Charlotte Brontë by Mrs Gaskell. Smith, Elder & Co., London, 1857, and numerous later editions.

The Letters of Mrs. Gaskell, edited by J. A. V. Chapple and Arthur Pollard. Manchester University Press, 1966.

Anne Brontë by Winifred Gérin. Nelson, London, 1959.

Branwell Brontë by Winifred Gérin. Nelson, London, 1961.

Charlotte Brontë by Winifred Gérin. Oxford University Press, 1967.

Pictures of the Past by F. A. Grundy. Griffith, London, 1879.

The Four Brontës by L. and E. M. Hanson. Oxford University Press, 1949.

Anne Brontë by Ada Harrison and Derek Stanford. Methuen, London, 1959.

The Brontë Story by Margaret Lane. Icon Books, 1953.

The Brontë Family, with special reference to Patrick Branwell Brontë, by F. A. Leyland. Hurst & Blackett, London, 1886.

A Man of Sorrows by John Lock and W. T. Dixon. Nelson, London, 1965.

The Infernal World of Branwell Brontë by Daphne du Maurier. Gollancz, 1960.

Brief Life of the Brontës by Royston Millmore. W. R. Millmore, Bradford, 1947.

The Life and Eager Death of Emily Brontë by Virginia Moore. Rich & Cowan, London, 1936.

The Brontës' Web of Childhood by Fannie E. Ratchford. Columbia University Press, U.S.A., 1941.

In the Steps of the Brontës by Ernest Raymond. Rich & Cowan, London, 1948.

The Shakespeare Head Brontë, published by Basil Blackwell, Oxford, 1931–8.

Charlotte Brontë and Her Circle by Clement Shorter. Hodder & Stoughton, London, 1896.

Charlotte Brontë and Her Sisters by Clement Shorter. Hodder & Stoughton, London, 1904.

The Brontës, Life and Letters, by Clement Shorter. Hodder & Stoughton, London, 1908.

Emily Brontë by Charles Simpson. Country Life, London, 1929.

The Three Brontës by May Sinclair. Hutchinson, London, 1912 and 1914.

Emily Brontë, her Life and Work, by Muriel Spark and Derek Stanford. Peter Owen, London, 1953 and 1966.

The Brontë Letters, edited by Muriel Spark. Peter Nevill, London, 1954.

The Miracle of Haworth by W. Bertrand White. University of London Press, 1937.

Index

London, 53; unable to face
reality, 55, 87, 89–90, 154; dis-
illusionment, 55–6; return
home, 56–7; restlessness, 58,
85; poetry, 58, 65, 102, 156;
becomes a freemason, 63; impatience, 63; secretary of the
Haworth Temperance Society,
63; teaches in Sunday School,
63; writes to Wordsworth, 63,
65; lack of literary judgment,
65; religion, 67, 103, 120, 156,
201; school usher, 73; art
lessons in Leeds, 73, 74; studio
in Bradford, 73–4; portrait
commissions, 74, 75; taking
drugs, 85, 154; his friendships,
84–6, 102; subservience, 85;
romantic nature, 86–7, 149,
153; translates Horace's *Odes*,
86, 88, 91, 93; tutor in
Broughton-in-Furness, 86, 89;
relations with Hartley Coleridge, 88, 91; takes railway post
at Sowerby Bridge, 93; at
Luddenden Foot, 101–2; dual
personality, 103; moody, 115;
shifty, 115; poems printed,
116; nurses William Weightman, 116; effect of Aunt's
death on, 119–20; tutor at
Thorp Green Hall, 121, 142;
love for Mrs Robinson, 148,
154–7; dismissed, 153; sodden
condition, 153–6, 159, 167;
sees Mr Robinson's obituary,
172; visit from Robinson
coachman, 172–3; receives
money from Mrs Robinson,
173, 180; deteriorates, 173–4,
178, 198–9; deceived about Mr
Robinson's will, 180; meets
Grundy, 200; death 201
Brontë, Charlotte: rebelliousness,
21; at Cowan Bridge School,
21, 23–4; description of, 27, 29,
44, 46, 110, 147, 232–3; leader
of family, 25, 224; reads *The*

Imitation of Christ, 26; enthusiasm for writing, 26, 28, 179;
closeness to Branwell, 27, 33,
36, 39, 46, 65, 86, 131, 201–2;
neatness, 27; shyness, 28, 37,
40; at Roe Head School, 32–6;
anxious for father's health, 36;
leaves Roe Head School, 38;
artistic, 39, 60; teaches at Sunday School, 45; conscientious,
45; pride, 45, 79–80; creates
Angria, 46; satire, 46; restlessness, 47, 61, 72, 98–9, 107, 142,
144–5, 147, 151, 161, 197;
energy, 54, 121; governess at
Roe Head School, 57; home-
sick, 59; as teacher, 60, 70,
129–30; as writer, 60, 61;
writes to Southey, 63; poetry,
63, 147, 161, 225; quarrels
with Miss Wooler over Anne,
70; religion, 70; breakdown,
70–1; melancholy, 70–1, 76,
263; introspective 71; refuses
proposals, 77, 78; closeness
to Emily, 79; relationship with
William Weightman, 82–4,
86, 93, 101, 104; writes to
Wordsworth for advice, 92;
transition period, 92; driving
force in school project, 98, 144;
plans to go to Brussels, 99–101;
leaves for Brussels, 105; in
London, 107, 192–7; in Belgium, 108–14; at *pension* Heger
as pupil and teacher, 109–14;
opinion of the Belgians, 110,
129; relations with the Hegers,
112, 129, 143–4, 148; determination to stay in Brussels,
113; visits Martha Taylor's
grave, 119, 135; Aunt's will,
120–1; second journey to Belgium, 127; at *pension* Heger
again, 128; learns German,
130–1; writes to Branwell, 131;
critical of the clergy, 132, 152,
204, 226–7, 238; loneliness